Comments about
The Comfort Garden: Tales from the Trauma Unit

"*The Comfort Garden* is filled with authentic moments that are both caring and healing. Embracing life, the author helps herself and her patients re-pattern traumatic experiences. Inspiring and painful at the same time, *The Comfort Garden* reveals the real world of human-to-human caring at its highest level. This work shows how the route toward emotional healing transcends medical technology and lies within a patient's inner experience."

NURSE THEORIST JEAN WATSON,
AUTHOR OF *HUMAN CARING SCIENCE: A THEORY OF NURSING*

"Ms. Barkin's text should be on the recommended reading list for the range of professionals who work with survivors of acute trauma."

MARGARET E. BLAUSTEIN PHD.
THE TRAUMA CENTER AT JUSTICE RESOURCE INSTITUTE

"Laurie Barkin takes us into the taut, jarring world of the trauma unit where nurses and doctors face daily battles, both emotional and physical. Barkin tends these battle wounds with empathy, precision, and insight."

DANIELLE OFRI MD, PHD. EDITOR-IN-CHIEF,
THE BELLEVUE LITERARY JOURNAL

"The Comfort Garden is a beautifully written book, at times joyous and poignant, at times incredibly depressing and somber. But, above all, it is honest."

LUCIA HWANG, *NATIONAL NURSE*

"The Comfort Garden is the compelling story of one nurse's struggle to remain compassionate and sane while helping those whose lives have been shattered on the battlefield of the inner city."

Echo Heron RN
Author of *Intensive Care* and *The Story of a Nurse*

Barkin "makes a compelling case for why health care centers should attend to the emotional needs of their staff if they want to retain these caregivers and better serve their patients."

JILL SUTTIE, BOOK REVIEW EDITOR, *GREATER GOOD* MAGAZINE

"*The Comfort Garden,* an engrossing journey into the contemporary world of hospital psychiatry... speaks eloquently to the humanity, compassion, and vulnerability of mental health professionals who help their patients navigate through some of the most difficult crises of their lives."

JACK COULEHAN MD. PROFESSOR EMERITUS OF PREVENTIVE MEDICINE SUNY; AUTHOR OF *MEDICINE STONE*

"At once beautiful and profoundly disturbing, Laurie Barkin's voice is that of every nurse. Every working parent can identify with her ambivalence at leaving her children every day, every nurse, with her passion for practice."

MARIE MANTHEY RN, MNA,
AUTHOR OF *THE PRACTICE OF PRIMARY NURSING*

"This is an important book for any health care worker, but especially for those of us who consider ourselves traumatic stress specialists. It reinforces the values and the spirit that brought us into the field. And it reminds us of the obstacles we face every day: human cruelty, social injustice, dwindling resources. Laurie is no Pollyanna. She is realistic and she suffers from vicarious trauma. But she copes and learns and survives and uplifts her fellow travelers. Read this. You'll be better for it."

FRANK M OCHBERG MD, CLINICAL PROFESSOR OF PSYCHIATRY, MICHIGAN STATE UNIVERSITY

"Whenever we walk into a hospital or a doctor's office we often assume that the patients are somehow broken, sick or frightened and that the nurses and doctors are whole, healthy and brave. In stories that prove these assumptions false, Laurie Barkin shows us how permeable the line actually is between the cared for and the caregiver."

CORTNEY DAVIS, AUTHOR OF *THE HEART'S TRUTH: ESSAYS ON THE ART OF NURSING*

"In an age when hospitals have been turning to quicker-acting medications, faster discharges, and fewer deep and meaningful conversations with patients, Laurie Barkin takes the opposite position. She urges us to make the time to use our knowledge of psychodynamic psychotherapy to help traumatized people early in the course of their distress."

LENORE TERR MD, PSYCHIATRIST, AUTHOR OF *TOO SCARED TO CRY*

The
Comfort
Garden

Tales from the Trauma Unit

Laurie Barkin RN, MS

FRESH POND PRESS

San Francisco

The names of all patients and their family members have been changed.

Library of Congress Control Number 2010924787
The Comfort Garden: Tales from the Trauma Unit / by Laurie Barkin
ISBN 13: 978-0-9844965-4-9
Printed in the United States of America
First Edition, February 2011

Author photo and cover art by June Komater

Published by Fresh Pond Press:: San Francisco, California

For orders, contact:
Fresh Pond Press
P.O. Box 460651
San Francisco, CA 94146

www.lauriebarkin.com

For my parents, Ted and Sylvia,
and their spouses, Roberta and Ernie.

For Catherine Galvin RN, MSN,
mentor and friend.

And, for Jeanne, for making me laugh.

contents

Contents

foreword

Over a span of thirty years, I have trained thousands of medical professionals to provide psychological care for victims of trauma.

A most important issue, one too frequently overlooked in the field of trauma care, is the well-being of trauma professionals who are at very high risk for developing compassion fatigue and vicarious traumatization as the result of their empathic work with patients. Laurie Barkin recognizes these critical issues, and, in her book, struggles to deal with them institutionally and personally. Her work underscores the importance of stress-management strategies, policies, and resources for professionals in the trauma field.

Laurie is a fabulous writer and storyteller and this book is a "must read" for people in the field. Her narrative is alive, compelling, touching, sad, at times, and funny and poignant. Through her vignettes, she models a treasure-trove of skills: the art of empathy and therapeutic communication including the "therapeutic use of self;" assessing mental-status, psychological vulnerabilities, and resilience; crisis intervention; and, finally, stress-management techniques. While contending with arcane policies and politics prevalent in our health-care institutions, Laurie realistically depicts the challenge of providing compassionate, effective care in a chaotic hospital environment.

Laurie's personal journey—seeking to balance her busy home life and demanding professional life—resonates as an ever-present theme for those of us in the helping professions. In using *The Comfort Garden* as a metaphor, we are reminded of the necessity to trim, prune, fertilize, and care for our lives in order to be able to flourish and give to others.

I will emphatically recommend this book in the trauma and disaster mental health workshops that I teach. A powerful and moving story, it illuminates the impact of trauma on both victims and caretakers. *The Comfort Garden* should be required reading in every training program for health care and mental health professionals.

Diane Myers RN, MSN
Advanced-Practice Psychiatric Nurse
Board-Certified Expert in Traumatic Stress

preface

I began my job as a psychiatric nurse consultant at San Francisco General Hospital with the feeling that I had finally found my professional home. My colleagues were talented clinicians fiercely committed to providing excellent care to people in need. My patients were always challenging, occasionally frustrating, and frequently awe-inspiring.

Toward the end of five years working with trauma patients on a surgical unit, I began experiencing many of the same symptoms as my patients: nightmares, palpitations, intrusive images, shortness of breath, tearfulness, and fear for my children's safety. At a psychological trauma conference, I learned that my symptoms could be attributed to "vicarious trauma" which can affect empathic people whose work exposes them to survivors' stories of interpersonal violence, war, and traumatic accidents. Staff support groups were recommended as an antidote. When requests at work for such time were turned down, I resigned my position in order to take care of myself. Months after I resigned, however, my patients' stories continued to haunt me. I started writing *The Comfort Garden* as a way of coming to terms with the nature of trauma.

To protect the privacy of my patients, I have changed their names, altered some identifying facts, and in a few cases, created composites. I hope that anyone who might recognize aspects of his or her story will understand that my purpose in writing this book is to educate health care providers about vicarious trauma and the public about the social, physical, and psychological consequences of trauma, especially childhood trauma, left untreated.

A warning: the stories in *The Comfort Garden* recreate the fast-paced work and transient relationships with patients at San Francisco General Hospital. Due to the push to discharge patients sooner rather than later, our work together often ended abruptly. For that reason, the overarching story in *The Comfort Garden* is my own: how vicarious trauma developed in an experienced psychiatric nurse, forcing her to confront personal issues of identity, dependency, and survivor guilt.

Laurie Barkin
February 2011
San Francisco

introduction

On rare occasions, a book appears in print that has the capacity to captivate and to deeply touch the soul of the reader. Such books emerge from an author whose motivation for writing comes from experience with life-altering events and the need to tell the story of these events is both compelling and poignant. Laurie Barkin is such a writer.

Her book *The Comfort Garden* is about the plight of people who have survived staggering trauma long enough to get to a hospital. The real-life stories unfold to highlight the astonishing impact of trauma on patients, family members, friends, and the caregivers who treat them. The narrative is from her perspective and in her voice as a psychiatric nurse who works with those who have sustained unimaginable injuries. The context for the experiences is a high-powered urban trauma unit that serves the breadth of humanity. The stories are exemplars of compassion in dealing with misery, courage in the face of grief, and of human determination holding hands with fateful destiny. The reader is invited in as a participant in the stories. The writing skillfully draws you to the bedside, has you sit with the rawness of the experience of loved ones, and provides a chance to listen in on the conversations about life and death that are common to the way of life on a trauma unit. The reader has the opportunity to understand the complex and challenging experiences of all involved: patients, nurses, surgeons, social workers, physical therapists, and others. Each participant provides texture to the fabric of the trauma unit experience.

This book is essential reading for anyone who wants to understand the intricate and sometimes cruel challenges of trauma and the path to healing. Ms. Barkin's work makes a great contribution to the heart of understanding the experience of both the healer and the healed. Her writing comes from a place where there are no veneers to hide the stark reality of situations, which she so artfully describes. One cannot walk away from this book without being transformed by its content. As the providers from the trauma unit often say, and as she has been able to richly articulate, *"It is as real as it gets..."*

Geoffry Phillips McEnany, PhD, APRN, BC
Professor of Nursing, University of Massachusetts Lowell

Psychiatric/Mental Health Clinical Nurse Specialist
Private Practice in Boston, Massachusetts

1

Listening to trauma

They are dressed in bright orange jumpsuits. Seven prisoners
— four African-American and two Latino men, and one
very pregnant African-American woman, all handcuffed and
shackled together at the ankle — shuffling through the entrance
to the hospital emergency room. Three sheriff's deputies — two
white, one Filipino — joke with the prisoners while herding
them through the doors, past the ER waiting area, and down
the hallway toward the back of the hospital. The sight of seven
people, mostly black, handcuffed, and shackled together, raises
my hackles. I keep expecting to see German Shepherds and billy
clubs as if it were the sixties in Birmingham and not the nineties
in San Francisco. Each clink of chain rattles in my ears. Seventeen
years ago, I worked on a surgical intensive care unit where inmates
from the local prison were chained to their beds. I never got used
to that either.

Upon my arrival to 4D, the surgical unit where I have been
assigned, a loud male voice blasts, "Don't touch me! Get the fuck
out of my face!"

4D, also called The Trauma Unit, pulses with adrenaline. Nurses dash from doorway to doorway as flocks of medical residents and their students swoop through the halls, poking in and out of patients' rooms. Lab techs dart around them, grabbing opportunities to draw blood. No one looks particularly concerned.

Don't screaming patients warrant attention around here? At Presbyterian, the hospital where I used to work, security would have been paged the moment someone raised a voice, let alone hurled obscenities at a caregiver.

Another blast from the agitated patient: "I said get the fuck out of my face!"

This time the voice sounds more panicky than angry. I'm halfway down the hall looking for the source of trouble when Trudy, the day-shift charge nurse, intercepts me.

"He's OK for now," she says before ducking into the head nurse's office.

Just ahead, a transport aide from the recovery room angles an empty gurney out of a patient's room. He pushes it past four rooms to the double doors at the entrance to 4D and slams the gurney through metal doors where it crashes into a portable X-ray machine that a tech is pushing into 4D.

"What the hell?" he sputters.

Trudy emerges from the head nurse's office to help the transporter and the X-ray tech do-si-do through the doors. On her way back to the nurses' station, Trudy stops when another scream pierces the din.

"Owwwww! Sonofabitch! Leave me the fuck alone!"

"Uh oh," mutters Trudy. "Here we go again." She looks my way and says, "It's the IVDU in 14-1."

In nurse-speak she is telling me the troubled patient is an intravenous drug user (IVDU) in room 14, bed 1.

As the new psych nurse consultant, I should be doing something to help but I'm not sure what. While I hesitate, Victoria, the trauma unit's humorless head nurse, opens the door to her tiny cubicle, a former janitor's closet that is opposite the nurses' station. She makes eye contact with Trudy and shakes her head. With hands on considerable hips and jaw jutting below thin lips, Victoria strides through the ward where she has reigned for eighteen years. Trudy, a head shorter, older but energetic, quickens her pace to keep up. A few minutes later Trudy returns to the nurses' station and puts her arm around me, saying, "This is why we need you psych nurses! Give James time to calm down before you check in with him. This was not his fault."

Victoria marches into the nurses' station shortly after Trudy and waits until a tall blond surgical resident accompanied by a Chinese-American medical student reach the Formica counter that frames two sides of the nurses' station. The two stop and talk, seemingly oblivious to Victoria's relentless gaze.

"So what just happened there?" Victoria demands.

The surgical resident scratches his forehead as if newly bitten by a mosquito.

Victoria raises her voice slightly. "I am speaking to you, Dr. Murdock. I want to know what set that patient off."

Dr. Murdock's jaw muscles bulge. Without making eye contact, he replies in over-articulated speech, "The dressing was dry, so, in removing the old packing some of the healthy tissue must have been pulled out as well. Sometimes it's unavoidable."

"Hell it is," Victoria growls.

"What did you say?" This time the resident makes direct eye contact.

"You heard me." Victoria locks her eyes with his and doesn't let go. "That kind of pain is totally avoidable. My nurses give their patients pain medication before taking down dressings. If the packing is dry, they soak it in saline so they can remove it easily without ripping out healthy tissue. That's why you don't hear patients screaming when the nurses remove the packing."

"We did it the way we've always done it," counters the resident.

"Here, you mean," says Victoria. "I bet you don't do it that way to the private patients at University Hospital, do you? Let me be clear, Dr. Murdock. When a patient, any patient, tells you to stop, it means you do not have consent to continue. Do you read me?"

"You're out of line," retorts the resident straightening his body. "I'll be discussing this with Dr. Steinfeldt."

He opens the patient's chart, scribbles a note, slams it shut, and exits the ward.

Victoria rolls her eyes. "I get so tired of these baby doctors," she says to no one in particular before heading back to her office.

I pick up the chart that the resident left on the counter and turn to the last entry. His note reads, "Patient uncooperative with care."

A hand lightly squeezes my shoulder. "Now that you're off hospital orientation, are you ready to start seeing patients?"

Everything about Janice is soft. Her creamy voice, her honey-colored hair, her luminous smile, and her round body all remind me of being curled up in an overstuffed chair, drinking hot-spiced cider next to a fire and talking with an old friend.

"I am, but I have to confess I'm a little nervous. I haven't worked at the bedside with medical-surgical patients since graduate school and that was ten years ago."

"Should we interview a patient together?"

"Sure."

I look at my list and choose a young paraplegic woman hospitalized for treatment of a urinary tract infection and a pressure ulcer on her buttocks, both common complications of paraplegia. According to her chart, Shalimar Banks became paraplegic after she was stabbed in 1983. The nurses say she's been withdrawn and tearful for the last two days.

Janice and I scan her chart. Then Janice shows me the filing cabinet where old charts are kept. Five thick volumes of Shalimar's old charts dominate the drawer. "I know it's a good idea to begin a consultation by reading the old chart, but that will take more time than we have. Let's see her first."

The patient rooms at SFGH differ little from most I've seen. All of them look monotonous. Paint, porcelain, laminate, and linoleum span the color spectrum from ivory to ash gray. The dull blue of both the bed curtain and the patient's standard gown offer the room's only hint of color.

Shalimar lies on her left side facing cartoons on TV. Long ringlets of thick black hair cascade down her shoulders. Over-tweezed eyebrows sit high above a wide but tiny nose and full, Kewpie-doll lips. Shalimar is a mixture of Caucasian, African-American, and Filipino.

"Hi, Ms. Banks," says Janice, extending her hand to Shalimar. "Laurie and I are mental health nurses who talk to patients on the medical and surgical units. Your nurses asked us to check in with you because they're concerned about your mood. How have you been feeling?"

Shalimar switches the TV off and turns her head toward us. "Not so good," she replies while gesturing toward the dull-gray plastic chair in the corner of the room. Janice moves it closer to the bed while I pull a chair from the corridor.

"My butt keeps breaking down because MediCal won't pay for a KinnAir bed in my hotel room."

"What's a KinnAir bed?" I ask.

Janice motions Shalimar to explain.

"A bed that's made to shift air around in the mattress so people like me don't get pressure sores. They say it's too expensive—but then they pay to hospitalize me when my skin breaks down. Does that make any sense?"

Shalimar reaches for a tissue and wipes her eyes.

"None whatsoever," Janice replies. "That sounds so frustrating. I can't do much about MediCal but maybe I can help you improve your mood. Have you been crying a lot lately?"

Shalimar nods. Janice asks her questions that comprise the standard depression inventory, suicide assessment, and mental status exam. Does she have any problems sleeping or eating? Does she sometimes think that life is not worth living? Does she hear voices telling her to hurt herself or others? Seamlessly, Janice weaves the questions into the conversation. A picture of chronic, untreated depression begins to emerge. Shalimar often thinks about suicide but has no active plan to carry it out. Janice zeros in on the trauma that severed her life into before and after.

"May I ask about your injury?"

"It's OK. It happened nine years ago."

She looks out the window and launches into her story. "I grew up in the valley. When I was eleven, I ran away to the city with my friend. She was thirteen. She said she knew someone there we could stay with. Prince seemed OK at first. He gave us some weed, took care of us. Then he shot us with dope. It felt so good at first. Like the best hug you could have. I would say to him, 'Where's my hug, honey?'"

My mind struggles to comprehend Shalimar's story. I force my breath deep into my lungs and grip the seat of my chair. I need to be able to listen to the rest of it.

Shalimar runs her fingers through her long hair. "Then Prince made us be with older guys. By that time, we were hooked. You know. We give him money; he gives us hugs. No money, no hugs. It went on like that until I was sixteen."

Five years! Where were her parents? Were the authorities notified? Did anyone notice this child was missing?

"Then, I met a really nice guy who asked me to marry him.

When I told Prince I was leaving to marry this guy, he said I couldn't, that I belonged to him. When I turned to go, he stabbed me in the back."

While I struggle to push down the jagged-edged outrage rising in my throat, Janice continues the interview, her voice steady and smooth.

"That's a lot to cope with," says Janice. "But right now I want to focus on the present. Have you been having difficulty sleeping?"

Shalimar whispers, "I'm afraid to sleep. Sometimes I have the worst nightmares."

"How about during the day?" asks Janice. "How would you describe your general mood?"

Shalimar curls a long strand of hair around her finger. "Most of the time I'm real bitchy because I'm not sleeping. And, I'm still afraid to go out. They never got him, you know, so I'm always looking over my shoulder thinking I see the flash of a knife."

Shalimar shudders and claps her hand over her mouth. She grabs another hunk of hair and winds it tightly around her fist. "Sometimes I see someone who looks like him and I start to feel like I'm having a heart attack, you know? I can't breathe and I feel like I'm going to faint. It's real freaky, so I just try to stay in most of the time."

"It sounds like it's been a living hell for you," says Janice. "Do you have any family or close friends you can count on for help?"

Shalimar shakes her head. "No, not really. I'm pretty much alone."

The sound of clanking metal outside Shalimar's room startles us. The porter has arrived to transport her to the radiation department.

Janice tells Shalimar she will see her again tomorrow. In the meantime, she will ask a psychiatrist to consider prescribing an anti-depressant to improve her mood. We return to our office on the seventh floor. Antionette looks up from a journal as we fall into our chairs.

"Whew," says Janice. "That was rough. I haven't heard a story like that for a while. How are you doing, Laurie?"

"I felt like I was going to lose it. How did you stay so calm and controlled?"

"I felt the same as you," Janice says. "I guess I've learned to fake it pretty well. Fooled you, I see!"

Antionette swivels around to face us. She is dressed in an elegant wool suit, stockings, and stylish shoes. We're both in our late thirties but that's as far as our similarities go. Antionette is an African-American from Savannah, sleek and stunning as a model, single, and a major in the California Army National Guard. She is as controlled and private as I am spontaneous and open. She can't hide her love for clothes shopping. If I had Antionette's body, I might enjoy it too.

We met several years ago when we both attended regular meetings of Bay Area psych nurse consultants who, like us, work on medical/surgical units rather than psychiatric units. There were only fifteen of us working in Bay Area hospitals then. After hospital mergers and reorganizations, we are even fewer today.

Antionette looks stricken after we tell her Shalimar's story. "Prostituting at eleven? That poor child. No wonder you two look ragged." Antionette shakes her head and sighs. "Whenever I hear a story like that I say to myself, 'There but for the grace of God go I.'"

Janice smiles at Antionette and points a finger at me. "I think exactly the same thing. Take good care of yourself, Laurie. I know you've been a nurse for a long time but listening to some of our patients' stories can suck the life out of you."

"I'll be OK," I say, a little too quickly.

To get my hospital ID, I walk across campus to an old brick building, which used to be part of the original hospital and now houses the Department of Human Resources. Outside, San Francisco's famous summer fog has lifted its veil to reveal a sky of startling blue. A soft glow of light warms my face. We've been enveloped in fog for days and it's no wonder that all of us who have just stepped outside are lifting our faces for a smooch of sunshine.

After I leave Human Resources with my laminated ID, I exit the wrong way and find myself facing a garden wall covered in psychedelic orange flowers. I walk through the entrance to the garden and catch my breath. Across from me, in front of an old red brick building that houses the HIV and methadone clinics, stands an enormous Atlas cedar. Its lowermost branch sweeps the ground like the arm of a ballerina bowing at the end of her performance—bent at the elbow and curling softly up at the wrist. To my left, a twenty-foot wide swath of garden sweeps downhill a hundred fifty feet or so until it reaches the busy city street bordering the hospital campus. Five mature Monterey pines line the length of garden like colossal warriors ready to defend the young and innocent plants that lie at their feet. I recognize many of them—roses, camellias, princess plant, hebe, and dahlias—but there are many more I can't identify and some I've never seen before. If Shalimar's story knocked the wind out of me, this garden—enthusiastic and bursting with life—revives me.

Since the few benches in the middle of this mass of flora are occupied, I stroll the length of the garden. Half way, a wooden post with a brass placard rises from a circle of pink geraniums and blue forget-me-nots. The placard reads, "The Comfort Garden: This garden was created in June 1990 as a living memorial to those employees of SFGH who have died. It is meant to be a place of solace where nature's beauty can bring you comfort." The garden is only two years old.

"What do you think about the garden?" asks a compact, sandy-haired man about my age. His cheeks are sunburned and he's leaning on a shovel.

"I'm in awe especially of the pines and the cedar. That's what's missing in my garden—a big tree for my kids to climb. How old are these?"

"Oh, probably sixty or seventy years. If you plant a sapling now your kids could climb it in about ten years."

His name is Antoine and he has been a gardener at SFGH for twelve years. "I have the best job in the city," he says. "I'm outside all day; I can ride my bicycle to work and wear shorts most of the year. For me, it doesn't get better than that."

Antoine wipes his brow and checks his watch. "Gotta run, but I'll see you around."

A young couple, previously entwined on one of the benches, pulls apart and walks toward the clinics. I sit down on the vacated bench and watch the people walking by. They are a mix of body types, colors, and ages. Some move with determination; others seem lost in their thoughts. A young mother drags her unhappy two-year-old son. An emaciated young man, perhaps with AIDS, inches along with a walker. A much older man with a cane passes him by.

Until now, I wasn't aware of the tension in my body. But thinking about the morning, it's understandable. First, it was seeing people, mostly black people, in shackles. Then as if a rock were thrown through a window, my usual calm was shattered by the knowledge of the violence done to Shalimar. I feel a murderous rage toward her pimp.

How many others has he terrorized? Is he still walking free among us? No wonder Shalimar can't sleep at night. I'm not so sure I'm going to be able to sleep tonight.

While massaging the muscles in the back of my neck, I muse about how I've come full circle. Just out of school, I began my nursing career on a surgical, intensive care unit at a county hospital much like SFGH. It was in Phoenix that I learned how to be a "real nurse"—one who could maneuver a butterfly catheter into the scarred veins of a junkie, one who could slip a nasal gastric tube into the esophagus instead of the trachea, one who could suction thick phlegm from a tracheostomy without gagging.

In Arizona, my first ICU patient was a husky, twenty-four-year-old Latino male with a head injury. Tubes penetrated his nose, mouth, arms, and penis—draining, ventilating, and hydrating a body that offered no resistance. Pointing to his nearly flat EEG, Betty, the nurse assigned to orient me, declared him a good patient on whom to practice invasive procedures. She showed me how to insert a Foley catheter through his penis and into his bladder and how to inflate the balloon that kept it from sliding out. She watched my technique as I pierced his impressive veins with twenty-gauge needles and connected them to intravenous solutions. Throughout the lesson, she called my attention to such things as the color of his urine, the condition of the skin under the thick adhesive tape anchoring the catheter to his thigh, and the spongy puffiness of the area around an infiltrated I.V., one that is no longer positioned in the vein.

To her credit, Betty never told me that the patient had been hit over the head with a metal pipe by a man who had witnessed him raping a young woman in an alley near Arizona State University. I learned that later from a newspaper article.

After a few months of close supervision on the day shift, I was moved to the night shift where I became the low person in the unit hierarchy. While day-shift workers thrived on precision teamwork at a fast pace, night shift attracted a less gregarious and more independent worker.

I never quite got the polyrhythm of life on the night shift. Beginning with a 7 p.m. wake up call, I struggled to adjust. After eating "breakfast" in the evening, I could catch the first set at the El Bandito jazz club and still manage to arrive on the unit by eleven p.m. Fresh from the soothing swish of brushes on the snare drum and long, sonorous, saxophone solos, I entered a world of hissing ventilators and angry alarms in the ICU.

County Hospital was the area's trauma center. Many of our patients arrived after being stabbed, shot, beaten, or mashed in car accidents. One night, the recovery room nurse called to let us know we would be receiving a young man who had barely survived a motorcycle accident. Watching us settle the patient in, the surgical resident shook his head and worked his jaw.

"We shouldn't have saved him," he said in a monotone.

I've forgotten the patient's name but can still see his eyes and droopy eyelids. The unfocused daze of Post-Op Day One gave way to a look of utter bewilderment, then fear as his clouded consciousness cleared. Each of us oriented the patient to his surroundings: "You've had an accident. You are in the hospital. It's Friday, September 19, 1975. You can't talk because there's a tube in your mouth to help you breathe."

I remember how his eyes darted, desperate to find something familiar, something comprehensible, something acceptable.

It happened sometime before night shift on Post-Op Day Three. His gaze turned hard as a drill bit, boring into the faces of the doctors and nurses who gathered around his bedside speaking over him in the language of laboratory values and neurological signs. When they left, his eyes blazed with anger, the anger of a man who has just realized he would never again be able to move or even breathe on his own.

I averted his stare. I was twenty-one years old and without a clue as to what to say to the first quadriplegic I had ever met. I felt overwhelmed just trying to figure out how to turn him and his tubes safely on the Stryker frame, a bed that allowed us to invert him quickly onto his stomach in order to relieve pressure on his backside.

The patient's care became routine after a few more shifts and

I relaxed enough to feel his eyes following me. When he had been turned and suctioned and his blood work drawn and sent to the lab, I sat down and forced myself to acknowledge the person inhabiting the body.

He regarded me without expression. He did not glare, implore, or narrow his eyes. Nor did he look away. His face was rough and ruddy, wide with high cheekbones, a fleshy nose, and full lower lip. Wisps of chestnut hair hung past his shoulders. Feeling unveiled and inept, I looked down. Wasn't there another nursing task I needed to do for him? Shouldn't I offer to help one of the other nurses with her patients? When our eyes again met like headlights approaching each other too close and too fast, I panicked. To avoid a collision, I imagined reversing direction and driving parallel to him, looking out on the same terrain. Then, after calming myself, I jumped into the seat along side him.

"You must feel lonely," I began. "Everything must be so strange for you. I've only been working as an RN for a few months and this place still freaks me out sometimes."

I chuckled before I could censor myself. "Oh, God, I'm so sorry. I didn't mean to laugh. I'm just kind of nervous right now."

Idiot! This is about the patient's feelings, not yours. Try again.

"I guess you're probably having a lot of feelings about what's happened to you. It must be horrible not being able to talk about it. It's just not fair. This shouldn't happen to anyone."

Finally, I just said it: "I'm so sorry this happened to you."

I don't know who started to cry first. It was an awful moment for us both. I reached for the tissue box and started to hand it to him before realizing I had salted his wound again. *Jesus, he can't even wipe his own nose.* I watched frustration foam out of every pore as I did it for him.

Returning to the present but with my head still full of memories, I walk past the Atlas cedar on my way back to the main hospital. A part of me would love to climb that majestic tree, to be above the world, oblivious to the pain of others. But, I've never been able to stay in a place like that, alone and unengaged with the world.

At the entrance to the trauma unit, Janice's warning echoes in my mind. "Take good care of yourself, Laurie. Our patients' stories can suck the life out of you."

Being out of practice, I can now imagine how listening to stories like Shalimar's, day after day can warp a person's view of the world. But, as an experienced psych nurse who has heard lots of horrible stories, I know I will soon recover my ability to focus on the things I can do to help my patients instead of being dragged down by their tragedies. I will revive my skills of listening to their traumas with my head and my heart in equal measure—at the same time analytic and empathic. Symmetry doesn't always come easily but surviving this job will depend on finding and maintaining that balance.

2

"As real as it gets"

Each Tuesday morning I attend nursing rounds on 4D, the Trauma Unit. Ruby, the trauma nurse coordinator, holds court in the nurses' lounge joined by the head nurse, the day-shift charge nurse, a social worker, a physical therapist, a couple of staff nurses, a drug and alcohol counselor, the occasional trauma resident, and me. We sit squeezed together around a chipped, city-issued table in the windowless room while Ruby reviews the trauma and surgery cases. She announces each patient's name and diagnosis, the prognosis, an account of the surgery that was or will be performed, and an estimate of the length of hospitalization required. The social worker reports on the patient's living situation and insurance status before asking about the patient's aftercare requirements. The physical therapist reports on how close the patient is to independent ambulation, and the nurses give an update on the patient's overall progress and cooperation with the treatment plan. Good patients comply with their treatment plans. Those who don't are labeled "non-compliant." The nursing staff often refers "non-compliant" patients for psych nurse evaluations.

Trauma rounds give me an overview of the patients on the unit and helps me to prioritize my cases. This morning, Ruby reviews the cases of three people with stab wounds, four with gunshot wounds, someone beaten with a baseball bat, two who were in motor-vehicle accidents, one who fell two stories, and two pedestrians hit by cars. The most I can see on a good day seems to be five new patients. Interviews can last from twenty minutes to an hour. Current and old charts must be reviewed, phone calls made, and consultation reports completed. In a pinch, I can call on Antionette and Janice to help, but unless they're having a slow day, I try not to bother them.

After the meeting, I like to check in with the charge nurse. While the head nurse is responsible for hiring and firing, scheduling, staff evaluations, policy implementation, and the like, the charge nurse is responsible for minute-to-minute patient-care issues. On 4D's day shift, that person is usually Trudy. She knows who's being discharged, who's being admitted, who's going to surgery, who's expected back from the recovery room, who's in pain, who's still groggy, who's an assault risk, who's a little nutty, and who needs a little something extra. My patients fall into these last few categories. After checking in with Trudy, I review the patients' charts, old and new. Then I check the medication record to see when patients last received something for pain, or if they are heroin addicts, when they are due for the next dose of methadone. Finally, I try to nab the patient's nurse in the hallway for her impression of the patient and her opinion of when might be a good time to see the patient. In the morning, I have to work around bedpans, bed baths, physicians, dressing changes, radiology, and physical therapy sessions. In the afternoon, visitors start to arrive.

This morning, my list reads like this:

Reginald Carter—31 y.o. SBM (single black male), grad. student, beaten by 4 young men with baseball bats. s/p (status post) right scapula fx, (fracture) left clavicular fx and ORIF (open reduction and internal fixation) of left tib-fib fx. (left tibula-fibula fracture) No LOC (loss of consciousness) Evaluate stress and coping.

Melinda Grayson — 26 y.o. SWF (single white female), truck vs M/C (motorcycle). Open-book pelvic fx, (fracture) orbital fx, cheek fx and skull fx. +LOC. (loss of consciousness) Evaluate stress and coping.

Rose Manalo — 41 y.o. WDF (white divorced female) s/p (status post) MVA (motor vehicle accident) vs ped (pedestrian) with ORIF R. tib/fib fx. No LOC. Behavioral management problem.

Since Ms. Grayson's nurse is washing her up and Mr. Carter is with the physical therapist, I begin with Rose Manalo. The nurses complain that she has been "non-compliant with nursing care." This can mean that she is spitting out medication, ripping off bandages, leaving the unit on the sly, or break dancing when a doctor's order specifies bed rest only. From Rose's medical chart, I learn that a car hit her as she was jaywalking on a major street. Although she avoided internal injuries and did not lose consciousness, her right leg was mashed and she lost her front dental plate. The orthopedic surgeons performed an ORIF, or open reduction, internal fixation of her leg last night, stabilizing it with metal plates and screws and wrapping it in a cast that she will need to wear for the next eight weeks.

Ms. Manalo's nurse seems exasperated. "I keep telling her she has to keep her leg up, but every time I turn around she's doing everything but that!"

Most of the nurses here, while being concerned, seem to take things more in stride. For now, I will keep this observation to myself and meet with the patient.

In her room, a petite, strawberry-blond-haired woman appearing to be in her fifties, struggles to move herself from her wheelchair to her bed. I offer to help but she refuses.

"Are you Ms. Manalo?"

"Depends why you're asking," she replies in a low and cautious voice. Without her dentures, Ms. Manalo's esses swish instead of hiss. After she has managed to maneuver herself into bed, she needs a moment to recover from the effort. Then she breaks into a gummy smile and extends her hand.

"I bet you're the shrink lady they want me to talk to," she says in a bright voice tinged with a Southern accent. "Just call me Rose. Hey, how was my paranoid person imitation? Pretty good, huh? Think I can get myself committed to some fancy asylum with good food?"

Her knobby shoulders shake as she laughs. I laugh too, delighted that she has a sense of humor and relieved that she isn't paranoid. Paranoid patients have no sense of humor. No matter how careful you are about your choice of words, they will always find sinister intentions in them.

"Yes on both accounts. I'm here because the nurses told me you weren't abiding by your doctor's order to keep your leg elevated at all times. Is that right?"

"Well, I just had to get out of this room and into the sunshine. It's been so gosh darn foggy lately. You can understand that, can't ya? But this wheelchair's busted where it should hold my leg up. So I figured out a way to use my crutches underneath for support."

I could see she was proud of her inventiveness.

"Great idea!" I say. "But I can see why your nurse might be a bit worried that you'll hurt yourself. You just had surgery yesterday."

She purses her lips as if to whistle but blows out a short burst of air instead. "Honey, I've been takin' good care of myself since I was sixteen. Besides, I don't want to bother the nurses for piddlin' problems. They work real hard as it is."

Rose tells me that she was the youngest in a family of four girls. Her violent father killed her mother when she was four. He had been molesting her older sisters for years. When he threatened to abuse her too, she ran away. After being picked up by the cops, she was sent to an institution for the developmentally disabled where she didn't belong. During her four years there, a clergyman repeatedly raped her.

"No one believed me, of course. But they didn't believe that my daddy raped my sisters neither." She ran away from the institution and worked in strip clubs "shaking my titties for tips," before eventually marrying. "He was a foreigner. I didn't know then that he married me just to become legal."

Rose ended up on the streets, hanging out with dangerous men and getting herself into dangerous situations. At some point, she moved to the West Coast where she supports herself by cleaning houses. She makes ends meet by living in shelters or cheap hotels and still manages to find dangerous men to abuse her. When she feels lonely and overwhelmed, a frequent occurrence, she walks in the park. With this injury, she won't be able to do that for many weeks.

Rose understands she's supposed to keep her leg elevated to maximize circulation to the surgical site. Given her history, I can see that she prides herself on being independent but needs every bit of sunshine she can get in her life in order to stay a step ahead of depression. She and I work out a schedule that allows her to get outside but that will also meet with her nurse's approval. At lunch, I'll talk with Janice and Antionette about what support services might be available to Rose in the community.

A sweet violin solo greets my ears as I open the door to Reginald Carter's room. The man in bed two is wrapped in gauze and suspended in traction. Even so, an expression of rapture graces his face. Loath to interrupt such ecstasy where one would least expect it, I turn to leave.

"It's all right. I'm awake. Are you the psych lady? My nurse said you'd be in this morning."

"That's me. Sorry to interrupt; you look so serene; I could

come back later."

"Yes, well, music does that to me. And the pain medication they gave me before physical therapy helps, too." He grimaces a bit while trying to scoot himself up in bed. "But I would like to talk to you. I need to talk to someone."

I settle into a blue plastic chair and rest my eyes on Reginald's expressive face. Close up, I can see abrasions on his smooth, dark cocoa skin. He tells me that he was attacked last night on his way home from attending an artist friend's open studio in a rough part of town.

"The Muni bus broke down a few houses away from the projects. I really didn't want to be walking alone around there at that time of night so I asked the tow truck driver for a ride to a safer neighborhood. He said 'no' and left me on the street where four brothers with baseball bats asked me for my money. I told them all I had was two dollars. It was the truth but they didn't believe me."

Reginald squeezes his eyes shut. "So, they hit me."

Tears sneak down his cheek. We sit in silence while he tries to maintain emotional control. I use the time to do the same. *Will I ever be able to hear these stories without getting emotional myself?* After a few moments, his facial muscles relax and he resumes.

"How could they do that to me? How could I be so meaningless to them? I can still hear them laughing. They were laughing while they were smashing my body."

Again, he squeezes his eyes shut and presses his fist into his forehead. "I don't understand how they could have laughed."

"Sounds like you're feeling betrayed."

"That's right. That's the word for it. Betrayed."

"Maybe a little angry, too?"

"That would be an understatement." He shakes his head. "I could never even imagine treating someone like that. I'm lying here with a shattered shoulder and a busted leg and they probably haven't given it a moment's thought."

"It sounds like you expect more from people."

"Well, at least from my own people. These kids haven't grown up in the church. They got no respect, no manners, and no sense of morality. They're a pack of wolves."

"How about the tow truck operator?"

"White guy. Probably thought I was gonna rob him."

"Has there been any other trauma in your life?" How Reginald answers this question will tell me a lot about him and how he reacts to stress.

"Yeah, when my dad died."

Reginald holds his breath while he readjusts his body. "He was stopped by a white policeman because he was parked in a tow zone. He told the cop he would move the car. But when he reached into his pocket to get his keys, the policeman panicked and shot him. He died right then. I was seven."

Once again, a question blows the lid off Pandora's Box. "What happened to your family after that?"

"My mom says she didn't sue because she had enough on her plate with us kids to take care of. I wouldn't let her out of my sight. I used to get so nervous if she didn't come back when she said she would."

"Does she know you're here now?"

"Not yet. First, I needed to get clear in my own head. I appreciate your talking to me. I think I can call her now."

I hand Reginald the telephone and head to the nurses' station.

"Hey, Laurie," says Marta, one of the Filipina staff nurses. Her hands are full of clean linens.

"I'm done with the lady in 18-2. You going to see her now? She's here from ICU last night. A truck hit her motorcycle last week. Looks confused, you know? She's got a skull fracture, pelvic fractures, orbital fracture, and a crushed cheekbone. That's why I won't let my kid get a motorcycle."

Melinda Grayson thrashes her head from side to side in her hospital bed. Her tattooed arms are tied down because she has been monkeying with the external fixator, a steel contraption that immobilizes her pelvis and maintains her bones in proper alignment while they heal.

"Can you tell me where you are, Ms. Grayson?"

"I'm at DV8," she says referring to a trendy downtown night-club.

Maybe she was on her way there when the truck hit her.

"Do you know what month it is?"

"No."

"How about the season?"

"Spring?" she ventures.

"Actually, it's already July. What about the year?"

"1985," she says with a tone of authority.

"No, Ms. Grayson, it's 1992 and you are at San Francisco General Hospital. You were hit by a truck and have some fractures but you'll be okay."

She squirms on the bed, pulling against the restraints. "Spiders," she whispers. "I'm afraid of spiders."

"Are you in pain?" I ask. She nods vigorously. I check her vital signs: pulse, respiration, and blood pressure are all elevated.

Attempting a psychiatric interview with someone in pain is futile. In addition, Melinda appears to be withdrawing from drugs. I check her chart for a history of alcohol, heroin, speed, cocaine, and the like. With any luck, they did a toxic screen on admission. Or, the problem may be iatrogenic, something we've caused. Janice and Antionette warned me that sometimes patients who have spent weeks in the ICU receiving high doses of intravenous Fentanyl for pain and Ativan for agitation are tapered off these drugs too rapidly. Not uncommonly, a couple of days after being transferred from the ICU to a floor where less acute care is required, some patients start experiencing symptoms of withdrawal: anxiety, irritability, disorientation, and the sensation that bugs are crawling over them. After flipping through her chart and finding a clean toxic screen, I compare Melinda's present doses of pain medication and sedative to what she was receiving in the ICU two days ago. Sure enough, they halved both doses instead of tapering her dosage more slowly.

I call JoEllen, the pain nurse consultant, and run the case by her. She agrees with my assessment and outlines a more graduated medication schedule. Then I call Melinda's orthopedic resident. After explaining how I came to be involved in the case, I describe Melinda's symptoms and make my suggestion.

He hesitates, "Who did you say you were again?"

"I'm a psychiatric nurse consultant on the psych liaison service. JoEllen is the pain nurse consultant. Would you prefer to get a consultation from one of the psychiatrists?" I ask.

"No," he says quickly. "Let me call you back in a minute."

I know that he's checking with his senior resident. Antionette and Janice told me that the surgical and orthopedic residents at SFGH hate to ask for psychiatric consults. In their eyes, this guarantees a longer hospital stay and more work for them. After a few minutes, the young doctor calls me back and gives me the OK to change the order. Apparently, even the indignity of a nurse recommending medication changes is preferable to getting a psychiatrist involved in the case. I'll check in with Melinda again later when her delirium has cleared.

Antionette, Janice, and I try to use lunchtime for "peer supervision." Two wide windows offering views of the parking lot and freeway help make our cramped office tolerable. Over salad, sandwiches, and yogurt, we check in, review our patients, and offer suggestions to each other about difficult treatment issues. Since I'm new, they want to hear how it is going for me. I tell them about Rose's run-in with her nurse.

"I spoke with Esperanza once before when I noticed she had been short-tempered with a patient," says Janice. "She told me that in addition to sending money to relatives in the Philippines, she's the sole support of her two children, her alcoholic husband, and her parents who live with her. She also works two full-time jobs. I think the stress is catching up with her."

My graduate school professor would say this is an example of diagnosing the whole consultation, not just the piece that involves the patient. Maybe when I get to know Esperanza a little better, I'll be able to talk with her about the stress in her life.

Moving on, I tell them about how thugs beat Reginald with baseball bats and how a nervous cop killed his father years before. "Life just isn't fair. That's what I keep thinking when I hear these stories. It just isn't fair."

Janice nods. "When you hear what some people have been through, it really seems like they were born under a dark cloud."

I scrape the bottom of my blueberry yogurt. "I feel bad saying this, but working at Presbyterian, I forgot about how really shitty life is for a lot of people."

Antionette opens a bag of low-salt pretzels and offers them to Janice and me. "I remember feeling shocked too," she says and I recall that Antionette worked at Presbyterian Hospital on a medical unit before going to graduate school in psych nursing and ending up at SFGH. "Now, I almost expect my patients to be drug addicts with histories of abuse and neglect."

"I've worked here too long to remember anything different," sighs Janice.

"So can we refer patients like Rose or Reginald to an outpatient psych clinic? Both of them could use some therapy."

Janice smiles at my naiveté. "All of our patients could use therapy. When I tried referring someone to a community psychiatry clinic, someone who wasn't about to jump off a bridge and wasn't floridly psychotic, they laughed at me. The resources just aren't there."

"So where do I refer my trauma patients?"

"Good question." Janice sips her Diet Pepsi before answering.

"Because SFGH is a Level One trauma center and all serious trauma patients are treated here, some of your patients will have private insurance that pays for short-term therapy. These days no insurance company covers long-term therapy. Then it's a matter of finding therapists with experience and training specific to trauma, which isn't easy."

She motions for me to wait while she bites into a turkey sandwich.

"A few psychiatrists and other therapists will take Medi-Cal patients but that number is dwindling because of the low reimbursement rates and the hassle of dealing with mounds of paperwork. Our uninsured patients are on their own. Training programs would see them on a sliding scale, but none is located near where most of our patients live. Since mobility is a problem for trauma patients, they rarely get treated."

"Welcome to "The General," says Antionette, offering me more pretzels. "By the way, the motto here is 'SFGH: As Real As It Gets.'"

During the afternoon, I evaluate a middle-aged pedestrian who was creamed by a drunk driver and a psychologist who broke a leg and a wrist in a biking accident and seems far more interested in being a referral source for me than being a patient. Before leaving for the day, I revisit Rose and hand her the phone number to a mental health training program. Her resourcefulness will help her to find her way there if need be.

"Do you have children?" she asks as I am about to leave.

Although it goes against everything psychiatry has taught me, I answer her question. This is not the time to be asking about her fantasies of my family and me. This is not psychotherapy.

"My daughter, Corianne, is four and my son, Danny, is eight months."

"You must be a good mother," she says, "because you are a kind person."

Then her eyes well up with tears and spill over. "Do you know that to this day, all I ever really wanted was to have a mom who hugged me and asked me, 'How was your day, honey?'"

She sniffles and manages a crooked smile at the same time.

"Could you hug me before you go?"

I have mixed feelings about it, but I hug her briefly. I don't know what my hug means to her, but I know that no amount of hugs can fill the void in a motherless child.

I park my car in front of my daughter's preschool and take a few moments to collect the day's images before putting them to rest. Closing my eyes, I visualize my patients resting comfortably in bed while I walk from room to room, waving goodbye to each of them. Then I take a couple of deep breaths and feel my body relax. Soon, Corianne will run into my arms—relieved that I have not abandoned her— and we will hold each other close. I will say, as I always do, 'How was your day, honey?' only this time I will be thinking of Rose Manalo, who yearned to hear these words from her own mother, and never did.

3

Beginnings

My mother loves to tell the story of how I beat up Ross, the neighborhood bully, when I was four. "You lowered your head, ran toward him, and butted him in the stomach, knocking the air right out of him. When his mother called me to complain I asked her, 'Aren't you embarrassed that my four-year-old daughter beat up your six-year-old son?'" Every time my mother tells the story, she laughs.

What my mother never knew was that before I attacked Ross, he had been teasing my sister. She was two years older than I was, shy and delicate whereas I was bold and sturdily built. The more Ross teased her, the angrier I got until something exploded in my chest and sent me hurtling toward him. It would be twenty years before I would feel that kind of propulsive anger again, the second time in response to an unfaithful boyfriend. In the interim, anger became jumbled with guilt, shame, and sadness, and all but disappeared from my consciousness.

My parents met in New York City in the late 1940s when my mother was working as a registered nurse at Montefiore Hospital and my father was completing his master's degree in social work. One of her patients introduced them. On the surface, they shared a lot: both were young and attractive, bright and ambitious. Poor, uneducated Eastern-European Jewish immigrants in loveless marriages, their parents had barely scraped by during the Great Depression. After a brief courtship, my parents married in 1949 and moved to Connecticut where my father worked as a social worker and took classes toward a doctorate degree while my mother took care of patients on a medical-surgical floor. Two years later, pregnant with my older sister, she enrolled in a natural childbirth program—one of the first of its kind—at Yale New Haven Hospital. Although her pregnancy was uneventful, when labor began, my mother developed toxemia. In addition, the baby was in breech position—feet first. After more than twenty-four hours of labor, my sister was delivered by Caesarian section.

According to my mother, Leslie's developmental milestones were delayed and when she finally started to walk, one foot crossed over the other. Two years later, I was born; our brother arrived four years after me.

When I was five, my parents left our extended families in the Northeast and moved us to Arizona. My mother was especially devoted to my sister. I spent a lot of time reading, riding my bike, drawing, climbing trees, and training my dog to do tricks.

As the director of the Jewish Community Center, my father was well known in the community and made many public appearances. He was voted "best instructor" multiple times at the community college where he taught "Human Sexuality" and "Marriage and the Family." He hosted a local television show in which he interviewed couples in troubled marriages and was featured in several newspaper articles about family issues. On Friday nights, my father often invited company over to our house for Shabbat dinner. Even though my mother was working full-time teaching eighth grade civics, she managed to get a delicious home-cooked meal on the table by the time company arrived. After dinner, while my father smoked a pipe and held forth on topics of the day, my mother scurried around picking up dishes and putting out coffee and dessert. Although she had a master's degree in English literature, she ceded the floor to my father. When the company left, he went to bed and she stayed up cleaning the kitchen.

I never saw my father cry and he rarely raised his voice.

"Only dogs get mad," he would tell us. Of course, we knew when he was angry by the way he jutted his jaw forward, minced his words, and over-pronounced his words in a pitch slightly higher than usual. At our house, anger was to be checked at the door like backpacks in a record store. Once inside, only classical music was allowed. No fighting, screaming, or otherwise ugly sounds of unhappiness were tolerated. Embedded in my memory is the one occasion when my brother slammed his bedroom door.

Following my father's example, I banished anger from my consciousness and expressed my feelings through art and music: pounding the piano; attacking the cello; drawing crazy pictures of long-limbed dancers, their faces hidden by a tangle of hair, their bodies covered in tattoos. I wrote horror stories about runaway merry-go-rounds and odd, orphaned girls, and I sang my heart out while playing Barbara Streisand records.

I wished I could be as cool as my father was. Once while we were eating dinner, one of his psychotherapy patients called to say that she was about to swallow a handful of pills. My father's voice remained calm as he asked her a few questions and listened carefully to her responses. Then he spoke in a gentle tone: "I can hear how terribly frustrated and alone you must feel right now. I'd like to help you. The first thing we have to do is to get you to a safe place."

After a few minutes of negotiation, she agreed to meet my father at an emergency room. I remember thinking at the time that I wanted to be like him—a person who knows the right words to say, a person who helps other people.

Although my parents never yelled or criticized each other in our presence, in sixth or seventh grade, it dawned on me that they didn't tease or nuzzle each other in the way my best friend's parents did. I knew that I was partially to blame. My mother had often criticized me for dominating my father's time when he came home from work. To remedy that, I convinced my sister and brother to pool our allowances for as long as it took to buy a bicycle-built-for-two. On their next anniversary, we proudly presented them with a shiny red tandem bike. After an uncomfortable silence, they thanked us for the thought but declined to take it for a spin. They did not ride it the next day or the next. Soon I understood that they would never ride it together. The following year, when my mother asked me how I would feel if she and my father were to divorce, I registered no surprise.

"You should do what's best for you," I said. I don't remember feeling one way or the other about it. Maybe I had already learned to be "cool" like my father.

Because they wanted to do what was best for us, my parents didn't separate until my brother graduated from high school. I often wondered if their friends knew that their marriage was in trouble. On the outside, they looked so good: my father, movie-star handsome with a perennial tan, broad shoulders, and a muscular build; my mother, pretty and petite with an ample bosom and shapely legs. They attended my father's work-related functions together and regularly dressed up for cocktail parties. On a few occasions, they went to Las Vegas with friends to see Frank Sinatra and the Rat Pack. In the '50s and early '60s when divorce was uncommon and people didn't openly discuss unpleasant things like cancer or homosexuality, they kept their discord to themselves.

The summer after the tandem bicycle fiasco, I was particularly anxious to return to music camp in Flagstaff, Arizona. I had been playing cello, my father's favorite instrument, for three years. As we drove through the desert in July and climbed high enough into the foothills north of the city to see the first scrub pines, I felt a flush of excitement. When the air turned cool and the pine trees grew tall, my heart quickened. After arriving in Flagstaff and a lunch of sopapillas and tamales, my parents helped me settle into my dorm at Northern Arizona University. My mother, certain that I would begin my period during those two weeks, reminded me that she had tucked everything I would need into a corner of my suitcase. They kissed me goodbye and the car doors slammed shut. Their car turned toward home and I let my hair down. For two whole weeks, I experienced a delirious freedom. I was loud and raucous and flirted with boys who attended sports camp on the other side of the campus. Of course, I was still a good kid and this was still music camp where I played cello four to five hours a day, but to me it was heaven. At night, my friends and I attended concerts, watched movies, and went to dances. After one dance, I made out with a cute trombone player with turquoise eyes whose kisses made my body shiver and left me breathless.

I took my first singing classes that summer. Our teacher taught us how to breathe in by expanding our diaphragms, not our chests. To demonstrate breath control, he put a lit candle up to his lips and sang. The candle barely flickered. Then he passed it around the room for each of us to try. Outside of class, I worked on "If I Loved You," a soaring ballad of secret longing from *Carousel* that spoke to my heart. When I hit the high note at full blast, something in me opened up, a new sensation that made me feel alive and energized and giddy with pleasure. Although I played cello to please my father, I sang to please myself.

Ballet West, a dance company from Utah, was in residence at the Flagstaff Summer Music Festival, which coincided with camp. As often as I could, I slipped into the theater to watch their rehearsals and sketch the dancers. Sometimes I came early when the dancers were warming up, wearing leggings like elite racehorses. As the rehearsal director clapped his hands and counted, "one-stretch-two-deeper-three-hold-four-release," the dancers moaned and grimaced. I loved watching rehearsals more than the actual performance, witnessing how sequences of steps slowly became a fluid whole, how the director made small but significant corrections to the angle of a wrist or the arch of a neck. During one performance, I was allowed to sit backstage in the wings against the wall, out of everyone's way. At the end of his magnificent solo, the male lead leapt offstage toward me with his chest out and his arms extended. While the audience clapped madly, he yelled, "Shit!" in mid-air before crumbling to the floor in front of me. Two young male dancers rushed to his side with an oxygen tank, which he sucked as if inhaling life itself. After they pulled him to his feet, he inhaled more oxygen, puffed out his chest and strutted on stage for a round of bows. Upon his return, he collapsed again. This time when he had recovered enough to stand, the two young dancers supported his body as he limped toward the dressing room, the sound of thunderous applause still in the background. This scene remained alive within me because it captured what I knew to be the truth about my family and myself: that our public faces were very different from our private ones and that anguish lay underneath each polished performance.

After two short weeks, the high note of music camp ended when my parents came to pick me up. Over the next four hours, through the open window of my father's Rambler, the only car in Arizona without air conditioning, I watched as the tall green pines gave way to the scruffy high desert with its occasional Palo Verde tree and prickly spines of cholla and saguaro cactus. After we crossed the mountains that ring the city, the air felt like race-car exhaust. It would feel that way until the thunderstorms of late August washed it clean.

Beginnings

When high school began, I carried on as usual with my school-work, practicing piano and cello, singing and drawing. Every Sunday morning, my father drove me to my cello teacher's home for a lesson. During the forty-five minute trip, we listened to classical music and talked about the waste of young lives in Vietnam, his work with Mexican farm laborers, the classes he taught at the junior college, and sometimes, his patients.

"People are fascinating," he would say before presenting a case. I remember him telling me about a man with "sexual hang-ups"—the result of growing up with punitive, ultra-religious parents. Another time he described a young woman with poor self-esteem who always managed to find abusive boyfriends. He told me how prevalent the incidence of childhood sexual abuse was among his female clients and even some males, and how it affected them as adults. If he were working with a teenage girl, he would ask what I thought might be troubling her and what approach he should take. My father's attention made me feel valued and grown-up, but it also caused me to feel increasingly distanced from my mother.

"It's going to be hard for any man to compete with your father," my mother once said after he surprised me with an expensive opal and diamond ring for my sixteenth birthday. She was right. Throughout high school, I worshipped my father and ignored boys my own age.

I graduated from high school a half-year early and a few months shy of my seventeenth birthday. (Ever since my parents had mistakenly enrolled me in kindergarten instead of nursery school, I had been the youngest in my class.) Too young to leave home, in their view, I attended the local junior college. More than anything, I wanted to achieve financial independence from my parents as soon as possible. Lacking confidence in my musical and artistic abilities and needing distance from my family, I decided to transfer my credits to the School of Nursing at Boston University. I knew that my mother had been a nurse before she returned to school to become a teacher. She didn't tell me stories about her patients except for one about a two-year-old who died after choking on a peanut. After telling me this, she sighed deeply, shook her head, and said, "Some things you never forget."

Nursing school and I were not a good fit. I loathed the conformity of the dress code, the constant need to consult the clock, the bickering among nurses, the required obsessive-compulsiveness of charting—everything but listening to patients talk about their fears and concerns and for that, there seemed to be little time. During the summer between my junior and senior year, I called my parents and told them that a stained glass artist I had met in the Berkshires had agreed to take me on as an apprentice.

"Just get your degree," they counseled. "Then you can do what you want."

Reluctantly, I listened. During the second semester of senior year when I was assigned to Boston State Hospital for my psychiatric rotation, I finally found my place in nursing. Maureen, my on-site clinical instructor, was an older woman with bleached blond hair. She looked and sounded like she'd been swigging cheap vodka since her student days. She assigned me to work with a nineteen-year-old male diagnosed with depression and paranoia. He had been hospitalized after threatening to jump off a building. The "precipitating event" was his brother's suicide six months earlier.

Maureen told me that the only way to circumvent paranoia was to "go for the affect," meaning his emotions. She cautioned that this might be difficult since the patient came from an Irish-American family where both parents were alcoholics.

"Kids who grow up in these families learn that feelings are dangerous," she said.

I learned the same thing in my non-alcoholic Jewish family.

With Maureen's coaching, I asked Sean about his relationship with his parents and his brother, "going for the affect" whenever the opportunity presented itself but not having much luck. One day, weeks into my rotation while we were walking on the grounds together, Sean told me about the night his older brother went raving mad and destroyed their home while Sean hid in the basement. Sean knew his brother had problems but didn't know how serious they were until that night.

"You must have been so scared," I said.

"Yeah," he said. "I thought he might kill me."

"That's why you hid in the basement?"

"Yeah."

Big silence. I was stuck. I was taught that my every utterance had to be "therapeutic" not just conversational. When the silence occurred, we were sitting on a wooden bench under a maple tree. Above us, squirrels chattered and chased each other up and down the branches. When Sean looked up, his face suddenly clouded over.

"What is it?" I asked.

Sean shook his head and looked away, but I could see his chin quiver.

"Sean, something just made you feel bad. I can see it in your face. You might feel better if you talk about it."

After an interminable silence, he cleared his voice.

"A long time after the noise stopped, I was still afraid to come out of the basement. Then there was banging on the door — the police." Sean closed his eyes while his whole body trembled.

"They found my brother hanging from a tree in the park."

I was terrified of what Sean would do next. No one else was around. What if he went crazy on me? I sat there with him while his body heaved and shuddered and his voice made high-pitched choking sounds. When it was over and he was calm, we walked back to his unit. I knew that something important had happened and couldn't wait to tell Maureen.

"OK," she smiled. "Now that he's in touch with his feelings, you need to help him identify them and manage the intensity of them.

Reassure him that feelings don't kill people and that putting them into words will make him feel better because he will have more control over his actions."

Over the next few weeks, I did what Maureen said. Using the "therapeutic communication" techniques she had taught us, I helped Sean talk about his guilt, shame, and anger. On the last day of our rotation, during community meeting with students, patients, and staff all sitting in a circle, Sean told the group that he felt "released" even though he was still a patient in a mental hospital. When someone asked him what he meant, he said that after crying for the first time in a long while, he felt "freed up" inside.

From that moment, I was hooked. Knowing I helped someone made me feel better than I had ever felt in my whole life. "Being with" Sean in his suffering — witnessing and appreciating his pain — helped to crack open the frightening and lonely world into which he had retreated. I wanted to know more about that world, and how to help people like Sean. As an added bonus, maybe I would learn more about myself in the process.

4

"It ain't right"

Graciella is already ten minutes late this morning. Oh well. At least it gives me a few minutes extra to wipe Danny's drool off my shoulder and to slap on some lipstick. With the exception of three minutes allotted for a mommy shower and two minutes for throwing on work clothes, Danny has remained affixed to my hip all morning, even as I put dishes into the dishwasher. Brian tried to spell me before he left for work but Danny refused to budge. When Corianne tried to share my lap during breakfast, he squawked and grabbed her hair. She responded by letting Danny know he is fast wearing out his welcome.

I remind Corianne that it's dance day at Little Bear School and to put her leotard in her backpack. Then I hear Graciella opening the front door. *Thank-you, God.* I can't wait to be at work where I can use the bathroom in private, eat lunch sitting down without interruption, and have grown-up conversations all day.

After Graciella pries Danny off me, Corianne and I run out the door. But, Danny's screams grab hold of my heart and I stop on the steps unsure what to do. Part of me wants to run back up the stairs, prostrate myself on the floor, and promise to never leave him. I wait for a moment, hoping to hear his cries diminish.

"Come on, Mommy," says Corianne. "Graciella says he stops crying as soon as we leave." She's right, but I wonder if I will ever be able to feel OK about leaving my kids to go to work. Although I don't envy Brian the long hours he works each week as an attorney, I know that he never wrestles with this feeling because we depend on his salary. I work because I have always worked and because I cannot imagine not being a nurse. It's what I love to do.

At Little Bear School, Corianne finds her best friend and lets me off easy with a hug and a kiss. She's a big girl now, almost ready for kindergarten. She has her daddy's straight dark hair and my olive skin. Her dark brown eyes come from her grandfathers. My sister would say that her bossiness comes from me.

The General does not have an employee parking lot. Last week, an intern dressed in blue scrubs was pistol-whipped in the neighborhood behind the hospital where I usually park. This morning, I park in a residential neighborhood in front of the hospital, closer to the lobby entrance.

Just outside the lobby doors, a skinny white guy with straggly hair, bad skin, and darting eyes paces the sidewalk while sucking on a nub of cigarette. Closer to the lobby doors, a platinum blond dressed in a purple caftan sits in a wheelchair looking into a mirror. A Veronica Lake wave of hair obscures a quarter of her face. It's 9 a.m., and although she's tarted up like a newly painted Victorian façade, the generously applied layer of pancake foundation can't quite hide the dark cloud of beard gathering on her jaw line. Seated opposite Veronica, an elderly black man with watery eyes inhales deeply on a cigarette and releases a curl of smoke. Then he erupts into a cacophony of wheezes and sputters that nearly jostle his slight frame off the concrete bench where he's sitting. When his body recovers, he pulls out a folded white handkerchief, wipes his face, and drags on his cigarette again.

"It ain't right"

Two seven-story masses of concrete contain the main hospital. My neighbor, an architect and designer, told me it was built in the 1970s in a style called "Brutalism." The tower to the left houses administrative offices, clinics, and the outpatient pharmacy. The medical emergency department and the psychiatric emergency department inhabit the first floor of the other tower. Above them are the medical-surgical inpatient units. Four inpatient psychiatric units crown the top of the building.

The lobby gives me the creeps. Devoid of natural light, it feels airless and dank. Plastic plants stick out of plastic planters connected to single-seated plastic chairs. Most of the seats in the lobby have cushions. Some even have backs but they have been arranged such that people cannot possibly sleep on them.

At Presbyterian Hospital, where I worked before my position became a casualty of a merger, the sunlit lobby features a supersized impressionistic oil painting of a garden in full spring bloom. Real plants stretch toward the light and filter the air. It is carpeted and clean. Comfortable couches allow for rest and contemplation. This is not to say that the patient rooms at Presbyterian are similarly enlightened. In fact, for the most part they look very much like those at SFGH—sterile and crowded with gadgetry. Still, Presbyterian did manage to get the lobby right.

Toward the end of trauma rounds on 4D, Trudy places a hand on my back and whispers, "Do you have time for a little crisis intervention?"

"Of course!" I say. "Nothing like a little crisis intervention to start the day. I'm already getting a rush!"

Trudy gives me my payoff—a disapproving smile—and tells me about Hope, a young woman who fell two floors at a rave party and fractured her left arm and leg.

"The trauma team was just in to see her and she's been sobbing ever since."

When I enter the room, Hope is propped up in a semi-sitting position. Her eyes are closed and she is hyperventilating. Then, as if attacked by a swarm of killer bees, she claws her face with frenzied fingertips.

"Hope, stop! You are hurting yourself!"

Is she psychotic or is she detoxing from something?

"Here," I say placing a pillow on her lap. "Squeeze this instead of your skin."

Hope grabs the pillow and bashes it into her head repeatedly.

When she loses steam, I ask her to slow her breathing.

"That's better. Now take a deep breath in, hold it, and let it go slowly. Good."

Jesus Christ, there are scars up and down her arms like tiger stripes.

"Now another deep breath in."

Looks like old cigarette burns on her hand. "This time as you breathe out slowly, feel your shoulder muscles relax. That's it. Now let air in and fill your lungs as much as you can... Good. Now relax your neck muscles and breathe out slowly..."

Ten minutes later, Hope, a chubby, baby-faced twenty-three year-old with hair the color of straw, tells me she fell from a swing in the warehouse where the party took place.

"It's hard enough not to be able to move," she whispers, "but then they treated me like that."

"Who did?"

"The doctors. They barge in and lift up my nightgown like I'm a mannequin, not a person."

I hand Hope a tissue for her tears. "Then they talked over me and I couldn't understand if what they were saying was good or bad."

Does the trauma residency program make a point of ruling out candidates with good social skills?

"God, I'm so weird." Hope squeezes her eyes shut and crinkles her nose as if she's smelled something offensive. Then she beats her chest with a fist.

"Hope," I say sharply to interrupt the self-flagellation, "It might help if you breathe again."

After a few more minutes of deep and controlled breathing, Hope relaxes. "Sometimes I wake up in the middle of the night hyperventilating. I get so scared. And, sometimes, I do feel like a mannequin. Like I can't move or feel anything."

Tears begin to spill onto her ample cheeks. "Like this morning. Oh, I can't deal with this! I'm so sorry!"

"It's OK. You don't have to deal with it now."

Hope tells me she began psychotherapy after breaking up with her boyfriend on New Year's Eve but stopped therapy after a few months because she didn't like talking about her family.

"After that, I joined a gym and worked out every day. I was starting to feel better when this happened. Why is it that when my life seems to go right, I find a way to mess it up?"

Hope breaks into tears again. I wait until she has composed herself. At the end of our session, I encourage her to think about going back into therapy.

When I return to the trauma unit, I write a treatment plan in Hope's chart and show it to Trudy who will make sure Hope's nurses are aware of it. The plan stipulates that no more than two physicians may come into Hope's room at a time. A female staff member must be present when she is examined. They must ask Hope's permission to touch her and they must make a reasonable attempt to respect her modesty. Trudy agrees and says she will also make sure each team of physicians sees the plan as well.

Although Ruby mentioned in rounds that I would need an interpreter to see Mr. Rodriguez, a man who was assaulted during a grocery store robbery, I didn't realize that I needed to book one in advance. When I call the service, they promise to send someone as soon as possible but as the situation is not an emergency, it may be awhile.

Waiting for the interpreter to arrive, I review the symptom checklist on the trauma evaluation questionnaire. The list is divided into three groups of symptoms: those associated with re-experiencing the trauma such as flashbacks and nightmares; those that have to do with avoidance like feeling emotionally numb and detached; and symptoms of hyperarousal such as shortness of breath, startling easily, being unable to concentrate, and having difficulty sleeping. I will also need to get a trauma history and do a mental status exam to determine if I'm dealing with a sane person with a sound mind.

The interpreter arrives. He's a Latino man in his fifties with deep lines in his handsome face. I brief him on the kinds of questions I will ask Mr. Rodriguez. As Francisco listens, his brows furrow more deeply causing the pinched folds of skin between them to look like a fan.

While I am conducting my interview with Mr. Rodriguez, his wife enters the room and sits next to her husband. Dressed in a bright floral print skirt, she listens intently to my questions as interpreted by Francisco, and to her husband's responses. When I ask about his history of previous trauma, he shrugs. In halting, heavily accented English, Mrs. Rodriguez tells me that thirteen years ago, Raoul endured months of torture in El Salvador.

"He has many scars on his body and in his mind. Many times, he has bad dreams and wakes up screaming," she says while rubbing his hand.

I do not ask more about the torture. I'm not sure that I can bear hearing the details, or that it will serve him well to reopen those memories at this time. But, through Francisco, I suggest that he consider talking to a therapist in order to lay his demons to rest. Mr. Rodriguez waves me off but his wife asks if I can recommend someone. I tell her I will try to get him a referral.

After the interview, Francisco and I walk wordlessly to the nurses' station. The idea of torture has shocked me into silence. My mind simply won't imagine that dark corner of humanity. When I look up, I notice Francisco wiping his eyes.

"Someday maybe I will talk to you about my life in Guatemala, about my nightmares." He turns away and walks off the unit before I remember to thank him for his service.

When he leaves, I remember a patient I haven't thought about for a long time. During my training on a medical/surgical ward in Boston, one of my patients was a petite French Jew in her early fifties with flowing silver hair and a blue number tattooed on her forearm. Whenever I checked on her, she took my hand in both of hers and smiled at me with tears in her eyes. Perhaps my Semitic looks reminded her of someone who didn't survive. A doctor told me that Josef Mengele had performed experiments on her in Auschwitz. I did not ask for details and did not want to know.

I learned about the Holocaust when I was nine. My father called me into the den one night to watch the documentary, *Let My People Go,* on TV.

"I think you're old enough to see this now," he said. The image of emaciated corpses stacked in large piles about to be bulldozed into a mass grave became forever seared into my memory. He told me he had witnessed a similar scene when his army unit liberated the Ohrdruf concentration camp in Germany, the same one that General Eisenhower toured.

After learning about the Holocaust, I read *The Diary of Anne Frank* and the gruesome, *Black Book of Polish Jewry* in my father's bookcase, which contained the now familiar scenes of emaciated

corpses and pictures of elderly Jews forced to clean the streets with
their tongues. I asked my father how this could have happened. How
could people be so cruel? Looking for answers, I compulsively read
books and watched movies about the Holocaust until I burned out
and avoided the subject altogether.

My rabbi says that the American Jewish community could not
talk about the Holocaust for 20 years following the end of the war.
How could words do justice to such injustice? I wonder if this is why
Mr. Rodriguez waved me away when I spoke to him about psychotherapy. From everything I know about psychiatry and from what I've
read about treating trauma, telling the story—the process of putting
events and feelings into words—heals the soul by imposing order on
internal chaos.

In the nurses' station, I call a community mental health clinic
and ask to speak with Dr. Membrano, a Chilean psychiatrist with
whom I used to work. He understands human suffering. In the few
minutes he has between patients, I tell him about Mr. Rodriguez. He
takes Mr. Rodriguez's phone number and thanks me for my call, saying he will think about who might be the best person to work with
the patient. When I see Francisco again, perhaps I'll suggest that he
call Dr. Membrano as well.

While I'm in the nurses' station with Trudy, Ruby materializes
from a patient's room and yawns a hello.

"I'm beat," she explains. "I've been in the emergency room since
six this morning. There was a bad accident on 280. You'll be seeing a
few of the survivors tomorrow, I'm sure."

Like me, Ruby is in her late thirties. Her green eyes reflect all
that she has seen during years of caring for trauma patients.

Before I can say anything, Ruby grabs my hand. "I heard what
happened to Hope this morning and I want to apologize. I wish I'd
been there to intervene. I'll be bringing it up at this week's trauma-
service staff meeting."

"It ain't right"

The next morning, I arrive early enough to see Hope before medical rounds.

"There is no excuse for what happened to you yesterday," I tell her. "Sometimes people forget what it's like to be a patient, how vulnerable and scary it can be."

A pained look reappears on Hope's face.

"And since you can't avoid being examined by physicians, I want to teach you some ways to better cope with it."

To ensure that we are not interrupted, I post a sign on her door that reads, "Relaxation Exercise in Progress. Do Not Disturb."

Ten minutes into our session, tall blond Fred Murdock and a troop of medical students barge through the door. *Hasn't anyone spoken to him about Hope's care plan?* Ignoring me, he addresses his underlings. "This patient fell and injured..."

"Excuse me, but we're in the middle of a session," I say, keeping my voice as even as possible.

"We'll only be a few minutes," he replies, adjusting his stethoscope.

Since Murdock has not made eye contact with me, I stand up. Not that it helps much since he is a foot taller than I am.

"Sorry, but we need more time. You'll need to come back later."

I've taught the class on assertiveness for nurses many times and I know it's important to remain calm but firm.

Murdock ignores me and moves further into the room, close to Hope's bed.

Hey asshole, what pig farm did you run away from?

I struggle to keep my voice controlled even though I raise it a few decibels.

"Excuse me but you're interrupting a session. You need to leave right now!"

A look of contempt tells me that I have finally communicated my message.

"And exactly how much time do you need?" he asks, squeezing out each word.

"Twenty minutes."

"I see. And who are you anyway?"

I tell him. He regards me for an extra long second or two before herding his entourage away from Hope's room.

"Wow," says Hope, gripping the covers that are pulled up to her chin. "That was something."

"Yes, and it shouldn't have happened."

I am aware of needing to temper my anger in front of a patient. "I'm so sorry, Hope. I thought I had communicated better with the staff than I apparently did."

Hope touches my wrist lightly. "What I meant was how you stood your ground. I could never do that."

"I couldn't have either when I was your age."

"Really?"

"Really."

"How did you learn?"

"To tell you the truth, it took me five years of therapy to learn to stand up for myself instead of always trying to please other people."

"Five years!"

"Yeah. I started when I was your age. One year seemed like a lifetime to me back then too. But it was the best thing I ever did for myself."

Hope looks crestfallen. "My therapist wanted me to talk about my family. I couldn't do it. I don't want to think about them."

"Therapy is hard. I worked on a psych unit once where there was a sign that said, 'THE STRUGGLE IS THE TREATMENT.' It's true. Sometimes you have to fight against yourself to get healthy. But in the end, it's so worth it."

Hope does not look convinced.

I take a break in the nurses' lounge and review my encounter with Fred Murdock. At heart, I hate conflict. When, on principle, I can't avoid it, something inside me rallies the troops. Afterward, even when the mission is accomplished, I feel my body sag like it's doing right now.

When my composure returns, I leave the lounge for the nurses' station where I look for Mr. Rodriguez's name on the dry erase board. Not finding it, I check the transfer/discharge list near the chart rack only to find that Mr. Rodriguez was sent home this morning. That was fast!

At first, I liked that my patients rarely stayed for more than a week. That way, I reasoned, I could preserve my emotional energy for my young family. Now it seems like something is missing. Patients are discharged as soon as they can walk or use crutches, which may be before their wounds or incisions have healed. The nurses don't have the time to teach patients what they need to know about possible complications to surgery and the uses and side effects of prescribed medications. I often don't have an opportunity to follow up with patients after my initial evaluation. What happens to them at home? How will they adjust to disability? What if they develop post-traumatic stress disorder? Who will they talk to? Unbelievably, SFGH doesn't have a psychiatric outpatient clinic.

Walking down a long hallway a few minutes before our department's staff meeting is to begin, I come upon a Chinese-American social worker listening to a tall, thin, African-American patient in his thirties with a cast on his right arm. The social worker's hands are clasped on his potbelly. He looks down at the floor.

"You can't do this to me, man," the patient fumes. "It ain't right."

"Sorry, but that is all I can do for you," says the social worker. He turns away and hurries down the hall.

The patient pounds the wall once with his good fist and swears under his breath. Then he snorts in exasperation and leans his head against the wall. I approach him with caution, making sure to leave him a lot of personal space.

"Excuse me sir, but are you OK?"

His eyes pinpoint my ID badge.

"My social worker say I don't need the hospital no more. Ain't no beds in respite so I'm out on the street. Know what that means?"

I shake my head.

"On the street, you predator or you prey. With this cast, baby, I'm prey. Can you help me out?"

I'm brought up short. I've never heard of discharging patients to the street. Something must be wrong. "Wait here a minute."

I run back to the unit and grab Trudy. She cringes but nods her head. "That social worker would be Tim. He's been burned out for years. He didn't handle the situation very well but what he said is true. We have no place for this patient to go. He's ready to leave the acute care hospital and there are no beds in the city's facility for respite care. We may be able to give him a week in a fleabag hotel but then he's on his own. He says he has no family who can help. All you can do is send him to social services on the first floor."

I want to say to him, "Surely there is someone in this world who cares about you." But, he is not my patient and I refrain. Instead I repeat what Trudy told me. For an instant, his shoulders slump and his head bows. Then he gathers himself up and walks toward the exit. Midway he stops and calls back, "Thanks for trying."

What has this world come to? Discharging patients to the street? I thought things were bad enough in the '80s under Reagan's deinstitutionalization policy when thousands of mentally ill patients were discharged from state mental hospitals. They were supposed to be funneled into community-based treatment programs but since few of these were funded and provisions were not made for stable living situations, most of the patients became homeless. Now, it looks like medical patients have joined the mentally ill and the criminals on the streets.

"It ain't right"

I walk up three flights of stairs and down another long hall to get to the Psychiatric Consultation-Liaison Service meeting on the seventh floor. Waiting for the other members of my department to shuffle in, I wonder what happened to the idea of a "safety net" to protect the unfortunate and the vulnerable. True, there are shelters but patients tell me they are filled with people who scream in the night and others who steal everything that's not being worn.

"Is something wrong, Laurie?" asks Donald, our department chief, when all thirteen of us have gathered around the table.

When I tell them about the man with the broken arm, Barry, one of the psychiatrists, releases an exaggerated sigh of relief. "Oh that! I was worried it was something really serious!"

How am I supposed to take that? Everyone snickers except Antionette and Janice who wear pained half-smiles.

"That's why it's good to have new folks," offers Donald. "They remind us how jaded the rest of us have become."

I look at the people seated around the table — psychiatrists, neuropsychologists, and psych nurses — all nodding in agreement. Where is their outrage? How can we discharge patients to the street? Doesn't that violate our code of ethics? Are they all inured to this? Will I become jaded too?

Later in the meeting, Jared, a psychiatrist in his mid-thirties, announces that he will be leaving The General to work in private practice. He's worked here for three years. A few people wish Jared well. Then it's on to a new topic.

I figured this would be the case. San Francisco psychiatry is so different from my experience working in Boston in the '70s and early '80s. There, where psychoanalytic theory reigned supreme, whenever a nurse, doctor, or mental health worker announced he or she would be leaving, or "terminating" as they called it, much time was spent during staff meetings discussing how this decision came about and how each member of the group felt about it. As the termination date drew closer, people recounted their experiences working with the departing person and the qualities they appreciated about him or her. Toward the end, the focus usually shifted to how the group's dynamics would change in the aftermath of the person's departure.

Once we are walking down the long hall back to our office, I ask Janice if the way the group dealt with Jared's announcement was typical of how the department deals with termination.

"That's as deep as it gets," she says with a hint of nostalgia. "Termination was a big deal where I trained too. But it's not part of the culture here."

Antionette catches up with us from behind. "What do you mean by termination? It sounds so sinister." Antionette worked as a medical-surgical nurse for years before she entered a graduate nursing program in psychiatric nursing. Outside of her student experience, she has never worked on an inpatient psychiatric unit let alone one with a psychoanalytic bent. Janice, on the other hand, has had professional experiences that mirror mine.

Once we're in our office, I explain about termination. "It sounds intense," says Antionette, "and time-consuming."

"It's both those things," says Janice. "A lot of the psychoanalytic stuff was over the top but because it focused on feelings and on the unconscious, we learned to connect how these things played out in relationships and in behaviors."

I couldn't agree more. "No one talks about feelings these days. Psychiatry has abandoned psychodynamics for psychopharmacy. Trainees learn very little about what makes people tick."

During my lunchtime walk through The Comfort Garden, memories of working at McLean Hospital pop into my head. Working there was a life-changing experience for me. At twenty-two, I was the youngest nurse on my unit. The oldest was only in her late thirties.

"It ain't right"

In contrast to my first nursing position on the surgical ICU where I tended to injured bodies, at McLean my job as a psychiatric nurse was to provide support and structure for untethered minds. I worked with patients who were convinced that their rooms were bugged and their food poisoned; people who were furious to have awakened alive and imprisoned after a suicide attempt; and people whose spirits had soared out of the stratosphere or all but disappeared.

Before McLean, I had never used the word "process" as anything but a noun, and a dry one at that. At McLean, the word was routinely used as both a verb and an adjective. At staff process meetings, we processed our feelings about how our patients' issues affected us. These meetings were uncomfortable at first but they taught me a way of communicating that I hadn't learned growing up. When a patient set herself on fire, when a staff member's nose was broken by an angry adolescent, when a nurse with an addiction was caught stealing drugs, and when a psychiatrist was fired for billing sessions that never took place, these meetings provided a sanctum where we could express our feelings.

I wish things were different here. Although I can't help feeling sad that something important and essential has been lost, I know better than to try to change an entrenched culture, especially as a new employee. For now, I will concentrate on helping my patients to process their feelings about being ill or injured.

Before leaving the garden, I stroll among the roses in search of the one with the sweetest perfume. Antoine, the gardener, told me that someone had willed these roses to The Comfort Garden. Many of them are "old roses" with beguiling aromas that have since been sacrificed by breeders wanting to develop larger, shapelier hybrids.

"Isn't the essence of a rose its scent?" I asked Antoine. He agreed and had no explanation other than the American ideal that "bigger is better."

On the way back to the trauma unit, I wonder if psychiatry is going the way of classic roses, sacrificing essence by becoming big business.

At the end of the day, I walk through the dark lobby into the blinding light of late afternoon. "Senorita?" a female voice inquires. Shielding my eyes from the light, I recognize the woman in the brightly colored floral dress as Mr. Rodriguez's wife.

"Muchas gracias por su ayuda," she says. In her limited English, she explains that she has just spent three frustrating hours in the outpatient pharmacy waiting to pick up her husband's medications. "But now I see you and I am happy to tell you good news."

Dr. Membrano, the Chilean psychiatrist whom I contacted, has offered to reduce his rates to treat Mr. Rodriguez for the torture he endured in El Salvador. After many years of refusing to talk about his traumatic past, he now agrees to go to therapy. Hearing this makes my day. I walk to my car humming, "Make Someone Happy." Once in the car, I let loose with the last line, delivering it full throttle like Judy Garland: "Make someone happy, make just one someone happy, and you will be happy too!"

As soon as I arrive at Corianne's school, she shows me the dance steps she learned in class today topping off the demonstration with the splits. When was the last time I stretched my body? Maybe it would help to alleviate the tension in my neck and shoulders that accumulates after a day of listening to my patients' stories.

Climbing up the stairs toward my front door, happy to be home, I think of the man without a home who railed against being turned out onto the street. He and the heaviness of his plight soon give way to joy when I see Danny straining his body away from Graciella's, stretching his chubby arms toward me. When Graciella hands him over, he throws his arms around my neck with surprising ferocity and presses his exuberant body against mine murmuring, "Mama, mama, mama."

I stifle an urge to cry. How could I have left my baby all day? Am I a bad mommy?

After sitting Danny on my bed, I slip out of my work clothes and pull on my sweats. Before I make dinner, all of us stretch out onto the floor and play. I need this time before the next work shift begins to feel my children's vivacious bodies and to draw in the energy of their fresh lives so unburdened by the world's ills. When I pretend to be asleep, Danny crawls over to my head and pushes my eyelids open. I refuse to wake up until he gives me a magic kiss at which point he breaks out into giggles. I carry him upstairs to the kitchen where he plays with pots and pans while I begin dinner.

Sometime between dinner and clean up, I slip back into the day and see Hope hyperventilating and scrubbing her face. It wouldn't surprise me to learn that Hope had been sexually abused as a child like so many of my other patients.

What happens when you are a child and the predator resides in your home?

Sensing my preoccupation, Corianne asks me to put on her favorite music from the *Nutcracker Suite*. We have choreographed a routine to it and she beseeches me to dance my part, which consists of lifting her up while she does the splits in the air and twirling her as she lies across my shoulders, moves that we have expropriated from ice skating competitions we've watched on TV. Danny has pulled himself up to the couch and bounces with glee as Corianne races back and forth across the room during the frenetic Russian Dance.

Looking at Danny's mop of Shirley Temple curls, Irish-white skin and blue-green eyes, I wonder if two children from the same parents could look more different. I pick up the delighted Danny and give him a whirl on the dance floor. In no time, Corianne plants herself in our path and announces that she has figured out a new move for us and that I must put Danny down in order for her to demonstrate it. And so the evening goes until Brian arrives home at eight. He changes out of his work clothes, hugs the kids, and helps himself to the salad, roasted potatoes, and steamed artichokes I've left out for him.

We have a deal. Since Brian values food over sleep, I do my best to keep the kids occupied while he eats dinner in peace. Since I value sleep over food, he allows me a little extra snooze time in the mornings. Neither of us is particularly successful at protecting each other's space and time, but we try.

After dinner, Brian plays with Danny before readying him for bed. I listen outside Danny's room as Brian sings "October Winds," an Irish lullaby he learned from a Clancy Brothers album. With Danny settled in, Brian climbs up to Corianne's loft where she awaits the next Athena story, composed on the spot and loosely based on the labors of Hercules but featuring Athena as a strong-willed and clever young woman.

When it is my turn to cuddle, Corianne switches gears and launches into long-winded depictions of four-year-old female culture at her preschool. She doesn't know what to do because two girls were fighting about who got to sit with her at lunchtime. One girl, Ramona, seems particularly possessive of her. Corianne tells me she does not want to hurt anyone's feelings; she likes both girls but she wants Ramona to back off a bit. We talk about what she might say the next time Ramona gets too possessive. Soon, Corianne loses steam. She finds Po, her stuffed polar bear, and pulls him close. I watch as her breathing grows deep and heavy. She has no idea what a lucky girl she is. In the still darkness, I think about Hope and others like her.

Even animals protect their young. I remember a middle-aged female patient I worked with in Boston who had been hospitalized for years, courtesy of a trust fund. Throughout her childhood and teenage years, she had been sexually victimized by her father and her brothers. In the hospital, she was extremely assaultive and unpredictable and, at times, psychotic. It didn't occur to me then to wonder why she was the only one in her family to be imprisoned for life. Now, from the lens of trauma, I understand her better. She had lived every second of her young life poised for an assault.

Upstairs, Brian spreads a stack of legal documents over the dining room table. Before he starts working again, I tell him about Hope and the trauma resident, how my treatment plan was ignored, but how it worked out in the end because she got to see the result of five years of psychotherapy in action.

"Did you tell her that I benefited from those five years too?"

"No, we didn't discuss you," I tease.

Brian has heard me say that, without therapy, I never would have been able to marry someone as emotionally healthy as he is. Sometimes I think he is a little too self-sufficient. On the rare occasion when he's been sick, he refuses my efforts to fuss over him. Maybe it comes from his being the third in a middle-class family of seven kids raised by an alcoholic dad and a mom who has battled depression much of her life. Somehow, he emerged from that with a strong ego, a strong sense of justice, and a discriminating and confident intellect. He also learned to distrust feelings as "irrational." This difference between us both strengthens our relationship and stresses it. Although I have tried to sell him on the idea that feelings are just as valuable as logic, he doesn't buy it. He attended Swarthmore College and Harvard Law School on the strength of his ability to analyze and reason, not because he was attuned to his feelings.

After kissing Brian good night, I check on the kids. Po is still tucked into the "V" of Corianne's elbow. Danny lies sprawled on his back with his mouth open, as relaxed as a cat stretched out in the hot sun. I breathe in his peacefulness and slide into my own bed. Soon, sleep blankets me the way the summer fog obscures the silhouette of the city, softly and in the blink of an eye.

5

"For an easy fix, get yourself admitted to General Hospital"

At this point, the doctors aren't sure whether the bullet that grazed Jamar Terry's eighteen-year-old lumbar spine did permanent damage. Trudy wishes me luck. The kid hasn't said a word to anyone for the last two days.

I introduce myself and wait for acknowledgement that never comes. Staying outwardly calm, I quickly refigure my strategy. How am I going to connect with this kid? Not by asking questions, that's for damn sure. I flash on my classes with Leston Havens, an existential psychiatrist who taught a yearlong seminar at Cambridge Hospital on the uses of language in psychotherapy. He taught us that questions are intrusive—that they thwart the process of patient and therapist coming together to work collaboratively. He developed an art form out of obtaining a patient's history without asking a single question and regularly assigned medical students to this task. Quickly, I summon forth some of the techniques I learned ten years ago.

"I heard you took some bullets in your back. Must be pretty tough."

"As if you would know, bitch."

OK, he's talking. What do I do now, Les?

I remain silent for a few seconds. Jamar's shaved head is turned away from me. He stares out the window to the courtyard. He is tall and lean with muscular arms and smooth dark brown skin. There are no cards or flowers in his room. An untouched lunch tray sits on his bed table.

"You're right," I say softly. "I'm goddamn lucky I'm not you. I'm lucky I'm not a young black kid living in the projects. We see a lot of you guys messed up with bullet wounds."

"You happy 'bout that." A statement, not a question. A question would have indicated his willingness to engage in a conversation and he's not about to give me that. He could have said nothing; I am encouraged.

"No, I'm not happy about that because I don't like talking to young men about being paralyzed, about losing their manhood, about not being able to go to the bathroom like a normal person."

I know that I am hitting him hard to make my point but I sense that a kind and empathic approach to this kid will fail. He could maintain this veneer of hostility and indifference all day but that wouldn't help either one of us. I have other patients to see and he needs to be able to connect with someone who can help usher him through this new and frightening detour in his life. I am relieved to see a tear trickle down his cheek. He sniffles, swallows, and works his jaw.

"You don't know nothin' lady," he mutters.

Progress! We've gone from bitch to lady! It is even more

encouraging when he steals a furtive glance at me for the first time.

"I seen a lot in my life. Once, I seen a little girl and a man in the bushes. He was doin' it to her."

"You mean he was raping her?"

"Yeah. But I didn't do nothin'. Ain't worth my life cuz he coulda had a gun. I only care about my own people. Why should I care if someone else get his head blowed off? I seen that too. It don't bother me none."

"But this time you got it in the back."

"Shit," he says soft and low, then begins his story.

Jamar was shot for being the messenger of bad news. The fifteen-year-old kid who shot him had broken into his cousin's apartment the previous week. The cousin sent Jamar to tell the kid he had better be looking behind his back at all times. When he delivered the message, another kid was present; a struggle ensued and Jamar was shot.

If Jamar agrees to file a police report, he will be eligible for Victims of Violence money. This fund pays for hospitalization, rehabilitation, and mental health care.

"No way," he says when I bring it up again, "I ain't gonna be a snitch." He turns his head toward the window again.

"So, Jamar, you're telling me that this fifteen-year-old kid who shot you lives across the hall from you and you're not worried about going home?"

"Nah. Whatever happens happens."

Before I can censor myself, a mommy tape plays. Foolishly I ask, "Do you think you could at least talk to him before you go home? Maybe you could reach some kind of truce."

"You crazy? I'm not kissin' anyone's ass!"

"Let me get this straight, Jamar. Your neighbor shoots you in the back and you won't consider going anywhere but home after you get out of the hospital. You refuse to get the police involved and you refuse to talk to this kid to sound him out on whether he plans to finish the job. How else are you going to feel OK about going home? I'm thinking you don't care much about your own safety."

"I don't want to hurt him 'cuz of that three strikes law, you know. But if we have to shoot it out, we shoot it out."

I am acutely aware of the cultural chasm that divides Jamar and me. His experience in the world is limited to the housing project where he lives and where, years before, his father left his wife and sons to fend for themselves. Although it's only a few miles from his home, he has never even seen the Golden Gate Bridge. How can we connect?

During our lunchtime peer supervision, I tell Antionette and Janice how hard it is to find common ground with Jamar. "He's black, he's from the projects, and he's an eighteen-year-old kid. I haven't followed basketball since the seventies and I can't stand rap music. How can I relate to this kid?"

"Something to consider," says Antionette, "is that he might be having a hard time relating to you. In fact, you might be the first white lady who's ever really tried to have a conversation with him. It's not a one-way street you know."

She's right. It hadn't occurred to me that Jamar could feel as uncomfortable around me as I feel around him. I had better find a way to connect with these young black men from the projects because there is no shortage of them on the trauma unit.

Antionette interrupts my thoughts. "Do you want to come with me to a patient care conference on 3B about Mr. Alvarez? He's the one I found shooting up in his room the other day. Usually he's on the medical service with endocarditis. They understand what it takes to cover his pain but since he's on the trauma service this time, medicine isn't writing the orders. And you know the trauma service's approach to pain management."

"Why is he on the trauma service?" I ask.

"He has abscesses from shooting up that need to be incised and drained. When he kept complaining that he was in pain and the trauma service refused to up his pain med dose, the patient had someone bring in a fix for him."

Antionette brushes the crumbs of organic rice crackers off her size six purple wool skirt. "If you're coming, we have to leave now."

An unpleasant odor hangs in the air as we walk through the 3B corridor to the conference room in the back of the unit. Although 3B is a medical floor, surgical patients are occasionally placed here.

As we take our seats around the brown laminate table, I notice that someone has pushed the broken beds, IV equipment, and wheelchairs into one corner so we don't trip over them. If this conference were taking place at Brian's law firm, a cart with gourmet coffee and teas, fruit drinks, and bottled water would be offered. The table would be made of mahogany and the chairs would be uniform and cushioned, not a motley collection of plastic and metal. Our professional worlds are so different, Brian's and mine.

Antionette and I sit as people begin to trickle in. Most wear white lab coats—the medical students in short ones just below the waist, residents in longer ones below the hips, both with requisite stethoscopes around the neck—while the medical attending staff and the consultants, with the exception of Antionette and me in our street clothes, wear the longest white jackets with their names embroidered on the breast pocket. Then I notice that the trauma resident in attendance is tall, blond Dr. Murdock, with whom I tangled on 4D. For a moment, I feel flustered. Even so, I force myself to nod to him. He does not return the acknowledgement.

Salma, the head nurse, a Filipina like most of her staff nurses, begins the meeting. "Does anyone know if Dr. Callahan is planning to come?"

"I just got off the phone with him," says JoEllen, the pain management clinical nurse specialist who works closely with Dr.

Callahan. "He'll be late but says we should proceed without him."

Salma introduces Antionette as the moderator and asks a medical student to recite the patient's medical history. After that, Antionette recounts how she found the patient shooting up in the bathroom yesterday.

Dr. Murdock is the first to respond. "I don't think there's much to talk about. The patient should be discharged for this infraction, period."

"Well now, that's not how it works around here," drawls JoEllen in her best Texan inflection that almost disguises the fact that she's poised for battle. "You see, we believe that if you're trying to medicate a patient's pain, you gotta give 'em enough pain medication to make a difference. Otherwise, the patient's gonna take matters into his own hands."

"Gimme a break," scoffs Murdock. "The guy's an addict. He's always going to say he needs more medication than what we give him. That's what addicts do."

The head nurse concurs. "The nurses on each shift say that he exhibits drug-seeking behavior. And he is rude to them when they tell him he cannot have more pain meds."

"Well, of course he does and of course he is," says JoEllen. "I called his methadone program and they confirmed that he gets eighty milligrams of methadone every morning. You trauma folks have seen fit to cut that dose in half without upping his morphine. Of course he exhibits 'drug seeking behavior.' You would too if you were an opiate addict in withdrawal."

Murdock leans back into his chair and sighs in exasperation. "Sure, we can give him all the dope he wants. Then you know what will happen? Word will get out on the street that for an easy fix, get yourself admitted to General Hospital. How is that going to address the public health problem of drug addiction? At least we're trying to do something about it, not give in to it."

Antionette tries to intervene but JoEllen can't let go. "Ah see," she says with more than a hint of sarcasm, "Ah guess ah didn't understand that the trauma service has taken upon itself the goal of curing addiction. Are you planning on detoxing all of your IVDU's before you discharge them? And who's gonna run your aftercare program—Nancy Reagan?"

Before Murdock's red face explodes, Antionette steps in. "OK everyone, this is a tough system-wide issue. Let's not make it personal. The fact is that SFGH, as the hospital of last resort, cannot abandon its patients, even when they misbehave. We're not going to be able to cure a twenty-five-year addiction in a six-week hospitalization. So, let's focus on what we can do to keep this patient safe and the unit safe until he's run through his course of antibiotics."

Bob Callahan, MD, director of the pain clinic and head of the ethics committee, rushes in and sits in a broken wheelchair. "So what's the story?"

While Dr. Callahan scans the patient's chart, Antionette gives a neutral recap of the discussion thus far. "Clearly, we need to match his methadone dose," he says. "Anyone have a problem with that?"

Murdock snorts and gets up to leave. "Anyone who shoots up while they're a patient in this hospital ought to be discharged. If they don't appreciate all we're doing for them, they can leave."

"Or face the firing squad," mocks JoEllen after the door closes behind him.

"That's the way it is around here," says Antionette after the meeting has ended and we're out of earshot. "Sometimes we butt heads. But I try to remember that each of us is just trying to do the right thing."

I don't think Fred Murdock did the right thing when he tried to remove a dry-packed dressing without offering the patient pain meds. I'm still pissed at him for interrupting my relaxation session with Hope.

"You're a generous soul, Antionette, and I'm a cynic. This is the second time I've seen Murdock withhold pain meds from an addict and I just got here. I have to wonder if that's his way of punishing them for complicating his life."

Before I see my next patient, I take a ten-minute break in The Comfort Garden where a path brimming with orange and yellow day-lilies leads me to my favorite bench. In front of me is a miniature fuchsia laced with hundreds of tiny red and purple-ruffled blossoms. To the left, spread like an umbrella, is a mound of maple-shaped leaves blotched in green and yellow with bell-shaped peach flowers. In front of these, a light green ground cover with delicate lavender flowers spills over and through an edging of cut branches woven like a basket.

Thinking about the care conference now, I feel ambivalent. I admire the passion JoEllen has for her pain patients and agree with her that they should receive adequate doses of pain meds. I also know that Murdock probably spent the previous night on call dealing with abusive patients in alcohol withdrawal, crack-smoking asthmatics, and other "frequent flyers" who get into trouble when they abuse their bodies or neglect to take their prescribed medications. As Antionette says, the hospital is the place of last resort for our patients and we can't abandon them. Does that mean we shouldn't have any behavioral expectations of our patients? Not that anyone here should expect "please" and "thank-you" but neither should the hospital be used as a shooting gallery.

I get up and stroll further down the length of the garden. Ahead, shimmering stars of bright white Shasta daisies rise above a dark green tangle of foliage. Light mauve blooms of cosmos and end-of-the-season-dahlias—dark reds, yellows, pinks, and oranges—throb with mounting intensity in the late afternoon sun. Sitting in this garden, I find it hard to imagine the world of addiction and violence that is home to so many of our patients.

I take some deep breaths and do shoulder rolls. Soon, my thoughts turn to Jamar. The nurses say that no one has come to visit him. He acts tough but he must feel alone and frightened. He's only eighteen, a soldier in the inner city wars waged each day over women, drugs, and turf. Like a soldier, he has distanced himself from his feelings. No wonder I can't find a way to connect with him. Remembering my public health rotation in Boston's Roxbury neighborhood, I shouldn't be surprised.

I was among a group of nursing students, all but one white, that was assigned to a health clinic in a rough section of Boston. A black social worker—an older, slight woman with tired eyes—cautioned us about working with the children at the clinic.

"Our young black moms don't want you well-meaning nursing students coddling their kids. They say they need to teach their kids to be tough to survive in this neighborhood. You need to respect their request."

Their request disturbed me. It went against everything I had been taught and believed about raising emotionally secure and healthy children. I was glad I had been assigned to work with the older adults. I don't think I could have held a child without crossing the coddling line.

While I walk under the Monterey pines, I wonder if Jamar's mother had also tried to toughen her son. Now, even though he needs to be cared for, he can't accept care-giving from me or from any of the nurses, even the African-American nurse on nights. How does he soothe himself? His world is violent, chaotic, and random. He has no future and no dreams. He has only a mask of bravado. Jamar says he doesn't care that he may be paralyzed. That's hard to believe. Of course, he cares. Who wouldn't? I decide to see Jamar one more time before I leave for the day.

When I knock and enter his room, Jamar looks irritated. "Why you back? You already axed me too many questions."

"That's what I want to say, Jamar. I came back because I want to apologize. I think I was too hard on you this morning. I may have asked you too many questions. It's tough enough to be here and you probably have a lot on your mind."

His young face looks hard and suspicious. His eyes regard me with disdain for so long I start to think I made a mistake. Why did I bother coming back? Jamar wets his lips. "If you're thirsty I can get you a soda," I say, just to break the silence.

He seems to consider my offer, and although his expression seems just as severe, I perceive the slightest of nods. I find a Coke in the unit refrigerator and bring it to him.

Jamar snaps off the top and takes a long, slow drink. Then he points to a lone banana on his bed table. "You want that?" he asks.

"Sure," I say, jumping up and down on the inside but staying cool on the outside. *Jamar, you just made my day.*

I savor this moment as I've learned to savor any small success in my work. I learned this lesson in my first job out of graduate school when I worked in a psychiatric day-treatment center affiliated with Cambridge Hospital. Many of our patients suffered from chronic schizophrenia and some of them had been institutionalized for years. Most of them lived in group homes supervised by graduate students in psychology. The combination of a secure living situation and a day-treatment program provided the structure our patients needed to avoid hospitalization. Even though we used an innovative approach to therapy that could best be described as "somatic treatment" of psychosis, the chronic nature of our patients' illnesses ensured that progress would be slow. Our director, a talented clinician, could have had a career as a stand-up comedian. In addition to creating a buoyant work environment and hiring energetic and idealistic staff, he taught us to exaggerate and celebrate miniscule moments of success with our patients. I have applied that lesson to my work with all patients ever since; hence my great pleasure in receiving a "gift" from Jamar.

When my friend, Jeanne, calls that evening, I tell her about Jamar's gift. Jeanne is a psych nurse friend from graduate school. She works with geriatric patients in Connecticut.

"Whatever floats your boat, babe," she says. "For you, it's a banana. For me, I'm thrilled when a patient has a good bowel movement!"

Jeanne called to say that she's planning to vacation on Cape Cod this summer. She knows that we attend Brian's family reunion there each year and wants to arrange it so that our vacation times overlap. We catch up on each other's work and families until Danny tugs on my pants, a reminder that it's time to hang up the phone.

At the hospital the next morning, Trudy asks me to see a patient who fell from a four-story building. Before being transferred to 4D, she spent twelve days on the ICU. It's unclear whether the fall was a suicide attempt or an accident.

"Ms. Hall?" I whisper.

"Ya," she says without moving her lips. She lies supine with her head hanging over the back of her pillow and her mouth open as if she is ready to receive communion.

"Are you awake?"

"Ya." Her short brown lashes flutter over white sclera visible under half-opened lids.

"I'm here to talk with you about what happened."

"They say I fell four floors," she says in a sleepy voice giving equal stress to each word. "Don't remember nothin' though." I would bet from the way Gina Hall pronounces the long "o" sound in "though" that she is from eastern Pennsylvania or Delaware.

When I tell her I'm a mental health nurse, she yawns. While her mouth is open, I notice that she is missing many teeth. Automatically, I scan her pale arms and wrists for cuts or scars. None is visible.

"You were in the ICU for twelve days, unconscious for a week.

Now you're on 4D. That means you're getting better."

Instead of responding to this news, she moves her right hand over the metal screws that poke out from her left arm. Then she touches the cold metal cage encasing her hips.

"Damn," she says with a sigh, "I was hopin' you were part of my dream."

Gina tells me that she was abandoned as an infant. "I grew up in an orphanage. Then, it was group homes. I was raped in one of them places when I was only seven."

For Gina, it was the beginning of a lifetime of exploitation.

It's always jarring to hear these stories. Over the years I have worked with women like Gina—women whose fathers, uncles, grandfathers, brothers, stepfathers, or foster parents encroached on their bodies; women who, in their search for love, reenacted these relationships with other men. Most sink into a life of depression, psychosis, and addiction. A few, like Gina, have problems but manage to bob back to the surface.

Gina talks about her past as if she's telling someone else's story. She speaks slowly in even tones without pausing the way people do when they are overcome by emotion. She denies being suicidal. Then how did she happen to fall four stories that night? Was she pushed? Was it drugs? She says she can't remember.

When I ask about her general mood, Gina replies, "I always been teased for bein' so ugly but I been with Cecil for seven years now. If one day I'm down, he pulls me up. Then if he's down sometimes, I pull him up. We're like a see saw, I guess. Neither one of us is down for too long."

While she speaks, Gina tries and fails to find a more comfortable position in bed. "Every day, we collect bottles and cans. That's our job. The both of us drink too much but we take good care of each other."

She breaks into a grin that reveals a mouth that looks like an ear of yellow corn picked over by field mice.

"I'm glad you've found someone who treats you right, Ms. Hall. You've lived a tough life but you've come out better than a lot of other people would have."

Gina looks at me and tears up. "Am I gonna see you tomorrow, too?"

"If you like."

"Ya, I do. I like talking to you."

"Then I'll see you tomorrow."

I want to be there for her. If there are many new consults tomorrow, it will be hard to keep my word. I promise myself to try. Gina has had too much experience with abandonment and disappointment in her life and I don't want to be one more person who lets her down.

After seeing a few more patients, I check in with Jamar before leaving for the day. According to his chart, his neurologist is "guardedly optimistic" about his recovery. Jamar has some feeling in his lower extremities but will need to be discharged to a rehabilitation facility where he can learn how to perform ADL's, or activities of daily living, while he is recuperating. Before I see him, I retrieve a Coke from the unit refrigerator.

"Hey," he says when I enter the room and hand him the Coke. "I be leaving soon." Jamar almost smiles. "I hope they got better food at this other place."

I tell him what I know about rehabilitation and how his recovery will depend a lot on how hard he is willing to work. Then I wish him luck.

"Later, man," he says. He extends his arm and we bump fists in a hip version of a handshake.

6

Maiden Voyage

I grab my book bag from the back seat, lock the car, and run four blocks to the hospital where I slow to a fast walk through the emergency room, race up five flights of stairs, and arrive on the trauma unit sweating but on time for nursing rounds with Ruby. Bursting into the nurses' lounge, I am greeted by an uncharacteristic silence. Nine or ten people are crowded around the table. Victoria, the head nurse, sits with her arms tightly folded over her chest. Trudy, the day-shift charge nurse, and Lou, the heavyset, substance-abuse counselor, flank her. Ruby, sitting opposite Victoria, shuffles through a stack of three-by-five cards, one card per patient, each filled with medical history notes, lab values, medications, and treatment plans.

She smiles briefly and begins. "OK folks, the bad news is necrotizing fasciitis. Three patients are here on 4D. Their wounds were incised and drained in the OR last night. Another three patients are on the ICU and two more are in surgery now."

"Necrotizing fasciitis?" I ask. "It sounds like a disease that affects dying fascists."

No one cracks a smile. Ruby takes a breath and recites the

information I need. "Necrotizing fasciitis is a bacterial infection of the fascia, the membrane that covers muscle. It kills healthy tissue so fast that without immediate treatment a person can lose entire muscle groups in a matter of hours. A bunch of these cases came in over the weekend, which is why the health department is here investigating. They think it has something to do with black tar heroin from Mexico."

Ruby sips her coffee and wipes her forehead with the back of her hand. She's been up and working long before the rest of us.

"So far, most of the patients are white addicts in their forties and fifties. Rick Walters in 20 bed 2 is a homeless diabetic, a drug abuser with one of the worst wounds I've ever seen. Both buttocks are gone. Once the muscle is destroyed, that's it. It doesn't grow back. The OR surgeons said they scooped out handfuls of decayed tissue during surgery."

Everyone groans. I'm about to gag. I can deal with blood and urine but forget the other body substances, especially the slimy ones. I'll take a paranoid schizophrenic over a pus-filled wound any day.

"So what's the treatment once the dead tissue is removed?" I ask eager to change images.

"Skin grafts. Rick was just grafted. Because his wound is enormous, they used a large patch of healthy skin from his back. Then they made tiny cuts in it and stretched it to cover the entire wound. As the new cells grow, they will fill in these holes. But, patients have to remain on strict bed rest for ten days in order for the graft to 'take.' Laurie and Lou, any emotional support you can give these patients will be appreciated."

Lou, the substance abuse counselor, whistles and shakes his head. "I feel for the staff nurses. These are hard-core addicts. Keeping them in bed is going to be tough. If the trauma docs don't give them enough morphine, they'll be out of here and on the street long before the grafts have taken."

Janine, a thin, dark-haired, forty-two-year-old woman with deep-set eyes and a crisscross of lines on her face, sits atop her bed linens, legs stretched out in front of her, hospital gown rolled up to her crotch. With the phone nestled in between her head and shoulder, she files her dark red, inch-long nails. On her thigh, exposed to the air and all who pass by, is a wound the size and color of a raw steak. Janine has refused to allow her nurse to redress the wound with clean gauze. She puts down the phone soon after I walk over to her bedside.

"That wound looks very painful," I say, keeping my eyes focused on her craggy face to stifle the feeling of acid rising in the back of my throat.

Janine looks at me as though I'm crazy.

"Just a boo-boo. No big deal. It'll get better by itself."

Whoa. Beam me up, Scotty. I can almost see bone and she's talking boo-boos? We've got some major denial here, Captain. Possible dissociation.

"Look, if you don't mind, I gotta call someone," she says.

Really, I don't mind at all.

The next "nec-fash" patient, also in her forties, has a large bandage on her left upper arm but refuses to talk to me until she gets her morphine. I don't blame her. It's hard to concentrate on anything else when you're in pain. I'll make sure her nurse hasn't forgotten about her. Before I leave, I notice that her left arm is hanging limp as a rope. I hope she is right-handed.

Rick Walters lies prone on his bed, his butt covered with snowy white bandages. There are patches of rosy pink rectangles on his back where healthy skin was removed for the grafts. His long silvery ponytail is bunched up and secured at the nape of his neck.

"Helluva way to meet a pretty lady," he says after I explain why

I'm there. Rick's deep brown eyes, both sad and mischievous, target mine. When he smiles, I notice that his yellowed teeth match his yellowed fingernails. *God, I'm glad I can't see his toenails. Gnarled and dirty toenails gross me out.*

I move the head of the bed away from the wall and position my chair in front of it such that Rick, lying face down and propped on his elbows, can see me. It no longer shocks me that someone with such a lined and leathery face is only forty five.

"How are you doing pain-wise?" I ask.

"It'll do for now," he replies. "They said seeing as I got a big hole back there—the biggest they've ever seen—they'd make sure I was comfortable."

So that's what it takes to get a decent dose of pain meds around here.

Rick passes the mini-mental status exam and other questions I ask him to determine his cognitive functioning. When we get to the "social history" part of the psychiatric evaluation, I ask him why he started shooting heroin.

"Ah, my maiden voyage. Every junkie chases after that first high. The problem is that it's never as good after that. We never stop hoping. Guess you could call us optimists."

Rick's chortling provokes a prolonged coughing spasm. When it ends, he seems to grasp the memory as greedily as air. "Back in the sixties, my father's brother lived in the Haight with his wife and kids. He was a hype freak; shot anything and everything into his veins. I was a messed-up kid. Just didn't seem to fit in anywhere. He thought he'd do me a favor, bring some joy into my life. After that, I was hooked."

As a young teenager, I watched newscasts of *The Summer of Love* in San Francisco's Haight-Ashbury neighborhood, usually with Jefferson Airplane's "White Rabbit" playing in the background. Although tamer today, the streets are still lined with runaways and dropouts huddled together asking for handouts and peddling drugs.

"You're probably too young to remember, but that's how it was," Rick continues. "One of the bedrooms in the front of the house was the neighborhood shooting gallery. All kinds of folks stopped in at any hour of the day. They all knew that the rest of the house was off limits. My aunt worked and took their six kids to church every Sunday. She had to know what was going on in the front room but ignored it. Do you know that all of those kids are upstanding citizens today, not a dropout in the bunch. My uncle was one lucky guy, a dope freak with an old lady who worked, raised the kids, and left him to his vices."

"Hmmm," I respond, thinking about the situation Rick has described, "So what did she get out of the deal?"

"You must be one of those modern women, eh? Back then, Catholic girls weren't raised to expect much. That was the beauty of it."

God love him, the guy is buttless and he can still joke.

I banter with him a bit, then clear my voice. "What about your folks?"

"My mom's a saint. My old man passed on twenty years back. Besides being a liar, a cheat, a drunk, and a bully, he wasn't too bad. Used to call me every name in the book."

Rick cups his hands around his mouth like a megaphone. "Hey Pops," he calls to the floor. "You'll be happy to know you were right. Your son really is just an asshole."

Rick starts to laugh. "That's what I've been thinking. All I am is an asshole." His shoulders shake and I can't tell if he's laughing or crying.

For a few moments, I stand there speechless. The whole thing is too damn much for words.

At the end of the interview, we talk about the skin graft and how he will endure ten days of bed rest. Rick says he loves listening to the blues and playing harmonica. A friend can bring him some tapes and his "harp." His mother, who lives in Oakland, will be bringing him a stack of sci-fi novels tomorrow. She's even agreed to allow him to recuperate in her home. Family support and a sense of humor. That's a rarity in this population. Maybe Rick won't be "just an asshole" after all. Maybe, he'll have a chance to turn his life around.

I promised Sarah, an enthusiastic young social worker, that I would evaluate a patient — another heroin addict — right after our staff meeting. She's found an opening in a residential drug treatment facility and needs a psychiatric evaluation to clear the patient of any co-existing psychiatric disorder, a program requirement.

As I'm reviewing Keith McSorley's chart, a high-pitched voice exclaims, "Hey! You're here!"

I look up to see Sarah.

"The treatment facility is waiting on your assessment. Keith is SO motivated to stop using EVERYTHING," she says, her energetic voice skipping with hope. "This is the EXACT right time to get him into TREATMENT. He was admitted for pneumonia, got septic, and ended up on the ICU for three weeks. While he was there, they WITHDREW him from heroin! Isn't that GREAT!"

Then she lowers her voice and whispers in my ear. "He seems happy to be clean but I want you to check him out on the depression front. There's a little something about him that feels sad to me."

Sarah's enthusiasm makes me smile. I don't feel as hopeful as she is, but maybe Mr. McSorley saw that tunnel of bright, white light while he was in the ICU and decided to make some changes if he woke up alive. Although I've never worked in recovery per se, over the years I've worked with many people with addiction problems. Addicts who have been withdrawn from drugs start to feel so good for the first time in years that they convince themselves and everyone around them that they'll never use drugs again. As soon as they hit an emotional snag, the chance of relapse skyrockets. Addicts just don't know how to manage bad feelings without reaching for a drink, a pill, or a needle. That's when they drop out of treatment programs.

According to his chart, Keith has been using heroin daily for over twenty of his forty-six years. *(At least he doesn't have necrotizing fasciitis!)* He also drinks and uses crack regularly. He has no family and no history of employment. Where did Sarah uncover this wellspring of hope? So far, I can see only a long-term polysubstance abuser with no social support and no marketable skills. In a stretch, one could say that the life of a successful junkie does require certain skills: meeting your dealer at the designated time; panhandling or stealing to get enough money for the daily fix; and shooting up in safe places at regular intervals all preoccupy a junkie's every waking minute and require personal organizational skills and creative financing.

At least Keith has a private room. All patients should. I imagine he hasn't slept anywhere as clean and quiet in a very long time. I open the door and ask his permission to enter.

Although the chart said Keith is HIV negative, he sure looks like an AIDS patient. Blue eyes ringed with dark gray and sunk deep into their sockets acknowledge my presence. He offers me a limp hand to shake. A weak smile reveals the poor dental hygiene of poverty and neglect. Paper-thin white skin hangs from his cheekbones like drapery. I have the sensation that were it not for the covers pulled up to his chin and tucked under his mattress, his body would float toward the ceiling and vanish through a wall.

"Sarah told me that you want to go into a residential treatment facility. Are you sure you're ready for it?" I ask.

"I'm ready," he replies in a barely audible voice.

"How do you know?"

"Because I'm so tired of living by my wits."

Keith pauses as if he's waiting for my response. I wonder if he's figuring out whether talking to this psychiatric nurse is worth the effort. He looks like he can't afford to waste a calorie.

"Twenty years of shooting heroin is a long time." I say.

"Hey, I've been high since I was ten. First, it was glue. Then I started drinking. At twelve, it was speed."

I sense him monitoring my reaction. I know he's looking for disapproval or judgment. If he can look beyond my practiced professional demeanor, he will see only sadness in my eyes. A ten-year-old kid should be playing ball or collecting trading cards, not trying to anaesthetize himself. From what? Something bad must have happened early in Keith's life.

"When I found acid, I thought I had died and gone to heaven."

His dulled eyes are suddenly ablaze at the memory of dropping hits of "pure" LSD in the sixties. You would have thought I had just asked him about a new and promising romance.

Sarah, what were you thinking? This guy is still infatuated with chemistry.

"I'm impressed that you've managed to stay HIV negative all these years."

He cocks his head to one side and looks at me with one eyebrow raised and one lowered. "I may be a junkie," he says in a serious tone, "but I've got my standards. I don't buy junk on Ellis Street, I have a reputable dealer, and I don't share needles."

This is good news. Maybe Mr. McSorley has retained some self-worth to build on. "I'm glad you've been able to take such good care of yourself," I say, "because I've heard of some addicts getting infected with that flesh-eating bacteria. They've traced it back to black tar heroin from Mexico. Have you practiced safe sex, too?"

"No," he answers, "I've practiced no sex. Haven't had a sex drive in years."

"Sometimes people who are depressed lose interest in sex. They can't concentrate; they sleep poorly and often lose weight. Have there been times when you have felt that life wasn't worth living?"

"No," he says, "I'm not depressed."

"Any family history of depression?"

He hesitates and turns his head toward the window.

"I guess you'd have to say my mother was depressed."

Keith stares out the window at nothing in particular that I can see. When he resumes speaking, his voice has changed. It sounds far-away and less articulate.

"We lived in the projects in Philly, my mom and me, on the twelfth floor. There was a playground in front. I was playing there when she jumped. She landed right in front of me, broke her neck. I was six."

A pain shoots through my own neck as he describes the scene. My stomach lurches at the thought of a child witnessing such a thing and, for a few moments, I cannot speak. In my thoughts, I have left Keith and retreated inward for a place to be alone. His words yank me back to his side.

"She had no right to do this to me!" he cries, his jaw quivering as he struggles to form the words. His face and body contort into newly exhumed agony. He pushes away the bed linens, draws his knees to his chin, and freezes.

I watch, as his eyes grow wide with the memory of being a child of six, confused and desperate to find a place to hide, to make it not so. Holding his head in his hands, he begins to rock his body.

"She took my life too," he whispers. "She killed herself, but she took me with her."

While he rocks and sobs, I put my hand on his bony shoulder and wonder who comforted him that night so many years ago.

Then it dawns on me. This is the first time in thirty-six years that Keith has been clean and sober. His emotional growth slowed at age six and stopped at age ten when he started using drugs. He's had no chance to understand his feelings or to learn how to manage them. Without those skills, he is defenseless against such a dangerous and intolerable memory. I didn't mean to open this door, to inflict this pain on him. If he refuses to see me again tomorrow, I'll understand why. Meanwhile, I talk to him in caressing tones while his six-year-old self grieves for the mommy who destroyed both of their lives.

A few minutes later, he stops crying and lies back with his face pursed as if to seal off all emotion once again. I wet a clean washcloth and ask permission to wipe his forehead and cheeks. I tell him he has done a lot of work for the day and can now take a break. I lead him through a relaxation exercise followed by a suggestion to imagine a place where he feels safe and utterly at peace. It occurs to me that he might never have experienced such a place but as I ask him to focus on the sights, smells, sounds, and textures of this wonderfully peaceful place, I notice that he has already fallen into a deep sleep.

"Forgive me," I whisper. I didn't mean to open up this memory before he was prepared to deal with it. I pull the linens back up to his chin and tuck him in again, just as his mother should have done that night and every night.

Can I, in good faith, say that Keith does not suffer from a co-existing mental illness? True, he's not schizophrenic, bipolar, obsessive-compulsive, or even actively suicidal, but he still suffers the effects of untreated childhood trauma. With so many years of addiction, his neurological system must be a royal mess. Even though I suspect he's headed for a big depression, I give him a pass on the mental health front. Otherwise, he'll be out of here, on the streets, and back on heroin in a nanosecond. Not that I think that won't happen anyway.

I don't have to struggle too hard to understand the lure of heroin. At twenty three, shortly after my stint in the ICU, I found myself in an emergency room awaiting surgery for an abscessed cyst. After a few hours, I became very thirsty. Forbidden to take liquids by mouth, I decided to quench my thirst by speeding up the rate of IV fluid dripping into my arm. In those days, nurses timed the IV drip to their watches, manually regulating the flow of fluid. What I didn't know was that a nurse had just injected 100 milligrams of Demerol, an opium derivative, into my intravenous line by way of a buretrol, a cylindrical container filled with a few ounces of IV fluid. When I opened the flow of the IV to quench my thirst, Demerol gushed into my vein catapulting me into the stratosphere. I remember float-ing—feeling lighter than a hydrogen balloon—surrounded by spar-kling sunlight, lifted upward toward the sublime, happier and more at peace than I have ever felt.

Like the act of smoking a cigar, psychoanalysts used to talk about the act of shooting heroin as sexual. If anything, shooting dope seems to me to be a pathetic form of self-nurturing, more milk than semen, a substitute for the bliss of being loved, and feeling secure. In the absence of self-love, heroin is self-nurturing. In the case of necrotizing fasciitis, the milk itself is toxic.

Before I go to my next patient, I sit down with a cup of tea in the cafeteria and pull out some paper. Although I used to keep a journal, since having kids, I've only written gooey sentimental stuff. This time, I write in breathless, sloppy prose about Keith, and how he was playing by himself in the playground in front of his apartment in the minutes before his mother jumped. I imagine her gazing out the twelfth floor window. Does she even see him down there playing with his toy trucks? Does she wonder what will become of him or who will take care of him? How his life will change if she dies? I want to yell, "Stop! Think about your son!" I imagine myself shaking her, yelling: "Suicide is an excellent way to achieve immortality. It forever screws up the people who love you. It will echo through your family for generations. Can you under-stand that? Is that what you want?"

At home, I am restless. The usual routine of picking up toys, sweeping floors, wiping tables and counters, and folding laundry helps to ameliorate the feeling of mild agitation in my body, but when it's done, I still feel antsy.

After we put the kids to bed, Brian hits the refrigerator for some pecan praline ice cream before beginning work on tomorrow's deposition. I'd like to tell him about Keith but I refrain. Brian does not like to dwell in sad places. As soon as the ground below him gets squishy, he leaps toward a stable ledge, or cracks a joke.

I have come to appreciate how Brian uses humor to deal with stress. In 1989, on the morning of the Loma Prieta earthquake, I hopped a flight to Boston for a mini-vacation, my first break since Corianne was born twenty months before. When I arrived at my friends' home and watched the TV news coverage, I saw that the earthquake had caused some homes and a section of the freeway and the Bay Bridge to collapse. The phone lines were down for hours.

Late that night, Brian finally got through to me. After establishing that he and Corianne were fine, I asked about the house.

There was a pregnant pause before Brian said, "I'm sorry to tell you this, but I came home to a scene of utter devastation."

I caught my breath. Before I could ask, Brian continued, "But then I realized that's how I had left the house in the morning!"

I smile at the memory.

Leaving Brian to his work, I pull on my sweatshirt and walk out into the cool, clear night. At the end of my street, I have to make the choice to go uphill or downhill. We live in a hilly neighborhood where uphill cannot be avoided. The question is whether to begin downhill and end uphill or vice versa. I start with uphill, one of the steepest in our city of hills. Leaning forward, I start trekking. Climbing the hills reminds me of our backpacking days. Brian wanted to move here from Boston in order to be close to the Sierra. Although I had camped with my family, I had never set out into the wilderness with everything I needed on my back. A tomboy at heart and with Brian, an intrepid and experienced backpacker in the lead, I was up for the challenge.

We started with easy weekend trips, south to Big Basin in the Santa Cruz Mountains and north to Point Reyes in Marin County, both a reasonable distance from the city.

As soon as I swung my pack onto my back, I understood why Brian had fretted about every ounce of weight. Foot blisters soon taught me about the importance of good hiking boots, and a couple of sweaty days and cold nights convinced me to invest in warm clothes made of fabrics that whisk moisture away from the skin.

With new clothes and new boots, I was ready for our third backpacking adventure, a three-day trip into the Ventana Wilderness along the Big Sur Coast. After hoisting our heavy packs, we began our journey on the Pine Ridge Trail. Although the midday sun beat down on us, the air was redolent with the sweet and spicy odor of black sage. Along the trail, we marveled at the red smoothness of madrone trees and how they feel as polished as the neck of a violin. Brian had hiked this trail in the past.

"It might be a little challenging at first," he said, "but I know you can do it."

While it took me some time to find my hiking legs, Brian's long strides soon carried him out of sight.

The Pine Ridge Trail runs alongside the Big Sur River. Many tributary creeks flow into it, each one with its own small canyon to traverse. We descended steep switchbacks to a place where we could cross the tributary and the trail shifted uphill. The pattern—steep downhill followed by grueling uphill—continued for miles. Sweating and weary, I rested at increasingly frequent intervals. At Logwood Creek where we descended four hundred feet only to have to go up again, I lost it.

"You LIED!" I yelled when I caught up with Brian. "You told me there would be SOME uphill, not miles and miles of uphill!"

"I guess I forgot how tough this part is," Brian conceded. "But any minute we'll start heading into the valley."

Any minute became another hour. "You KEEP lying!" I exclaimed when I caught up with him again. "How can you do that? Just tell me the truth and don't ever lie to me again!"

"I don't mean to lie to you," said Brian. "Really, I just forgot about the hard part."

Upon reaching a vista that heralded the beginning of a downhill trek into a lush valley, my mood improved instantly. Within an hour or two, we found a beautiful spot near a creek, set up camp, pumped water, and made dinner. After cleaning dishes and bear-bagging the rest of our food—hanging it high and out of reach—we drank hot cocoa and looked at the stars while Brian, a history buff fascinated by ancient Rome, regaled me with stories of Theodosius and Caesar.

I must have forgotten about the hardship early in that trip because over the next few years, before Corianne arrived, we backpacked whenever we could. Brian learned to level with me about the degree of difficulty of each trip and I learned to prepare mentally for long stretches of uphill climbing.

Other than a brush with a rattlesnake, the only dangerous situation I encountered was crossing a rushing creek in early spring. In the Trinity Alps, a six-hour drive north of San Francisco, we drove down a bumpy dirt road for miles toward the trailhead only to find the bridge over Coffee Creek had washed away. We doubled back to the ranger station where the embarrassed ranger who had sent us to Coffee Creek, suggested we try the Union Creek Trail.

Maiden voyage

Hiking up Union Creek, we mistook a major tributary for the creek itself and continued along the tributary instead of crossing it. We lost our trail, and ended up in Bullard's Bar basin. When we figured out what had happened, we still had to find a place to cross the tributary in order to rejoin our trail. Once again, the turbulent water of early spring impeded our journey. The only possible way to cross was via a downed tree that spanned the creek. Brian, normally sure-footed and confident, hesitated. The tree's surface was rounded and slick with water. Before I could question him, he started across. I didn't breathe until he stepped safely on the other side. When I realized it was my turn to do the same, my legs went hollow. Brian shouted words of encouragement but I couldn't hear them over the roar of the water. I remember thinking that I didn't want to ruin our precious three-day weekend. Nor did I want to slip and crack my skull. I looked up to see Brian gesturing, 'You can do it.'

Relacing my boots, I took a couple of deep breaths and imagined myself crossing in one fluid movement. I pulled the straps of my pack tight and picked up my walking stick—a tapered branch I'd found along the way. Taking one more deep breath, I started across. Two thirds of the way, my foot slipped and my heart lurched. My walking stick landed in a depression on the log, offering resistance against a tumble into the chilly water. Ignoring the rushing water, I righted my footing and focused on the physics of balance. When I finally stepped onto the creek's soft bank, I was wiped out.

A few minutes later Brian found a blaze—a diamond-shape carved into a tree marking the trail we had lost. We knew we were on our way to Union Lake where we would camp for the night.

If I were backpacking now instead of climbing hills in my neighborhood, I would be reading topographic maps to prepare for the next day's uphill challenge with its payoff in scenic views. At night around a campfire, I would be thinking about my job at

SFGH—how fortunate I am to work with the people there and how much I learn about life from my patients. On the trail the next morning, I would be looking for blazes cut into trees that assure me of taking the right path. At the end of another hard day of climbing, and after finding a beautiful spot to set up camp, I would loosen my shoulder straps and slip off my backpack and notice how good it feels to shed its weight.

7

'How can you bear to listen?'

I take a pregnancy test and am shocked when the stick turns pink. Brian is jubilant. From the beginning of our marriage, we had hoped to have three children, but when conceiving Danny took almost three years, I figured my baby-making days were over.

Months pass. At thirty nine, I've become happily reacquainted with the less charming aspects of pregnancy: nausea and fatigue, though neither has been severe and both are finally waning.

I worried about telling people at work about my pregnancy, especially my boss, and Antionette and Janice, who will have to cover the trauma unit for me. I make sure that my boss, the Director of Psych Nursing, understands how much I love my job and that I intend to stay for the duration of my career. When I ask for six months maternity leave, she is unfazed, saying, "Fine, whatever you need."

Antionette and Janice seem happy for me but one says, "We'll get through it the best we can."

I know it won't be easy.

On my way to the seventh floor, I congratulate a former patient who has progressed from wheelchair to crutches following a motor-cycle crash. She has endured four surgeries and needs at least one more.

"Sometimes I think this will never end," she says. "It's hard to keep my spirits up."

She is on her way to an orthopedic appointment. I give her my card and ask her to call me. "Maybe we can sit and talk for a few minutes the next time you're here."

"That would be great," she replies.

Even though General's trauma department is world renown, the hospital offers patients no psychological follow-up. This seems to me to be a huge omission. I make a note to ask Ruby about it. Perhaps she would be interested in leading a support group with me.

My first patient today, Jimmy Boudreau, is a fifty-two-year-old African-American admitted two weeks ago for a "sucking chest wound." He is twelve days post-surgery for the debridement of dead tissue from a large, infected wound in his chest wall. Three months earlier, surgeons removed one of his lungs because it was the site of "a large arteriovenous malformation."

The nurses say Mr. Boudreau vacillates between being anxious and being angry.

"I feel like I'm in prison!" he tells me at the outset of our conversation. His breathing sounds labored and his eyes are wide. Between his southern accent and his Cajun patois, I make out a few key phrases: "They don't know what's wrong with me. I don't want to be their guinea pig. They keep telling me I shouldn't smoke or drink. I'm not a child. I only listen to God, not to man."

I can understand his frustration. Mr. Boudreau's doctors are not sure why his recovery is so slow. According to his chart, they think that he may have a "bronchopleural fistula" which may require another surgery. Since he does not understand what this means and I am not exactly clear myself, I grab a nurse who explains that a fistula is an abnormal, tube-like connection between two parts of the body that are not supposed to be connected. In his case, the fistula is between a bronchus and his remaining lung. She draws a diagram for him of a trachea branching into two bronchi that carry air to each lung. She shows him where a fistula between the two might occur.

After she leaves, Mr. Boudreau calms down and I ask about his life. He has suffered many losses beginning with his father who died when Mr. Boudreau was eight. Suddenly, he bursts out crying. With difficulty, I make out that his cousin, with whom he lives, died in a fire over the weekend.

"If I'd been home there wouldn't be no fire because I don't let my cousin smoke in bed!"

"It sounds like you're blaming yourself for his death," I say softly.

"I can't help the way I feel." He has tensed up again but when he talks about his cousin—how close they were, how they fished together, how they were the "blackest" members of the family—his body relaxes.

"You loved him very much."

"I did," he says, tearing up. "We was closer than me and my wife ever was."

He looks at me and narrows his eyes. "I ain't never told anyone so much about myself as I told you—a stranger and a white lady!"

"Does it feel OK?" I ask him.

"Yeah, I guess so," he says patting my arm. "It just seem a little strange."

This is what I love about my job: that I get to talk to all kinds of people I would not otherwise get to know. In getting to know them, I am constantly reminded that no matter how dissimilar we appear on the surface, we experience the same feelings. When we share them, the distance between us shrinks.

I let Mr. Boudreau's medical team know that if it's at all possible, he would like to go to his cousin's funeral. I also communicate to them that their admonishments about his drinking and smoking make him feel infantilized and won't change his behavior. I'll drop in as often as I can to offer him "supportive emotional care."

My next patient, Christian Whitcomb, expects to be arrested at any moment. "I'm wanted for a parole violation but I'm not going anywhere with two broken legs. That's fine by me. I'm going to use the time I have to confront what I've done. That's why I asked the nurses for someone to talk to."

This is an ex-con talking? So far everything about Christian Whitcomb is striking: his words, his chiseled good looks, his Lou Rawls baritone, and his sincerity. "Pull up a chair," he says. "Things are weighing heavy on my mind. Drugs didn't help. Maybe talking will."

Immediately, I feel myself being charmed. All I know about Christian is that he is a forty-four-year-old African-American with a lower-left extremity fracture and an upper-right extremity fracture sustained after a thirty-foot fall.

Christian tells me that a judge gave him the option of five years in prison or a stint at a well-known rehab facility in the city with a reputation for working with the most serious offenders.

"The program was b.s," he says. "Pardon my language, but that's what I think. If you have a problem with someone there, you can't confront them. You have to write down what happened on a piece of paper. Three times a week they have what they call "games" where they set you up with the person who bothered you and you're supposed to tell him why you're ticked off. He can say anything he wants back to you and you have to sit there and take it. This is supposed to teach me how to manage my anger? I've spent a lifetime trying to control my anger because I can become very violent. All that did was provoke me."

Christian left the program after being chastised for holding the door open for some women. "I wasn't being sexual," he says. "I was just doing what I was taught to do."

Shortly after that incident, he split and headed for the Tenderloin, San Francisco's red light district. This is where his story gets murky. Christian says he met some "associates" who let him stay in their hotel room after they had finished conducting their business. Early the next morning, he noticed a white man in the next building looking through a window and putting on a flak jacket.

"I didn't want to go back to prison so I ran to the top of my building and looked for a way down. There were water pipes to hang on to but I didn't see the barbed wire at the access point. I grabbed it, lost my footing, and fell right into a group of policemen!"

Christian laughs at the absurdity of the scene. "They called the paramedics who brought me here. I know they'll find out that I have a parole violation. I can't run. So, I'm waiting for them to take me to jail."

I am curious about Christian, and, I admit, attracted to him. He tells me his life went downhill ten years ago when he started smoking crack. "Have you done crack?" he asks.

Do I really look like someone who smokes crack? Hey, maybe I don't look as square as I am! Maybe there's even an air of mystique about me! I can already hear Brian laughing when I tell him this.

"Let me tell you about crack," he says. "You know how good an orgasm feels?"

Whoa! Can I be professional and sexual at the same time? I nod because he's caught me off guard and I'm at a loss for another way to respond.

"Well, compared to the most intense orgasm you've ever had, the first time you smoke crack is one hundred times more powerful than that!"

I'm blushing and way more turned on than I should be.

"The problem is…"

"I know, I've heard. You spend your life chasing that feeling because it's never as good after that."

Christian laughs, "You heard right."

"So then what happened?"

"One day, I decided to make a break with who I'd been. I got sick of the game. I left the accounting firm where I'd worked for twelve years, the only black guy there. I cut up all of my credit cards, my driver's license, even my Social Security card. I took the name 'Shay' and worked the street breaking bones of people who didn't pay their dealers. I'm not proud of it. I was bad and that's what I did."

OK, Christian. Now I find you less attractive. It's the violence thing.

"You didn't say why you started smoking crack."

"I was depressed only I didn't know it at the time. My wife and I had broken up. I lost my house. Everything went downhill after that."

Antionette says that the Tuskegee experiments on African-American men who were denied treatment for syphilis still ripple through black America. I wondered about it when I detected distrust from Mr. Boudreau toward his surgeons, most of whom are white. Now I wonder if that's a factor in why Christian didn't seek psychiatric help for depression.

Does psychiatry only hold sway with middle-class white people?

I talk to Christian about depression, and how talking—sometimes combined with anti-depressant medication, in the case of major depression—can help.

"It seems to me that you didn't give yourself time to understand why your marriage broke apart. Instead of working through all of your feelings and mourning your loss, you started smoking crack. Basically, you ran away from your feelings instead of confronting them."

I know that Christian already knows this but sometimes it helps to hear it from another person. His social worker is trying to get him transferred to the city's rehabilitation hospital. The question is who will arrive first: the ambulance to take him there or the police to take him to jail?

"I told you I have a lot to think about," says Christian. "If I'm still here tomorrow, could you stop by?"

"Sure," I reply.

Meanwhile he waits.

I've heard the psychiatrists in our small department talk about the new doc who has been hired to fill in for another shrink's year-long maternity leave. Apparently, the new doc is "a star." In a few minutes when our psychiatric consultation-liaison service meeting begins, I'll find out what that means.

Janice, Antionette, and I walk down the long corridor to the meeting room. Slowly, the others trickle in — five psychiatrists, four neuropsychologists, and two medical students. Donald, our department head, takes a seat and clears his throat motioning for the meeting to begin. "Miranda Lowenthal should be with us momentarily. Ah, that must be her."

A tall woman with a long face, strong jaw, slightly protruding teeth, and large green eyes enters and takes the chair next to Donald.

"Welcome to clinical rounds." says Donald. "Everyone, this is Dr. Lowenthal. She joins us from Yale where she completed her psych residency a few years ago and where she worked on the psych liaison team until recently."

Miranda smiles like a news anchor who suddenly realizes she's on camera. Her dark frizzy hair is pulled into a bun. When her eyes sweep the room, she directs her gaze slightly above our heads.

Donald continues, "Dr. Lowenthal is the editor of a psychopharmacology textbook that will be coming out in a few months. Maybe you could tell us a little about the research you conducted at Yale."

Psychopharmacology text? Research? My hope for a fellow process queen just died.

Miranda speaks in well-articulated flurries of words that remind me of the Czerny piano exercises I practiced as a child. Her voice projects competence and supreme confidence. I cannot avoid feeling a twinge of envy. OK, more like a tug.

When I was ten, my father suggested that I might want to be a doctor though I planned to become a veterinarian. In fifth grade, my friend Leah and I dissected baby birds that fell from their nests in our mulberry trees. "In the name of science!" we exclaimed before making the first cut with a steak knife. When I found out later that getting into vet school was even more competitive than medical school, I abandoned the idea. Had I been serious about medical school, so-so grades in math and chemistry would have thwarted my ambition.

After introductions, we get down to business. Everyone groans when Antionette announces that Troy Gerard is back in the hospital. For Miranda's benefit, Antionette lists Mr. Gerard's medical problems. "We're talking about a forty-two-year-old African-American man who's been a paraplegic since a fall in 1981. Mr. Gerard is a crack addict with chronic osteomylitis, chronic foot and sacral ulcers, chronic bladder infections, and a personality disorder. He's often verbally abusive, and if people get in his way, he's been known to mow them down with his electric wheelchair. He leaves the unit whenever he wants and returns intoxicated. Like many of our patients, he routinely leaves the hospital on the first and fifteenth of the month to collect his General Assistance paycheck. Typically, he parties until the money runs out. Then, he's back on our doorstep via the ER for treatment."

"And we continue to admit him?" Miranda asks.

Antionette sighs. She has worked with Mr. Gerard for years. Each new crop of residents or medical students asks the same question and each time she patiently explains the hospital's position. "SFGH is the end of the line, the hospital of last resort. As such, we cannot refuse to treat anyone who is in need, even when the patient leaves against medical advice and comes back higher than a kite."

"That's ridiculous," says Miranda.

Everyone snaps to attention. It's too early for a new person to voice such a strong critical opinion, even if part of me agrees with her. I know from my work with many personality-disordered patients on inpatient psychiatric units and day-treatment centers that setting clear and consistent limits with enforceable consequences is the only way to modify anti-social and manipulative behaviors. But people here see things differently. To them, setting behavioral limits is punitive, not therapeutic, and forcing people into substance abuse treatment programs "infringes on their civil liberties." This being San Francisco, we have a certain reputation to uphold.

Miranda freely comments on the other patient issues that we discuss. Our styles are very different. Having had a lot of experience entering new work groups, I've learned to act the part of the tourist for a while, observing the people and the culture before imposing my opinions on them.

In our office after the meeting, Antionette plays the latest messages on our message machine. The last one is from a nurse on 5A, the AIDS unit. "I'm calling about a patient who's been extremely anxious on nights. He's a paramedic who got AIDS from a needle stick during a resuscitation in the back of an ambulance. His wife is a nurse. He gets anxiety attacks when she's not here."

Since we share cases on the AIDS unit and it's been a while since I've worked there, I volunteer to take the consult.

What's strange about this request is that the nurse mentioned exactly how the patient was infected. Most of us assume that patients acquire HIV through sex with an infected person or by sharing dirty needles. On a few occasions, I have read admission notes in charts that seem to take pains to explain that a patient became HIV positive after a blood infusion. That Wade Rawling was infected while saving someone's life in the back of an ambulance knocks denial right out of its den.

Famous 5A, the first AIDS unit in the world, has remained the premier model for inpatient care of HIV-related illnesses. When the unit opened in 1982, most of the patients were gay professional men. Since most members of the nursing staff were gay men or lesbians, they felt like they were caring for their own community. Staff members approached their work with missionary zeal and their patients rewarded them with gestures of appreciation. Since then, many of the gay nurses have themselves died of the disease and been replaced by straight white and Asian women. The AIDS virus has found its way into the intravenous drug-abusing population, a group not known for gestures of appreciation.

Before moving to San Francisco from Boston in the early eighties, I had little experience with gay culture. To me "cruising" was a word for what ten-month-old babies did before they could walk independently. Each time Brian and I strolled through the gay Castro District, he held me like a shield proclaiming his heterosexuality. By that time, a few cases of Kaposi's sarcoma and pneumocystis pneumonia, both previously rare diseases, had emerged; the alarm had yet to be sounded. Day and night, disco pounded through open doors and windows of bars on Castro Street. One morning while I was walking home on Castro Street after working a night shift, a man wearing leather chaps—only leather chaps and cowboy boots—emerged from a bar in front of me. Before the doors swung shut behind him, I heard a blast of Sylvester and Two Tons of Fun singing "Do You Wanna Funk?" Strutting bare-cheeked up the street, the cowboy entered the next pulsating bar that was blasting a disco hit and the doors swung shut behind him.

At Presbyterian Hospital in the late eighties, I saw the bony faces and sunken eyes of young men and the shocked faces of their Midwestern parents who had rushed from the airport to the hospital only to be confronted with their son's disease, his homosexuality, and his lover eyeing them from the opposite side of the room. At SFGH, my first AIDS patient was Denny, a forty-three-year-old who, as evidenced by his photo near the bed, was a teddy bear of a man before he became ill. He was admitted to the hospital with a host of HIV-related illnesses that he sideswiped with a sense of humor.

"I was born without a gag reflex," he told me in a solemn voice. "It made me a very popular fellow among my crowd."

He took my laughter as a green light for more.

"My doctor told me he wanted to give me a drug holiday. 'A drug holiday?' I said. 'Sounds great! How about a little crystal meth with a sinsemilla chaser?'"

I am still smiling at that memory when I enter the AIDS unit where a powerful odor of diseased excrement sends me reeling. Patty, one of the nurses, makes a face and then says, "I know, I know. It's even too much for me and I'm used to it. Let's talk in the lounge."

Patty, Wade's nurse for the day, is a straight woman who comforts and cares for her patients as if they are close family members. Patients respond well to her jokes and her gentle teasing to get some of the most resistant patients up and moving and taking their treatments. Today, she looks frazzled.

"What can you tell me about Wade?" I ask.

"You know how he got infected, don't you?" she asks, tucking errant strands of bleached blond hair into a barrette.

I nod.

"Scary, isn't it? His wife arrived a few minutes ago if you want to speak with her. She's an RN at St. E's night shift. He calls her constantly and begs her to stay with him."

Patty grimaces. "Poor thing. I don't know how long she can keep it together. Who could?"

Patty tells me that Wade is having a better day today than yesterday. When she leaves, a medical resident, who entered while we were talking, takes the chair across from me.

"Is that the chart of the paramedic who got stuck?" she asks. When I nod she says, "We were just talking about him in rounds. He's DNR you know."

I open the chart and see the Do Not Resuscitate order signed in Wade's shaky hand. This means that no heroic measures will be taken to save Wade if his vital signs — blood pressure, pulse, and respiration — begin a fatal dive. He will be made comfortable on a morphine drip. He will not receive medication to coax his heart to beat nor will he receive oxygen to inflate his lungs.

"He's only twenty-nine," I say, more to myself than to the resident.

"I know," she says. "He and I were born on the same day in the same year."

I look at her for the first time. She is a Latina with long hair swept back into a half-assed French twist. Dark circles under her eyes testify to a tough night on call. She glances at my ID badge.

"Psychiatry? We could use some of that on our service. It's so damn hard seeing people our age die. Everyone wants to quit but no one can afford to because of our med school loans."

"Doesn't one of the shrinks lead a support group for medical residents?"

"It's only for fourth year med students. Residents are on our own."

"Sorry to hear it. Maybe you all should request your own support group."

"Hey. We're docs. We're not supposed to have feelings."

She pushes her chair back abruptly. "Good thing I didn't go into psychiatry. Dealing with other people's emotions all day? No way! I can barely handle my own!"

I walk out onto the unit and notice the original artwork hanging on the walls, contributions from people in the community. Since the unit opened in 1982, patients and staff have received more support than have other units in the hospital. The first head nurse, Cliff Morrison, made staff support groups mandatory. After he left, however, the group became elective and gradually disappeared. That's too bad. Nurses who deal with death and dying on a daily basis could use an ongoing support group. Meanwhile, the head nurse has asked Antionette and me to facilitate a staff retreat.

Rochelle, a young woman dressed in blue hospital scrubs, sits by Wade's bed holding his hand and staring out the window. I doubt that she sees the pink blossoms of the tree that grows from the atrium one floor below. They look spectacular against the clear azure sky but her eyes are focused into the distance. Wade appears to be sleeping. I whisper an introduction.

Rochelle strokes Wade's black wavy hair. "He called me six times last night. I tell him he's in good hands here but he panics when I'm not around."

Rochelle has delicate features and short auburn hair. A fringe of feathered bangs nearly obscures her eyes. I hear the emotion trapped in her chest as she groans in frustration, "All I want to do is go shopping with my girlfriend. Is that asking too much?"

"Sounds reasonable," I reply. "You need time for yourself too."

"I wish I could believe that," she says, twisting a strand of hair.

Still holding her husband's hand, Rochelle tells me about their life since Wade contracted HIV. "We only found out about it because his friend needed surgery and he wanted to donate blood."

She strokes Wade's arm and glances at the monitors. "For a long time he was in total denial. He refused all prophylaxis medications. He still won't take them because he hates the side effects. He wants to feel as good as he can with the time he has left."

Rochelle's voice seems flat, as if she expended all emotion on this issue long ago and has no more in the bank. She tells me that initially Wade had insisted on being hospitalized at St. Elizabeth's so he could be near her. "You know how confidential things are in the hospital. When the nurses I work with found out he has HIV, they assigned me to all of the HIV patients, probably because they thought I was infected too. Well, I'm not!" Rochelle's nostrils flare. She presses her lips with so much force, they blanch.

Wade startles awake, his blue eyes wild until Rochelle says calmly, "I'm here, honey. Go back to sleep." Dutifully, he obeys. Rochelle strokes his arm and glances at the monitors above his bed. This time she whispers. "His nurses used to call me to come down every time they needed to start his I.V. His room was always dirty and they wouldn't change him so of course his skin broke down."

She wipes away the tears pulsing down her cheek. "That's why we came to General this time. The nurses know what they're doing here. They let me be his wife instead of his nurse."

"How have things been at home?" I ask.

"Not so good." Rochelle tears up again and wipes her eyes. "We had to move in with my parents. Between the bed and Wade's medical supplies, there's no space left for me."

I spy a tissue box on the bed table and hand it to Rochelle.

"How have you been sleeping?" I ask.

"Sleep? Every time he coughs, I jump. Sometimes he strikes out when he's dreaming. With the pneumonia, he has trouble breathing. He won't let me sleep on the couch. But I'm OK. I manage."

She glances at the monitors again.

Rochelle is clearly not as OK as she says. After she tells me more about Wade, the course of his illness, and her life, I ask how long she plans to stay.

"I just want to be sure he gets some sleep."

"What about your sleep? You just worked a night shift."

"Actually I did a double. I slept a few hours before I came here. I'm fine."

There's a word for people like Rochelle: counter-dependent; people so phobic of being weak and dependent on others that they deny their own normal needs. Lots of nurses are counter-dependent, caring for others but unable to care for themselves or to allow others to take care of them. I should know. I'm one of them.

I put my hand on her shoulder, "Rochelle, go home. You need more than a few hours of sleep. Patty is a great nurse. If anything changes, she'll call you. Go home. Take care of yourself."

"But he needs me. When he wakes up he gets so anxious."

"I promise we'll get him something for the anxiety. You won't be able to help him unless you take care of yourself. Go home and get some rest."

The trick to using the broken record technique is patience and gentle persistence. "Go home, Rochelle, you need to sleep."

I hold out my hand. She eyes it and slowly lifts her body from the chair.

Since my conversation with the Latina medical resident, someone has placed a batch of brownies in the nurses' lounge. Averting my eyes from temptation, I page Dylan—the psychiatrist covering our service—to let him know that Wade will need a med consult. Then, while I'm listening to my internal debate about the brownies, Bodie, a young gay nurse, enters and searches for a patient's chart.

"I suppose you've heard the story about the paramedic," he says.

"I have."

"What really bothers me," he says, "is how bad everyone seems to feel about HIM. It's OK if WE'RE infected because we're fags doing dirty, disgusting things. But somehow because HE'S straight and got a needle stick on the job, HE'S a saint."

Bodie grabs a chart and leaves without waiting to hear my response.

If he had stayed, I would have asked if he'd heard about the ER nurse who got stuck last week with an HIV infected needle that someone had left in a patient's bed after a procedure. To my mind, Wade is just another health care worker who got stuck, a reminder of the risk frontline health-care workers take every day. Each time it happens, everyone feels more on edge.

While waiting for Dylan, I notice a bulletin board covered with newspaper clippings of recent obituaries. I recognize one of them as Denny, the guy without a gag reflex who made me laugh so hard last summer.

When Dylan arrives to do the psych consult, I fill him in on what I know. He wears his curly dark hair to his shoulders and sports a tiny gold earring in his left earlobe. Recently, I found out that Dylan plays drums in two different rock 'n roll bands. At first, it was surprising because he's such a mild mannered guy; then it made perfect sense. He's mild mannered because he pounds drums seven nights a week.

Dylan asks me to see Wade with him. "Mr. Rawling?" he asks, knocking softly at the door.

Wade startles awake, eyes popping in terror. "It's OK, Wade," I say. "Rochelle was just here. She needed to go home to get some sleep." Wade calms down at the mention of his wife's name. I put my hand on his arm and introduce us.

Wade is alert and oriented but becomes easily agitated. When that happens, he breathes too fast, which depletes his oxygen supply, which causes him to panic and require even more oxygen. After I calm him down, he tells us how badly he feels that he and Rochelle had to move in with her parents.

"Shel's mother won't come into my room," he says. "She makes me feel like a leper."

When the respiratory therapist enters, Wade becomes tremulous again. Seeing this, Dylan tells Wade he will order medication to treat his anxiety. "Nice meeting you, man," he says shaking Wade's hand on our way out the door. I also make sure to grasp his hand before leaving. We will wash our hands after we leave his room, as we do before and after contact with any patient.

On my way to the trauma unit, I get in the elevators with Roberto and Nestor, buff young men with thick leather belts around their waists who comprise the hospital's "lifting team." When too many nurses injured their backs moving patients, the hospital got smart and hired these guys to help out. Where Nestor is strong and silent, Roberto is strong and effusive. Gay and Cuban, he normally speaks with a pronounced Spanish accent that he magnifies for effect.

"How ees going for zhou, Laura?" he asks pronouncing my name "La-o-da."

"Estoy bien, Roberto. ¿Y tú?"

"Fantastico, Laura. Especialmente por que I see you today. We go out clubbing later, yes?"

"Muy bien, Roberto. Hasta luego."

Roberto and Nestor leave me at the nurses' station and zigzag through groups of medical trainees to a patient's room. One of the staff nurses, Dolores, taps me on the shoulder and motions me to follow her into the medication room.

"I'm so upset," she huffs once the door closes. "The surgeons just walked out of Mrs. Escobar's room after telling her she was too full of cancer to operate. They didn't even have the decency to give her a moment to react."

"Is anyone there with her now?"

"No, her husband can't come in until after work. I need to take care of my other patients. Can you see her?" Dolores grabs the medication record and makes a notation. "Oh, I almost forgot to tell you that she's monolingual Spanish."

By now I can do a rudimentary trauma evaluation in Spanish as long as the patient answers "si" or "no" but there's no way I can see this patient without an interpreter.

"I'll try," I tell Dolores while mentally reviewing my options. Dolores locks the med room door behind us and hurries off to a patient's room. When I call the interpreter service, they tell me they are short-staffed and cannot send anyone until much later, if then.

Down the hall, I see Nestor and Roberto talking to a patient. When they pass me, I corral Roberto.

"Roberto, mi amor, could you translate for me? I am so sorry to have to ask you but I need to see this patient now and they can't send me an interpreter."

"Para tu, por supuesto," he says, bowing his head. Roberto follows me into Mrs. Escobar's room.

With the curtains drawn, the room is half-dark. Crayon drawings by small children decorate the walls. Framed pictures of smiling family members crowd the nightstand. When we enter, Mrs. Escobar is sitting up in bed wearing a crisp, flowered bed gown from home. Her black hair is pulled back into a long braid. She sits forward on her bed grasping crumpled tissues in both hands. I am thankful her roommate is elsewhere.

Mrs. Escobar offers a sad smile after Roberto explains why we have come. Since there is only one chair, she motions for him to sit next to her on the bed. Later, I'll have to teach Roberto about maintaining good boundaries with patients. I begin by asking her what she understands about her medical condition. She knows she has little time left. Then she begins to cry. Roberto gets off the bed and kneels down on the floor next to Mrs. Escobar. He takes her hand between his and looking up at her with tears in his eyes, coos to her in Spanish. I am horrified. Maybe I shouldn't have assumed that I would remain in control of the interaction and that Roberto would know how to maintain a "therapeutic relationship" with a patient. Now the two of them are crying in Spanish and I have no idea what they are saying and what I should do. Asking Roberto to translate was a mistake. He has not been trained to listen to such sadness without becoming immersed in it himself. He doesn't know when to draw the patient out and when to help the patient maintain control. Watching him respond to her predicament, I kick myself for exposing him to her pain and suffering. This is not in his job description. Then Roberto moves closer to Mrs. Escobar until he is inches from her face. He murmurs to her in Spanish and touches her cheek with his hand. I am aghast. *Boundaries! Boundaries! No merging and fusing with patients!* I reach out to pull Roberto away by his belt but before I grasp it, Mrs. Escobar starts to laugh. She kisses Roberto's cheek and holds his head in her hands while she blesses him. He rises up and after many "graciases" are exchanged, she tells me she feels better. Thoroughly confused, I shake her hand goodbye and follow Roberto out of the room.

Roberto runs into the linen room. I follow him there and close the door behind us. He stares at me for a moment. His eyes fill with tears. I hand him a washcloth from the laundry cart.

"I am so sorry, Roberto. I should have explained what you were walking into." Roberto gives a final heave and straightens himself up. Holding my arms, he looks deeply into my eyes. "How you do this? How you listen to such pain all day?"

It is not a rhetorical question. I can tell by the expression on his face that he really wants to know how I can spend all day listening to other people's pain without going crazy myself. How can I answer him? He would need to understand that I welcome real emotions the way a parent welcomes a baby's first breath. He would need to know that I've worked with schizophrenic patients who can't feel their feelings at all; manic patients whose feelings are obscured by gale force energy surges; borderline patients who cut themselves in order to feel human; obsessive-compulsive patients whose repetitions distract them from feelings; and depressed patients whose fatigue drains them of feelings. He'd need to know that my work is to help patients find their feelings, claim them, live with them, understand them, and share them with others. Maybe then, he could understand that listening, being there, navigating for someone in the squall or stillness of deep unadulterated emotion is for me, as satisfying as being a midwife ushering in new life.

"It's what I do," I explain. "I listen because I can. Because I know that it helps people."

Roberto regards me with curiosity and maybe a touch of sympathy. "Ees good for you," he says. "No good for me."

He is gone before I remember to ask him what he said that made Mrs. Escobar laugh.

The next morning, I head to the AIDS unit to check on Wade. Patty is his nurse again today. When she sees me, her face clouds over. "He's taken a downward turn," she says. "Spiked a fever yesterday afternoon. Today, his O2 saturation stinks and he's talking ragtime. Rochelle is with him now if you want to check in."

The head of Wade's bed is slightly elevated. An oxygen mask encases his nose and mouth. His eyes are closed as if it takes all of his concentration to accomplish each labored breath. Rochelle sits by his bed with her upper body resting on the edge of Wade's mattress, next to his flaccid arm.

I touch her shoulder and whisper, "Rochelle?"

She raises her head and glances at the monitor. Then she looks at me with knowing, grieving eyes. "He doesn't have long."

"I'm so sorry."

"At least I slept some yesterday."

"That's good to hear."

She whispers, "Can we talk somewhere?"

I direct her to the visitor's lounge, a feature unique to 5A. Above a piano, a giant picture of a young Elizabeth Taylor nearly covers one wall. The aroma of fresh brewed coffee almost masks the unit's odor of disease and decay. I pour us each a cup from a collection of ceramic mugs. After we settle into the upholstered chairs, Rochelle talks and talks.

After five years of caring for Wade — losing sleep and personal space, staying strong through each indignity of his illness — with the end now in sight, she no longer needs to be a rock. Although Rochelle admits feeling angry that Wade refused to take meds, exhaustion, not anger, fills her body. This is not a good sign. Anger, at least, makes a body feel alive. I grow more alarmed when Rochelle tells me she's been hospitalized twice for depression. In response to my question about follow-up treatment, she tells me that she discontinued outpatient therapy two years ago.

It soon dawns on me that I have a new patient. With a dying husband, impaired sleep, and a history of depression severe enough to have required hospitalization, Rochelle is at high risk for another breakdown. "Have you thought about seeing your psychiatrist for support?" I ask.

"Yeah, I thought about it but," she shrugs her shoulders.

"But what?" I press.

"I don't know. I guess I don't think it's necessary."

"Oh."

I give the moment some silence in which I hope she will hear my subtle "I beg to differ with you" and come to a more reasoned conclusion. She doesn't. My next strategy is the "psycho-educational" approach. I list her symptoms and suggest that therapy and medication could head off a major depression at the pass.

"I know you're trying to be helpful," she says, "but I'll know when I need to do something."

"You may and you may not. You've been so focused on Wade and on work that you may be out of touch with your own needs. If there ever was a time for support, it's now."

Rochelle does not react.

OK. This is going nowhere. New approach necessary. She's a med-surg nurse. Speak her language.

"It's like when one of your patients starts having TIA's," I say, pleased that I remember about transient ischemic attacks—ministrokes—from my ICU days. "You know you have to do something or the patient is headed for trouble, right? Well, you could be headed for the psychiatric version of a stroke. That's why I'm pushing you hard to call your doctor now."

Rochelle tilts her head backward until it rests against the wall. With her eyes closed, she looks as if she is praying. When she opens them, I can see that she was trying to stem the flow of tears. "I'll think about it."

So typical. Too many of us nurses are bad about self-care. We're overweight; we smoke; we overwork; we slip into addiction. We're so used to being the helpers that we can't see when we ourselves need help.

Early on in my family, I trained myself to become a self-contained, no muss, no fuss machine. For many years my nightly mantra was, "I will never need anything from anybody ever." I never told my parents about the ornery, old cocker spaniel that bit me on the leg when I was in third grade or the strange man who tried to lure me into his car on the way home from school the following year. I have since learned that many of us with "family issues" avoided bothering our overburdened parents with our own needs. Uncomfortable with the notion of being anything but totally self-reliant, we become counter-dependent. That's why I'm doubtful that Rochelle will take my advice. I tell her I will check back with her later. Right now, I need to follow-up with my trauma patients on 4D.

"Did the police come for Christian?" I ask Trudy when I notice that Christian Whitcomb's name has been erased from 4D's census board.

"The police? No, he was transferred to the rehabilitation hospital a few hours ago. Why would the police be involved?"

I tell Trudy the story of how Christian, a parolee who had violated the terms of his parole by leaving a treatment facility prematurely, had fallen from the top of a building onto a group of policemen below, the very folks he was trying to avoid.

"He may get lucky," she says. "We'll never know."

This part of the job is becoming increasingly hard for me—not knowing what happens to my patients. Again, I consider the idea of offering a support group, perhaps as much for me as for them.

I check in with a couple of other patients before I see Mr. Boudreau, the Cajun man who blames himself for his cousin's death in a house fire last week. When I pull a chair over by his bed, he narrows his eyes at me.

"What the hell," he growls. "I don't like talking much but seein' as I chewed your ear last time, I may as well tell you I'm none too happy with my doctors."

Mr. Boudreau is mostly upset at them for refusing to grant him permission to attend his cousin's funeral. On top of that, they want to take him back to surgery to repair the fistula. "I ain't inclined to do it," he says. "I'd rather be home smoking and drinking."

"It's your decision," I say. "But it's important that you understand the consequences either way."

This is the kind of situation where a care conference might be beneficial to everyone. After our conversation, I place calls to members of Mr. Boudreau's treatment team and arrange a meeting for tomorrow with all of the players.

Hours later, I return to the AIDS unit.

"It's over," says Patty, Wade's nurse.

"Was Rochelle here?" I ask.

"To the end," says Patty. "She made sure his doctors made him comfortable. Do you want her phone number? She kind of fell apart afterward."

"How about you?"

"This is an AIDS unit. He had a good death. That's what's important to me."

Although I tried, I wasn't able to get in touch with Rochelle until the following day. "I'm fine," she said. "At least I'll be able to sleep now and go shopping."

"Have you contacted your psychiatrist?"

"No, I'll be OK," she said. "I just need to go shopping."

When I was a kid, I didn't talk to anyone when I was feeling bad. Instead, I climbed trees. I preferred being by myself high above the world, beyond feelings. Therapy, and later, marriage forced me to climb down a few notches from my perch. Raising children and being such a part of their lives has forced me down a few more notches. Now I realize what I couldn't feel back then, that being up there by myself was a very lonely place to be.

8

Balancing the big scale in the sky

On the last Sunday in June, while my kids and I were feeding ducks in Golden Gate Park, Luk Hui crossed Lincoln Avenue and was hit by a speeding car. "I had too much good luck in my twenties," he says. "Now I have bad luck." He states this as a fact, one that he accepts.

I wish he hadn't said that. Six months into my pregnancy I'm worried that because life has gone so well for me, asking for three healthy children would be asking for too much.

Luk Hui, a forty-one-year-old man with sharp but playful eyes, says that his good luck began in China twenty years earlier at the end of the Chinese Cultural Revolution when he returned from the countryside where he had been forced into hard labor. After performing well on state exams, he was "pushed" into medical school, eventually landing at Stanford University for graduate training. His run of bad luck began four years ago when he was fired from his job as a medical researcher. In his view, life is a balance of good luck and bad luck. Given his long run of good luck, he knows what's in store.

Many patients theorize why bad things have happened to them. Some believe in karma. Others believe they did something to anger God; perhaps the lie they told a parent or the affair they had years before. Consuela, an eighty-year-old grandmother who worked as a medical aide up until the time a car mowed her down while she was crossing the street with the light, refused to accept that she, a caregiver for all of her working life, had earned the wrath of God.

"I don't know what to think," she cried while squeezing a crucifix. "I go to church; I do good in the world but God did not protect me."

As someone who does not believe in a god who watches out for me personally, I am not one to handle these spiritual crises. When Consuela refused my offer to call a priest for her, all I could tell her was that bad things sometimes happen to very good people for no discernable reason. This seemed to upset her even more: the idea that trauma can occur randomly.

"No," she countered. "I must have done something very bad. But I cannot remember." She grasped my hand tightly. "There is a reason for everything."

On my way to the medical psychiatric area to see my next patient, I remember my work with chronic schizophrenic patients. They too came up with theories to explain what went wrong in their brains. "Aliens implanted radio waves in my mind" or "Bugs crawled into my brain through my ears and can't get out." Even theories like these are preferable to accepting that things in life sometimes happen randomly and without a greater purpose.

The hospital recently created a four-bed mini-unit called the medical psychiatric area, or MPA. The new unit was established after the hospital realized it was spending too much on sitters—non-licensed staff to sit at the bedside of suicidal or mentally ill patients with concurrent medical or surgical problems. The MPA was formed

by knocking out a wall between two double rooms on an orthopedic unit. That allows one nurse to continually observe four patients,
thereby saving money.

The only problem is that the ward's orthopedic nurses are experts
in repairing broken bones, not broken minds. The hospital's solution
to this has been to give the nurses classes in psych nursing: therapeutic
communication, psychiatric assessment, psychiatric illness and diagnosis, seclusion and restraints, and psychiatric medications. After Janice,
Antionette, and I taught a series of these classes, it was clear to us
that the ortho nurses had yet to morph into bona fide psych nurses.
In fact, many of them were frightened of psychiatric patients and
rankled that their ambitious nurse manager had volunteered his unit
to house the MPA.

When I was asked to see Serena Deaver on the MPA this morning, my heart sank. Unlike Luk Hui, Serena—a patient with whom I
had worked years ago in a day-treatment program—has known only
misfortune her entire life. As soon as I heard her name, I remember
her history. Why is it that I can't remember what I made for dinner yesterday but can recall former patients' psychiatric histories in
astonishing detail?

When I enter the medical psychiatric area, a female patient in
four-point restraints is writhing naked on the bed closest to the door.
Her sheets and blankets lay in a heap on the floor. A male X-ray tech,
who must have just taken a series of films of the patient in the next
bed, steals glances at the writhing woman as he flirts with a young
female nurse sitting outside the doorway to the four-bed ward.

"The show's over," I announce while walking over to the patient
and placing a sheet over her body. Up close, I recognize Serena's square
jaw, broad nose, and broad forehead. Her severely cut straight hair is
streaked with yellow. Although she is awake, her eyes ping pong around
the room. Mumbling and thrashing on the bed, she does not respond
to my presence. Probably, she is hallucinating. Leather restraints secure

each limb to a corner of the bed so that she doesn't take off running or tear out the I.V. in her arm or pull the nasogastric tube from her nostril.

Serena's life began with a mother who abandoned her and a father who made her young body available for the sexual enjoyment of his buddies. Typically, she latches onto people in her life with such ferocity that they get scared and abandon her, the usual precipitant for her self-destructive behavior and suicide attempts. One day in women's group, Serena told us she had survived a jump off the Golden Gate Bridge. When a passing fisherman pulled her from the water, she realized that God wanted her to remain among the living for a reason. Apparently, between then and now, she and God have stopped communicating.

This time, Serena overdosed on Tylenol, a drug whose potential lethality is well known to experienced psychiatric patients. According to the psychiatry resident's admission note, the precipitant to this suicide attempt is the upcoming graduation and relocation of Serena's student-therapist. In her eyes, this is another abandonment.

A wonderful psychiatric nurse I knew used to read Shakespeare to patients in four-point restraints when she worked the night shift. She swore that the rhythm of the verse calmed people better than drugs and without the side effects. Now, even though Serena is attending more to internal experiences than external ones and in lieu of Shakespeare committed to memory, I pull my chair close and speak softly to her about where she is and why.

When I am finished, I speak with the young nurse charged with Serena's care. She is a registry nurse, meaning that she is employed by a nursing agency and not by the hospital itself. Most likely, she's replacing a regular nurse who has called in sick. The registry nurse tells me she has no psych experience and is angry that the regular staff has assigned her to the med psych area. I would be too. Unfortunately, this kind of mistreatment happens all too often.

I pull out a copy of a mental status exam and give her a brief tutorial on how to assess Serena's state of mind. Then I encourage her to speak with Serena at frequent intervals to remind her where she is and why she is in restraints. The nurse promises to page me when Serena's delirium clears.

I smell Mr. Reeves before I see him wheeling past me on 4D.

"You tell 'em they can kiss my ass, sister. I got more education in this here pinky then any of them doctors do. An' you can tell 'em that for me too!"

"Good Morning, Mr. Reeves."

Mr. Reeves is not officially my patient. He refuses to see anyone from psychiatry. I interact with him briefly each day with the hope that he might someday be able to tolerate a serious conversation about his mental health issues.

He glances at me briefly. "They keep threatening me with amputation. I tell them to just fix the goddamn leg. They don't need to take it off. If they do, I'll sue 'em just like I sued Stanford and St. Mary's for thirty million each. All I gotta do is call my lawyer. These people will have to learn the hard way they can't mess with me."

Mr. Reeves stinks, plain and simple. His foot is the color of an eggplant and smells like a rotten egg. A second whiff reveals the competing fragrances of old urine, old sweat, and soiled clothes. His face, the color of Sedona red clay, is a topographic map of craters and ridges. His greasy, color-depleted hair clumps together and sticks out from his large head. A week's worth of stubble, like prickles on a cactus, dot his face and neck. His blue eyes, though, cut clear and sharp through the layers of grit and odor.

"Hey sister, can you get me a cup of coffee?"

"Take a shower and I'll buy you coffee for a week," I say, but he's already wheeled himself down the corridor.

Mid-afternoon, most of the televisions on the unit are tuned to cartoons. Sometimes I have to ask patients, "Do you mind turning this off so we can talk?" Usually people comply, but not always. One patient grunted and turned the volume down the teeniest bit. Actions, or lack of them, say so much.

On this afternoon, 4D hums with a different din than the frenetic popping, whirring, and zooming noise of cartoons. Voices, some feminine, some masculine, controlled and modulated, emanate from the black boxes that swing out over patients' beds. Curious as to what accounts for this change, I stop by the room of Mr. Monroe who was shot in the gut two days ago under circumstances he refuses to discuss.

"White dude with a gun downtown," he growls in response to my "what's up?" gesture. "Buncha people shot up in a law firm. Hear them ambulances? That'll be them now."

Oh my God. Brian.

I step out to call him. The phone rings four times before his voicemail picks up.

Damn it! Where is he?

Mr. Reeves wheels past me. "Gotta go down to the ER," he grumbles. "Gotta warn these people of their rights."

How about the right of everyone in this hospital not to be assaulted by the odor of your putrefying foot?

"Save your breath, Mr. Reeves. You won't be able to get near those folks until they're stabilized. Go get yourself a cup of coffee instead." I hand him fifty cents.

Victoria, 4D's head nurse, comes up to me. "You heard the news? They'll be in surgery this evening. You'll have your work cut out for you tomorrow."

I step back into Mr. Monroe's room to catch the details. "Repeat, there is an armed man in the law offices of Pettit and Martin at 101 California Street. We think he is alone. So far, ten people have been evacuated."

Thank God, it's not Brian's law firm. Then I cringe. It may not be my husband but it's someone else's loved one. I call again to no avail.

"Hey," grouses Mr. Monroe. "I got shot and nobody puts me on the goddamn news." He switches the channel back to cartoons. Since tomorrow will be busy, I spend the afternoon following up on patients I've already evaluated.

Serena's nurse pages me late in the afternoon. "She's awake and alert and asking to get out of restraints."

"I'll be right down." Before I leave, I call Brian's office again. This time he answers on the first ring. "Oh Brian, I was so worried."

"It's a couple of blocks down the street, not here."

"I know. But I needed to hear your voice anyway."

"I remember you," says Serena when I pull up a chair next to her bed. "I liked that day-treatment place, even if it was in the Tenderloin. I felt pretty good then."

Since the day-treatment center closed for lack of funding, stability has eluded Serena. She's been in and out of hospitals and vocational programs and supervised living situations. For the last three years, with her student-therapist's support and weekly AA groups, she's managed to stay out of the hospital. When Scott told her he was leaving, the voices in her head started screaming that she was no good, that she deserved to die.

"I'm so tired," she says. "Every time I get a leg up on my life, something goes wrong and I slip off the deep end."

It seems Serena's fate in this world is to teach psychology students about what happens when children are neglected, abused, and abandoned. How ironic it is that in the course of training students, we replicate that abandonment and re-traumatize the same patients we purport to treat.

Looking at Serena, I feel a huge sadness. Her arms tally up rendezvous with knives and cigarettes. Her neck gleams with a necklace of scar tissue. When dissociated from her own body, she panics and draws blood to prove her existence, to know she is human. When she remains conscious she feels despicable, a worthless creature with no hope in this world.

What did she do to deserve such a wretched life? Wouldn't Luk Hui say she's due for a round of good luck?

Miranda, the new star psychiatrist from Yale, thinks that psychotherapy is "bogus."

"No study has ever proved its effectiveness," she declared at a recent psych consult meeting. Others pointed out that just because scientists don't yet have the tools to prove that psychotherapy can be effective doesn't mean that it should be abandoned. Patients like Serena with serious personality disorders are notoriously difficult to treat. At McLean Hospital in the mid-seventies, these patients were hospitalized for months, even years at a time. Ten years later in San Francisco, they were discharged after three days with the rationale that hospitalization more often than not results in behavioral and psychological regression instead of growth. There was a lot of truth to that charge. However, long-term outpatient therapy with a competent therapist can significantly improve these patients' lives. The process is slow, requiring eight to ten years of work with highly skilled and committed therapists. In the end, such therapy can be cost effective in allowing patients to lead productive lives. Still, very few therapists and clinics are willing to make such a commitment to treatment. Lacking this option, people like Serena must make do with rotating student-therapists.

Now that her mental status is clearing, Serena will be discharged soon. Before leaving for the day, I will call Scott, her student-therapist, and his supervisor to inform them about Serena's overdose attempt. I will impress upon them the importance of finding her another therapist, another hand to hold to keep her afloat for another school year. And I will suggest to the supervisor that students ought to address termination issues early in therapy, especially a course of therapy that must end in nine months. That could allow the patient time to anticipate the loss and to develop coping skills that could prevent a future suicide attempt.

That night, after the kids are fed, bathed, and put to bed, Brian and I turn on the news. "This afternoon, Gian Luigi Ferri, a southern California businessman and disgruntled client of the law office of Pettit and Martin, walked into the building at 101 California Street armed with two semi-automatic weapons and 250 rounds of ammunition. He got off at the thirty-fourth floor where he roamed the halls and fired indiscriminately. Fourteen people were killed or wounded before he turned the gun on himself."

The baby kicks me as if in protest. "Hey, enough of that," I say rubbing my swollen abdomen. Brian places his hand on the baby in time to feel the next round of impressive kickboxing. Maybe the news, or my reaction to it, is stressing this baby out. I leave Brian and head downstairs to watch a "Cheers" rerun in our bedroom.

The next morning, Brian takes Corianne to preschool so I can get to the hospital before the media zoo arrives. Silly me. At 7:30 a.m., 4D is already crammed with press people, hospital officials, and family members. I push through them to the nurses' station to check in with Trudy who briefs me on the status of three women patients who survived the gunman's bullets. Another more seriously injured victim remains in the ICU. Two other victims have been transferred to private hospitals.

Trudy surveys the crowd in front of us. "Go see the patient in room nine now, while Norma is finishing her dressing and the family is outside her room. Otherwise you'll be hard pressed to see her."

I take Trudy's advice and introduce myself briefly to the patient's family before suggesting that they take a coffee break in the cafeteria. Then I slip into the patient's room.

While Norma finishes her nursing care, I tell Yvette Carry why I'm here. She is pale and petite, in her late twenties with pleasant features and short, straight, sandy-colored hair. When Norma leaves and the heavy door separates us from the din outside, I tell Yvette what I know from the news and ask her to tell me everything she remembers about yesterday. I explain that piecing together and organizing her memories into a coherent story will help her to integrate the experience psychologically and emotionally. Yvette regards me evenly, considers what I have said, and agrees to revisit the details of yesterday's tragedy.

Like her husband, Michael, Yvette is a lawyer. She was visiting his law firm on her lunch hour in order to use the law library. Michael had set her up in an empty office on the thirty-fourth floor. When Michael heard the news that a gunman was in the building, he raced to her office only to find himself face to face with Gian Luigi Ferri. Michael threw his body over Yvette's like a shield. In doing so, he took the bullet that would have taken her life.

Yvette relates the story as if she is narrating a movie. "I called 911 and told them we needed medical attention right away. I kept talking to Michael telling him to hang on, that someone would come soon to help us. Then I called again. I remember saying, 'Where are the paramedics? Why aren't they here? I need them to come now.'"

Yvette remains dry-eyed, which helps me to stem my own tears.

"I am not an emotional person to begin with," she says, "but I think I'm in shock."

I don't doubt it. Yesterday, Yvette was pleading for the paramedics to rescue her and her young husband who lay dying in her arms while his murderer continued to roam the corridors of the law office with an automatic weapon. Today she wakes up a widow, injured, and surrounded by friends, family, and the press. Since she uses intellectualization as a way of coping with stress, I give her an intellectual explanation.

"Your psychological defense system will not expose you to more than you can handle. If you feel like you are removed from your emotions right now, it is a protective response though your emotions will catch up with you. I think it would be a good idea if you had the names of a few therapists to talk to when you're ready."

Yvette agrees. She will have to grapple with images of violence, the loss of a sense of security in the world, missing her husband, and knowing that he sacrificed his life for hers. All this sounds like more than the twenty sessions that an HMO typically allots to psychotherapy. Fortunately, Yvette has a supportive family, a career, and the means to pay for the treatment she will need after her insurance runs out.

As soon as I open Yvette's door to leave, her family rushes in. I close the door behind them and hope the media will respect their privacy. In front of me, seated in his wheelchair amid a sea of reporters and photographers, Mr. Reeves spouts off about injustice and incompetence. He wheels past two well-dressed young women standing outside a patient's doorway. They crinkle their noses in his wake. "We've got to get her out of this hellhole NOW!" says one.

I sidle up to them. "It's not the Ritz," I say, "But this is the best place in the city for treating trauma. The nurses and doctors here are trauma experts. This is where I would want my relatives to be."

They didn't ask me for my opinion but I just had to set them straight.

Over the morning, I manage to meet with the other two women who survived the massacre. Step by step, we recreate the sensations and observations of their ordeal. One woman is predominantly anxious and fearful. The other displays a sense of unreality. She giggles throughout the interview saying, "I thought to myself, 'These can't be real bullets!'"

Three different women, same gunman, three different reactions.

Looking up from the note I am writing in the medical record, I notice Miranda talking to Victoria, the head nurse, just outside her office. After she leaves, Victoria walks over to me.

"The new shrink wants to know why the psychiatrists were not asked to see the 101 California folks. I told her that we routinely call the psych nurses for the trauma cases and that just because these victims are white and carry briefcases doesn't change our protocol. Christ, I hate these goddamn high-profile cases! Everyone and their mother wants to get into the act."

Without waiting for an answer, Victoria marches back to her office.

In psychiatric-consultation rounds later in the morning, 101 California is on everyone's mind. Donald asks me to present the patients. I describe the different responses to trauma evidenced by the three patients I saw and since medical students are present, I include information about what can be predicted by three such distinctive responses. I remind them that statistically, most victims of trauma do not develop post-traumatic stress disorder, or PTSD, which can only be diagnosed at least one month after the traumatic event. Before that, it's called Acute Stress Response, or ASR. We review the diagnostic criteria of ASR and PTSD: re-experiencing the trauma (through intrusive memories, dreams, hallucinations, flashbacks, and intense distress after exposure to cues that recall the trauma); avoidant responses (feeling detached, uninterested in previously pleasurable activities, avoiding anything or anyone that arouses memories of the trauma); and, hyperarousal (difficulty sleeping, irritability, hypervigilance, startle response, and difficulty concentrating). In terms of risk, we know that people who have been exposed to previous trauma, especially at a young age, or those who have suffered from chronic stress are more prone to developing PTSD than those who have not. According to the most recent journal articles, people who dissociate in response to trauma are the most likely ones to develop PTSD. However, a good social support system can protect a person from developing PTSD.

"Any questions or comments?" asks Donald when I have finished.

Miranda notes that time is almost up and says, "We didn't talk about meds for PTSD. I'm also wondering why none of the psychiatrists were asked to consult."

It's more of a pout than a question but I answer her as if it were the latter. I explain to her what Donald already knows: that my predecessor originated the psychiatric nurse consultant role at SFGH in the early 1970s and developed an expertise in trauma over the next twenty years. She educated the 4D staff nurses to recognize signs and symptoms of acute stress response and post-traumatic stress disorder. Since then, the nurses have been automatically phoning in the trauma cases to the psych nurse consultants. We, in turn, ask the docs to consult if the patient requires medication.

"We see people with gun shot wounds every week, Miranda. If you would like to see some of these patients, there are more than enough to go around. Let me know and I'll be happy to call you."

Miranda shuts up.

"Other questions, comments?" Donald asks.

One of the new medical students half-raises her hand. "Does a person actually have to be hurt to have a diagnosis of PTSD?"

Barry, who coordinates medical-student classes for our department, responds. "Not necessarily. If a person witnessed or was confronted with a horrible event where there was a threat of great bodily harm or death, that person could also develop PTSD."

The student, a sturdy young woman with deep dimples and a shy smile, hesitates as if she has something more on her mind.

"Well, that's not exactly what was I was thinking."

She squirms in her chair and looks around the group. "I'm not sure if this is the place to talk about it but, well, working with AIDS patients last month really got to a lot of us. I guess I'm asking, could the things you see as a doctor traumatize you?"

From the mouths of babes. So how does being immersed in horrible images week in and week out affect us? We never talk about that. From the silence that has settled over this group, it seems we may never know.

"Let's follow that up in supervision group this afternoon," says Barry.

"So, how have you two coped with the effects of listening to war stories for so long?" I ask my officemates after the door closes behind us.

"Good question," says Janice. "Sometimes it's tough. Occasionally I lose sleep over a really bad story. But a couple of margaritas with my Girls' Night Out group usually improves my spirits!"

I look over at Antionette, who looks svelte and toned as usual, in a stretchy top and skinny skirt. "How much time have you been spending at the gym?"

"As much as I can," she says. "But I also have close friends in the Guard that I see a lot."

Antionette was recently promoted to Lieutenant Colonel in the California Army National Guard. Once a month over almost twenty years, she and her fellow reservists have driven to Sacramento for "drill." Each summer they spend two weeks at Camp Roberts, a four-hour drive south, for training exercises.

"How about you, Laurie?" asks Janice. "I know it's hard to get away with young children and one on the way."

I tell them that I stroll through The Comfort Garden when I need to clear my mind. "Then, when I heard Keith's story—the one where his mother jumped from their twelfth floor window and landed in the playground in front of him—I pulled out a pen and started writing. It helped to release my feelings but I still had to go climb the hills that night to wear myself out."

Antionette nods in agreement. "When I'm really stressed out, I run in the park or walk along the beach. Being in nature always makes me feel better."

"I spend a lot of time painting sets," says Janice. "Both of my girls act in a theater group so that's what I do to help out. You'd be surprised how soothing it can be!"

Overall, I seem to be bringing fewer images home with me than I did last year. Some nights, however, I still write pages and pages about the inequities of human experience. Talking with Janice and Antionette, I'm reminded of this morning's meeting with Luk Hui about good karma and bad karma. I tell them what he said about having had a long run of good karma and knowing he's due for a change.

"When he said that, I got nervous even though all of my prenatal tests have been negative."

"I've thought about karma too," says Antionette. "You can't work here and NOT wonder why you've been so blessed while others have not."

"Maybe that's why we work here," says Janice. "It's our way of trying to balance the big scale in the sky."

What if the scale never comes close to being balanced? Can we accept that for some people, life is unfair? People like Serena Deaver never had a chance at living a good life and probably never will.

9

A walking time bomb

T rudy is off and Noreen, an Irish nurse, is in charge. I am glad to see her back on the unit. She's been out for a few months with an injured back, the scourge of nurses who must lift and reposition patients. At times, Noreen can be a pinch critical of her co-workers, but she runs a tight ship and cares deeply about her patients.

"Ah, Laurie," she says, "I've got two gentlemen for you to see this mornin'. One, Mr. Herrold, just out of ICU, was shot in the heart two weeks ago in a club a few blocks from here. Don't you know an ambulance just happened to be circlin' the area when they got the call. Five minutes later, he was in the OR with Dr. Steinfeldt himself on duty. That's enough luck for a lifetime, I'd say. The other gentleman, well, I don't quite know what to make of that one. Isaac Abdul, he calls himself. He's got a compression fracture of the lumbar spine. According to him, a cop pushed him off a building. He says that this same cop has beaten him many times before and is probably looking for him right now. If you ask me, he sounds paranoid and delusional. See what you think."

Throughout our conversation, a tall and wiry young man has been pacing the unit like the Energizer bunny.

I ask, "Is that guy OK?"

"Pee Wee? Oh, he's a bit wired but he does what you tell him to do. Smoked some crack a couple of nights ago and collapsed his lung. He's been burning a path around the unit ever since he got here."

Noreen continues talking as I close Mr. Herrold's chart and search for Pee Wee's. "You know, Laurie, I was thinkin' I could do what you do, you know, talk to people, listen to their problems. Must be nice not to have to work weekends and holidays."

Pee Wee passes us again. He looks like Gumby with elastic legs and arms stretched as far as they can be stretched without breaking. His gait is jerky and his eyes are glazed. Pee Wee is Native-American. His long straight black hair is gathered into a ponytail. A large herpetic lesion on his full lips and dark circles under his eyes mar his otherwise clear but ruddy complexion. Chest tubes protrude from the right side of his upper abdomen and empty into a pleurovac, a hard plastic container the size and shape of a briefcase. It collects drainage from his chest wall. Pee Wee drags it with him as he paces, talking continuously and addressing anyone who passes by.

"I mean that's what you do, right? Talk to people. No heavy lifting and such," Noreen persists.

"None."

I open Pee Wee's chart. Sure enough, what we've got here is a twenty-year-old crack-smoking, HIV-positive, alcoholic, manic-depressive six-foot-five-inch kid with a collapsed lung. I shudder thinking about the things that can go wrong with a full-blown manic patient on any surgical unit amid IV poles, urine containers, traction equipment, wheelchairs, and crutches.

Noreen waits for me to say more. I can hear in her voice that she thinks I have an easy job, and in lots of ways, it is easier than what she does. But, one of the problems inherent in this job is its invisibility. Although all of us psych-nurse consultants continually assess the environment for potentially violent situations and take measures to prevent them from occurring, it's difficult to connect our actions directly to a situation that never erupts. Luck plays a part, as do the interventions of others. Unfortunately, clinical experience with violent patients that hones one's instincts and informs one's judgment is invisible and not easily taught.

"I think you could make a good psychiatric nurse, Noreen," I respond, hoping she doesn't hear the irritation in my voice. "If you're interested in doing what I do, get a masters degree in psychiatric nursing. It was the best investment I ever made. But I advise you to work on a psychiatric unit for a couple of years first."

If Noreen were a psych nurse, she would know to be very nervous about this kid. Although Pee Wee isn't full-blown at this moment, I remember working on inpatient units with manic patients whose bodies surged with unbridled energy. When I was working at a day-treatment center in San Francisco's Tenderloin district, a manic patient threw an oak chair at me because I would not give him the drugs that he demanded. Luckily, I ducked. Instead of shattering my head, the chair shattered the twelve-foot high wall of glass behind me that bordered the street. On the other hand, manic patients have entertained the night staff in hospitals by singing Broadway show tunes or by tap dancing up and down the corridors until daybreak. But, you never know when the energy will turn ugly.

The frequent sensation of pressure on my bladder reminds me that I'm seven months pregnant. Otherwise I'm feeling fine and still enjoying the second trimester surge of energy, which I know will diminish during this last trimester.

After emerging from the tiny bathroom near the lounge, I open the vertical filing cabinet and retrieve Pee Wee's old chart. According to these records, Pee Wee's nose and face have been busted at least three times in the last two years. He has been jailed and is *persona non grata* at a private hospital in town where he "ripped his room to shreds." A call to the Psychiatric Emergency Service confirms that they know him well. On a few recent occasions, Pee Wee has been committed to a locked inpatient psychiatry unit for seventy-two hours each time on grounds that he is a "danger to others." Once there, he has refused to take psychiatric medication. It's the same old story. At the end of the seventy-two hour psychiatric hold, Pee Wee pulls himself together for the commitment hearing in front of the district attorney at which time he denies being suicidal or homicidal and convinces the D.A. that he will eat fois gras from the dumpster behind Star's restaurant and sleep at St. Boniface Church. After Pee Wee presents an acceptable plan of self-care, the D.A. orders the hospital to release him.

I call Donald, the chief psychiatrist on our team. He's on afternoon call. "Listen Donald, this guy isn't losing it yet but he hasn't slept for at least three nights; he's walking into patients' rooms, and he's pacing nonstop. Can you take a look at him and make some medication suggestions?"

"I thought you said he's refusing meds."

"He is, but I'd like to have an antipsychotic on the unit in case he blows."

"The surgical residents haven't asked for a psychiatric consult," he protests.

"I know, but I'm involved with the case and now I'm asking you to co-consult about a medication recommendation."

"OK," he sighs, "I'll try to stop by before I leave this evening. But do me a favor and contact the psych resident on call tonight and fill him or her in on the situation."

Even though I know the nurses rarely get around to reading it, I write up a nursing care plan describing when and how to set limits on Pee Wee's behavior. So far, he's just being intrusive and obnoxious. If he becomes argumentative, controlling, and incapable of redirection, we'll be in trouble.

For someone who was just shot in the heart, Greg Herrold, a husky dark-eyed, twenty-five-year-old, looks glowingly alive. He jumps at the chance to repeat his story as if doing so gives him another opportunity to realize that yes, it really happened and yes, he really survived.

"I was working as a bouncer at the Oasis; been there for a few months; no major problems or nothin'. Friday night, this guy all dressed up in white—white pants, white shirt, white vest—wants to get in, but like, I smell alcohol on him. I mean the guy reeks so I'm not gonna let him in. He's got two friends with him. The guy's so loaded, they're propping him up. 'You two are OK,' I tell them, but not your friend. So all three of them leave. Half hour later, the guy in white comes back, only this time he's dressed in black. I got a bad feeling in my gut. Then he flashes a gun at me and it's lights out."

While Greg tells me his story, I marvel at his composure. When he finishes, his face clouds and he motions for me to move closer.

"Something really weird happened while I was in intensive care," he whispers. "Two guys dressed in them green doctor suits come in and look at the paperwork they got hanging near my bed. Suddenly I go apeshit 'cuz I know they're the friends of the dude who shot me. Look, I'm not crazy or nuthin'. In my business, you remember faces. Anyway, they got that tube down my throat and my hands tied down so's all I can do is rattle my bed to get the attention of my nurse. She's workin' on the guy next to me. I keep rattling the rails until she hears me but as soon as she turns in my direction, they split. You think I'm nuts, don't you? Go ask my nurse. Go ask Carol. She'll tell you! Those guys scared the shit outta me. All I could think was they've come to finish me off."

Greg is breathing hard as if he's seen a ghost.

"No, I don't think you're crazy," I say, in an effort to reassure him. "But sometimes morphine makes people hallucinate."

In truth, I am wondering what else might account for his altered perceptions. I have a hard time believing that someone off the street would know where to get hospital scrubs, and have the gall to enter the ICU where strangers are routinely questioned, and on top of that, to stand at a patient's bedside flipping through his chart. Greg was in the ICU for two weeks. For most of that time, he was in a coma. Sometimes patients under the influence of sedating drugs remember distortions of reality.

Greg shakes his head and says sadly, "I knew no one would believe me."

Isaac Abdul, as he calls himself, looks younger than his nineteen years. Maybe it's the Dutch boy bob and the freckles or his slightly smirky smile. Or, the way his words bubble over each other so fast that, like a five-year-old, he gasps for breath in mid-sentence. In any case, he pulls me right into his world.

"This cop has it in for me because I won't be a 'citizen informer' for him anymore and because I blew the cover of some narcs who'd gotten in with a group of people I know. He chased me onto a roof in the Tenderloin and pushed me down two stories. I mean the guy has it out for me. He's had me arrested so many times for possession of marijuana that the judge even told him to get off my case. I'm freaked that he's gonna find me here and I can't even move."

Isaac tells me that he has a "soft spot" on his head where he had surgery for a malignant glioma five years ago. Because he is HIV positive, he has refused radiation and chemotherapy. I do a mental status exam to look for problems of cognition but find none. Isaac organizes his thoughts and presents his ideas in a coherent manner. He can do math problems in his head and spell the word "world" backward. His short-term and long-term memory seem consistent and intact. During our conversation, he stays attentive and engaged, not preoccupied with internal thoughts or easily distracted. He demonstrates a full range of emotions and a good sense of humor. His speech is fast but not pressured as in mania. His judgment is questionable given his alleged frequent encounters with the law but he has insight regarding his medical conditions. Isaac has signed a "release of information form" that was sent to the hospital in Sacramento where he had brain surgery. I wonder if the records will corroborate all that he has told me.

Could Isaac's stories be paranoid delusions? Years ago, I worked with a man labeled "paranoid and delusional" who said, as these patients typically do, that the FBI was after him. As it turned out, he was telling the truth. Since that time, I've learned to keep an open mind.

At the end of the interview, Isaac admits he's no angel. "I used to sell drugs but I stopped when a woman wanted to buy crack for herself instead of milk for her three kids. I just couldn't do it no more when I saw that. Now I got me some trained rats. I taught them how to ride miniature bicycles. I can make up to eighty dollars a day at Fisherman's Wharf!

"What? You don't believe me? I'll show you the pictures tomorrow. My friend is going to bring them when he visits."

I'll believe it when I see them. Meanwhile, Isaac is very happy that I will make the necessary arrangements to give him an alias so that the bully cop won't be able to find him in the hospital. I'll have to give the nurses explicit instructions not to reveal Isaac's real name to anyone, especially to a police officer.

I take Pee Wee out to the patio to get to know him and to give the staff a little break. A few steps from the elevator, glass doors open to the blue sky. Various shades of green shrubs and a reddish-purple tree soften the gray concrete walls that edge the patio. The shiny green leaves of a large pittosporum tree shade a sitting area.

"What's your life like outside of here?" I ask Pee Wee, who is distracted by a group of men across the courtyard sitting in a huddle around an upright ashcan. All three are grizzled and tattooed. The only one wearing hospital clothes sits in a wheelchair and drags deeply on his cigarette.

"Huh? Oh, I hang out in bars on Polk Street. Get wasted. Turn tricks. I do pretty well too. I'm young and studly." He does a mock impression of a body builder posing at a competition.

I have to laugh. He notices and flashes me a grin. Perhaps it will be a thread of connection on which to build a relationship.

"Not only are you strong, Pee Wee, but I can see you've got a lot of energy. That's why I'm a bit worried about your being on the surgical unit."

The grin fades. "I'm not going to any psych unit," he says with conviction. "I'm not taking anti-psychotics. I know my rights. You can't force me."

Connection destroyed. "You're right. No one can force you right now. That's why I want to talk with you about how you can keep it together. I don't want you to do anything that will land you on the psychiatric unit."

Since the mood stabilizers take a couple of weeks to work, manic patients are often given antipsychotic medications to slow them down in the short run. But, these can have unpleasant and serious side effects.

Pee Wee starts pacing. He interrupts the three men to bum a cigarette. While he's getting a light, I visually sweep the area for objects that could be thrown. Two metal folding chairs and the ashcan jump out at me. I shudder at the possibility. While my uterus knots up into a mildly uncomfortable "practice" contraction, Pee Wee resumes pacing. When the contraction lets up, I place myself in between him and the door that leads back into the hospital.

"As long as I get lots of smoke breaks I'll be OK," he says.

Ah, the manipulation begins.

"I can't promise you that, Pee Wee. But we'll do what we can."

"He didn't sleep a wink last night," says Noreen as we watch Pee Wee drag his pleurovac around the unit the next morning. He stops for a moment and fiddles with one of the tubes coming out of his chest. I can see by the contents of the pleurovac that the tubes are still draining light pink stuff. Too bad. Psychiatric units won't accept patients with chest tubes. The sooner they can be safely removed, the better.

Near the nurses' station, Pee Wee spies a diminutive dietary aide carrying a breakfast tray into another patient's room. He reaches over her head and helps himself to the orange juice on the tray.

"Hey!" she barks, "That's not for you!"

As she stands glaring up at him—hands on hips, nostrils flaring—Pee Wee peels back the lid, empties the contents into his mouth, and wipes his lips with the back of his hand.

"Sorry," he says, replacing the now empty container back on the tray. Noreen motions the fuming aide away and deals with Pee Wee herself.

"Mr. Fortier, you may NOT do that."

Noreen can sound both stern and kind at the same time.

"In the future, if you would like some juice, let me know and I'll be happy to get it for you."

Pee Wee is already half way down the hall, poking his face in patients' rooms along the way. No doubt the other patients are mortified by his behavior and intrusiveness.

I'm glad to see Donald's note in Pee Wee's chart. He must have seen him yesterday afternoon. "The patient is exhibiting periods of agitation, restlessness, and increased irritability. His thought process is linear and at times tangential. He denies suicidal or homicidal ideation. There is no clear paranoid ideation. Currently he is not on neuroleptics or Lithium. Although he has tenuous control over his behavior, he has not been a danger to himself or others."

I know that Donald has to document his observations as objectively as possible but he can see as well as I can that Pee Wee is teetering toward a blowout. I'm worried that he may lose it tonight or over the weekend when only one psychiatrist from Psych. Emergency Services will be available for the whole house.

Although Pee Wee is not receiving any "neuroleptics," which is another word for antipsychotics, he's taking a ton of pain meds, anti-anxiety meds, and anti-nausea meds that should help to sedate him. Maybe that's what Donald is counting on. I hope they kick in soon.

In the afternoon, I take Pee Wee out to the patio for a cigarette. I met his mother yesterday when she brought him a carton of smokes. A lovely person, she is as short as her son is tall. When we spoke, she seemed at her wit's end. In a voice strangled by frustration, she told me that Pee Wee thinks that only crazy people take meds.

"As long as he doesn't take them, he can convince himself that he isn't crazy. He doesn't realize that he gets crazy when he's not on medication, even when every time it comes to this."

During our brief conversation, Pee Wee paced around the unit without acknowledging us. His mother's weary eyes followed him down the long corridor. "He needs treatment badly, but he never gets it for long enough to make a difference. Why is it that in this city, patient's rights win out over a mother's desire to protect her child from harm?"

On the patio, Pee Wee seems to be slowing down a little bit. His speech sounds a little slurred, and he moves less like the Energizer bunny and more like a bear looking for a place to hibernate. Maybe all the Ativan, Droperidol, Benadryl, and morphine he's been receiving have finally started to kick in. Thank goodness. The nurses need a break. I need a break from babysitting him.

Shortly after we sit, he begins to pull at the tape that secures the tubes to his chest. "Pee Wee, leave the tape alone. I know that chest tubes are uncomfortable."

Pee Wee pounds the arm of his chair. "You can't tell me what to do!" he yells. "I'm sick of everyone telling me what I can and can't do! Everyone here wants to control me!"

He moves his body off the metal chair so fast that it falls over and clatters on the concrete floor. My body tenses as I realize that Pee Wee has stationed himself between the exit door and me. When I spy the upright ashtray within Pee Wee's reach, a "practice" contraction almost doubles me over.

Pee Wee walks over to the opposite side of the patio. While he paces, and mumbles to himself, I focus on breathing slowly and deeply until my uterus eases up.

"Sorry," he says, walking over to the downed chair and righting it. "Can I have another cigarette?"

After handing him one, I sit in silence as he puffs and paces. Then, my uterus cramps again, uncomfortable as hell.

When we arrive back on the unit, Donald is hovering over Pee Wee's chart. I describe the scene that just took place outside.

"Pee Wee is a hair away from losing it. If he doesn't crash first, you can bet that over the weekend, someone will be hurt and he'll end up in four-point restraints. It would really be helpful for the staff to have an anti-psychotic on the unit ahead of time instead of having to go to the pharmacy in the middle of a crisis."

This time, Donald concurs. He writes a brief note in Pee Wee's chart with a recommendation for five milligrams of Prolixin as needed for a psychiatric emergency. Since Donald is a psychiatric consultant, a physician on the primary service—in this case a surgeon—must write the order that will be sent to the pharmacy. That shouldn't be a problem. Most of the time, the primary service orders the medications or treatments recommended by the consulting service.

Dr. Steinfeldt stands at the nurses' station writing a note in Greg Herrold's chart. Bald and bespectacled, Dr. Steinfeldt is about five feet ten inches and looks to be in his mid-fifties. His big chest, strong forearms, wide shoulders, and trim abdomen provide evidence of regular workouts. Dr. Steinfeldt is a legend at SFGH for many reasons not the least of which is that—unlike some surgeons who refused to operate on HIV positive patients during the early days of the AIDS crisis when the route of transmission was unknown—he operated on anyone who needed surgery.

"I'll take Mr. Herrold's chart when you're done," I say to Dr. Steinfeldt when he looks up from writing his note. I doubt that he remembers my name but I think he knows I'm from psych consult.

"That's one lucky kid," says Dr. Steinfeldt in a deep baritone. I can't help but notice his large hands and wonder how many lives he has saved with them.

"He took a bullet to the heart and survived. I can tell you that doesn't happen too often. The paramedics were in the area. They got him here in seconds. We slapped him on the OR table in record time."

Dr. Steinfeldt signs his name and hands me the chart. "Helluva lucky kid," he says before taking leave of 4D.

I peek in on Mr. Herrold. "Hey, didja talk to my nurse about those guys in the ICU?"

"No, I don't need to. I believe that you saw what you saw."

He looks disappointed but perks up when I ask him about other disturbing memories.

"I remember being so cold—must have been in the ambulance. Then I remember hearing someone say, 'We've lost him.' There was this white light and I was up in a corner somewhere looking down on the people who were working on me. Later—I guess it was a dream but it felt so real—I had an airplane ticket and someone was pressuring me to get on the plane but I kept saying, 'It's not my flight!' I guess that's true. It just wasn't my time to go."

A crowd of people who look like family enters Greg Herrold's room. I wish him a good weekend and good luck in case he is discharged before I return on Tuesday. On my way to check in with Isaac Abdul, I wonder what will happen to Greg and how this rendezvous with death will affect his life. Too bad, we don't have an outpatient trauma group. He would be a great candidate for it.

If Isaac hadn't fractured his lumbar spine, he would be bouncing on his bed. Instead, he waves a pack of photographs at me.

"Look at my rats! I told you they could ride bicycles!"

Sure enough, there's Isaac holding a hoop of fire through which the rats, dressed in vests and hats, are riding miniature bicycles. In the background, children and adults gaze in delighted wonder at the spectacle.

"OK, rat man, you win. I only half disbelieved you anyway."

We discuss his medical condition. Isaac's medical records from Sacramento confirm that he had surgery for a glioma five years ago.

"They told me the tumor will keep growing unless I do chemo or radiation but I decided to take my chances."

He tells me that just before he was diagnosed, he was locked up in the California Youth Authority. "They kept me in isolation because I have AIDS. For some reason, I started tearing up books. Then I started having seizures and auras and weird dreams and shit so they took me for an MRI. Since then, I've had two brain surgeries."

Isaac says that he's been lucky that the bully cop hasn't beaten him on his soft spot. "I got enough problems without having brain damage to deal with. My rats need me."

I check on Pee Wee one last time before leaving for a long weekend. Hallelujah! He is actually lying down on his bed. Nevertheless,

I leave word with Psychiatric Emergency Services that 4D may be calling them over the weekend. Then I page the trauma resident and ask him to order the Prolixin that Donald had suggested in case of a psychiatric emergency. The resident promises to do so as soon as he returns to the unit.

I walk past the surgical ICU on my way to the elevators. *What the hell.* After retracing my steps, I push open the double doors.

"Can I help you?" asks the first person I see. I recognize a few ICU nurses but not this one.

"Is Carol on today?"

"I'm Carol," she says. "How can I help you?"

I tell her who I am and what Greg Herrold told me about the guys in green scrubs. "I know it's probably the morphine or something else, but he really wanted me to talk to you."

I feel stupid for taking up her time in this way, especially when a patient's alarm starts beeping. While Carol turns away to tend the alarm, I turn in the other direction to leave.

"He's right," she calls after me. "Hold on just a second."

She repositions her patient and monkeys with tubes and wires until the alarm stops. Then she follows me to the door.

"This is freaky," she whispers. "I just assumed the guys in the scrubs looking at his chart were medical students. I didn't recognize them. I was taking care of my other patient when they were here. Then I heard Greg rattling his bed. His eyes were wide as saucers. He was on the ventilator so it took me awhile to understand what he was saying. By the time I could figure it out, the men were gone. You know, he could be right. Anyone can walk in here at any time."

"So you think it was possible that they were the assailant's friends?"

"Hey, like I said, anyone can walk in here at any time. Security is a joke. Once a guy came in packing a gun. Do you see any metal detectors anywhere?"

A walking time bomb

Before I leave my office, I begin to write a detailed note to Antionette and Janice who may have to deal with Pee Wee on Monday when I'm not here. On second thought, I scribble, "Call me at home Monday morning re: Pee Wee."

I've talked about Pee Wee in peer supervision so they know he's on shaky ground. Then, obeying yet another impulse, I dial the D.A.'s office and ask to speak with an attorney who knows Isaac Abdul.

"Yup, I'm very familiar with Mr. Abdul," says Jordan Vasquez. "What can I do for you?"

"Well, Mr. Abdul seems quite convinced that a certain policeman has it out for him. He tells me that this cop has beaten him a number of times and that he pushed him off a roof. Does this hold any water for you?"

I hear Mr. Vasquez sigh on the other end of the phone. "Most of the time, I wouldn't give any credence to these kind of stories, but in this case I know the cop in question, and to tell you the truth, I wouldn't put it past him."

I wake up Saturday morning feeling anxious about Pee Wee. To put my mind at ease, I dial the nurses' station on 4D and ask to speak with his nurse.

"After last night, I wouldn't be surprised if the entire night shift calls in sick tonight," she says. "This morning we're short staffed and no one has time to take him for a smoke. So of course, he's acting out. What's the matter with those psych nurses on the seventh floor? Why can't they handle a patient with chest tubes?"

Med-surg nurses don't consider us psych nurses to be real nurses, in part because psych units can't accept patients who come with intravenous lines and other medical paraphernalia. It's just not safe on a unit with psychotic people walking around in tenuous control of their behavior.

When I arrive twenty minutes later, Pee Wee is parading himself buck naked up and down the unit. I stifle a laugh and address him sternly, "Mr. Fortier, the only thing anyone here is impressed with is your lack of manners. I expect you to get some clothes on NOW. If your clothes are not on in ten minutes, I'm sure the security officers would be able to assist you. Is that what you need?"

"Ah, you're no fun." Pee Wee answers, then heads toward his room.

I slip into the nurses' lounge with Trudy who is in charge this weekend.

"You know," she says, trying hard to mask the 'I've had it up to here' tone in her voice. "Rightfully, Pee Wee belongs on the medical psychiatric unit. I know they're not totally ready for someone like him, but two beds have opened up in the MPA this morning. I think we should transfer him there."

I am reluctant to transfer Pee Wee to med psych for two reasons. 4D nurses are the best at giving good psychological care. They've developed this sensitivity because of their interest in the psychological aspects of treating trauma patients. They are also the most culturally diverse nursing staff in the hospital. Excluding 4D, the psychiatric units, the ICUs and the emergency department, most of the nurses on the other units, including the MPA, were trained in the Philippines where there are only two psychiatric hospitals: one connected with a university and the other, sequestered on some remote inaccessible island where psychiatry is still in the Dark Ages. From what the Filipina nurses have told me, mental illness in the Philippines is attributed to a weak will. Mentally ill family members are often kept secret and hidden from view. Nursing students there receive far less training in psychiatry than do American trained nurses. One Filipina nurse told me that her psychiatric nursing training had lasted two weeks. On the unit she was assigned to, patients were shuffling and drooling—the result of long-term antipsychotic use. I don't want

Pee Wee to become an object of fear and misconceptions.

"I just don't think they are ready yet to handle someone like Pee Wee."

Trudy purses her lips and shakes her head back and forth. "Last night, he was pacing and going in and out of patients' rooms. I understand that he's been doing this for the last few days. But, Noreen said that if she told him to stop, he did. After five minutes, he would be at it again, but at least he was redirectable. Today, he isn't. Last night, he screamed obscenities at anyone who tried to set limits on him. This morning, he's been fooling with the dressing around his chest tube site and pulling at the tubes. You and I both know he's headed for four-point restraints. We could do it here but we don't have the staff to keep him on constant observation. That's what they're set up for on the med psych unit, so I say we move him. Not to mention that he's driving all of us crazy."

I know she's right. I also know that Pee Wee could lose it when he hears he's being transferred there. I beep the psychiatric resident on call to discuss the issue of a unit transfer. While waiting for the phone to ring in response, I look at Pee Wee. At least now, he has his boxers on. I'm not going to struggle with him about what "getting dressed" means; I'm more concerned about how awful he looks. His gait seems less coordinated. His eyes are ringed and glazed. Pee Wee takes no note of me as he rounds the nurses' station, but he swipes a chart off the counter as he goes by. Was it an accident? Without security backing me up, I decide not to confront him. He's as fragile and volatile as a pile of dried pine needles near a lighted match and I don't want to set him off. When the psychiatric resident finally calls back, I state the case for transfer to med psych. She agrees and says she will come up as soon as she can. Then I call Flora, a med psych nurse, to arrange the transfer and give her a rundown on Pee Wee.

"Get out your leather restraints and make sure that you have the key for them," I caution.

I call security to give them some information about Pee Wee, but they cut me off.

"What unit did you say you're on?" As soon as I answer, they hang up. A few minutes later, three officers, dressed in police navy blue, swagger onto the unit looking for action.

Truth be told, it's been about ten years since I've been involved in a takedown. Suddenly I recall how difficult it was to remain calm and professional with adrenaline squirting into my bloodstream. The intervention has a better chance of going smoothly when handled by staff members who trust each other and communicate well. I have never worked with these security folks nor do they seem remotely interested in my input.

"We'll take it from here," they assure me. My internal alarms go off even as I'm relieved I don't have to be physically involved. As if to remind me that I have a good reason to avoid the inevitable scene, my uterus contracts hard.

With security present, I insist on informing Pee Wee about his impending transfer. When a patient sees people in uniforms, one of two behaviors occurs: he quiets down or he blows up. Luckily, Pee Wee acquiesces. He knows this scenario well. Maybe he's learned that it's best for him not to challenge the posse of people in dark blue with silver badges.

As he walks calmly off the unit accompanied by the three officers, I call the charge nurse to let her know they are on their way. With Pee Wee and his escorts out the door, Trudy wipes her forehead, rolls her eyes, and makes a "whew" sound.

"I feel for them," she says, "But boy, am I glad he's outta here!"

I follow Pee Wee and his entourage down to med psych to survey his new home. When we arrive, I hand his chart to the unit secretary, a guy dressed in drag who flutters his fake eyelashes at me, saying, "Thanks, darlin'."

A walking time bomb

The medical psychiatric area, or MPA, consists of four beds in one large room. A nurse sits just to the right of the open Plexiglas doors at the entrance to the MPA so that she can observe all four beds at once. Two patients are in their beds on one side of the room. Pee Wee has the other side to himself.

Flora, the nurse who has been assigned to Pee Wee, busies herself with routine nursing admission activities. She must inspect his chest tube dressing; check the intravenous fluids, tubes, and sites to make sure they are running well; take his vital signs, and do a general physical assessment of his body. Pee Wee stands quietly as Flora takes his blood pressure and pulse. With Pee Wee in good control, the three security officers walk away.

I watch as Flora checks the drainage in the pleurovac and inspects Pee Wee's chest-tube incision site. She and Pee Wee stand between the two freshly made beds with Flora near the head of the bed, against the wall that abuts the room next door.

Maybe she hurt him by lifting his dressing to look at the incision. In any case, it wouldn't take much. His voice rises from a place of rage and terror. "Get me outta here, I didn't do nothin' wrong. You can't force me to stay here. I want out NOW!"

Unbelievable to me, Flora ignores Pee Wee's outburst. In her calm nurse patter she tries to assure him, "I'll be out of your way in a moment, Mr. Fortier. Hold still now while I get your blood pressure."

I run out of the unit and yell, "Security! Come back!" The security officers stop, spin around, and sprint toward me.

"Get out of there, Flora," I hiss under my breath when I return. Then I notice that she is hemmed in by a wall, both beds, and Pee Wee. Stepping outside the MPA, I stop a nurse in the hallway.

"Where are your locked leather restraints?"

She doesn't know.

"How about a 5150?"

She doesn't know about that either. I check back in to see Pee Wee's arms flailing. This time I speak louder, "Flora, I need to see you right now!"

Forget the admission protocol and get the hell out of that room! Can't you see this guy is going to blow any second?

Pee Wee, physically unable to restrain himself any longer, screams, pushes Flora against the wall, grabs the pleurovac that is still connected to his chest wall by yard-long rubber tubes and hurls it over the bed and through the window. Glass shatters everywhere. The pleurovac bounces back into the room, barely missing Flora.

"I told you to leave me alone!" he raves. He grabs the bottom of the bed near the window and knocks it over on its side. Then he picks up the portable blood pressure machine and hurls it through another supposedly unbreakable window.

Flora scuttles over the untouched mattress closer to the door. When she is out of the way, the security officers grab it and use it to push Pee Wee against the wall.

Pee Wee hollers, "Illegal imprisonment! Assault!"

"Where's the 5150?" yells one of the officers. "We don't touch him without a signed 5150!"

Exactly on cue, the on-call psychiatrist arrives. She is a short, stocky Chinese-American woman that I don't know but dimly recognize. "I'm Dr. Chen, your on-call shrink. OK, where are you guys hiding the patient?" she asks wearily.

From behind the mattress Pee Wee shouts, "I'm taking all of you to court!"

"And where would that 5150 be?" she asks without flinching.

"I was hoping you would bring one. They don't seem to have any up here."

"You know what I always say?" asks Dr. Chen.

I shake my head. "A psychiatric unit without a 5150 is like an ortho unit without traction. Twice before, I've been up here and no one could find the 5150s. This time, I brought my own."

She whips one out from a folder. Then she lowers her voice and whispers to me, "How is it that orthopedic nurses are suddenly psychiatric nurses?"

"You've been through medical school. Couldn't you repair a fractured clavicle in a pinch?"

"Not if my life depended on it, or the patient's either, for that matter."

Dr. Chen scribbles her name on the 5150 and shows it to the officers who are struggling to keep Pee Wee behind the mattress. Satisfied that the psychiatrist will take full responsibility for any issues of liability, two officers lunge toward Pee Wee. Before he can register what's happening, he's lying face down on the same mattress that pinned him to the wall. One officer holds his arms behind his back while the others hold his legs.

"You're killing me, man!" screams Pee Wee. Meanwhile, Flora has located the leather restraints and assists the officers in securing Pee Wee to the bed.

The nurses on this unit, like most units in the hospital, have some experience taking care of patients in leather restraints. But, as orthopedic nurses who are just learning the skills of psychiatric nursing, they may not know that psychotic patients can easily misinterpret a posse of staff securing their limbs to a bed as a prelude to rape. Others lie rigid with fear as childhood scenes of sexual abuse flood their minds. For now, I will encourage the nurses to reassure Pee Wee that he is safe and that he will not be violated in this most vulnerable position.

Dr. Chen orders an intramuscular injection of Prolixin, the antipsychotic that Donald had suggested and that, it seems, the trauma resident never called in. I run the order over to the pharmacy myself so as to impress upon the pharmacist that we're in the middle of a psychiatric emergency.

When he feels the needle pierce the skin near his hip, Pee Wee screams that he is allergic to antipsychotic medication. Having read through his old chart, I know this is untrue. However, I will alert the nursing staff to possible side effects of the drug. When Pee Wee has calmed down, I follow Flora into the med room where she is having the ohmygodthatwasclose post-incident jitters. It is a time to soothe, not a time to be critical. In a few days, I will review with her an important rule of psychiatry: never let a patient come between you and the nearest exit. For now, I'm relieved that the crisis is over and that Pee Wee and the staff are safe.

As we exit the med room, I see Pee Wee's mother hunched against the counter of the nurses' station. Her hands cup her eyes. She must have watched the institutional police rush her son with a mattress and slap the leather cuffs on his ankles and wrists. She must have cringed as they pulled the leather straps taut and anchored them to the four corners of the bed's metal frame. She must have heard him scream, "I have rights!"

I put my hand on her back as she weeps. Her sobs carry me to an abyss where I glimpse the depth of helplessness a parent feels when unable to relieve a child's suffering.

When I told my obstetrician my fear that the universe will not allow me to have three normal kids, she addressed me sternly: "I have three normal kids. Many people do. There is no reason that you can't be one of them."

I don't believe her. The cosmic scales have been ridiculously unbalanced to my advantage for too long. My good karma is bound to change.

10

Sweet interlude

We have vacationed on Cape Cod every summer since Corianne was born. When Brian's grandmother died fifteen years ago, Brian's mother sold Nana's house and used the money to build a home on Cape Cod in the hope that it would become the hub of annual family reunions. Her plan worked. Each August, all seven kids and their families meet here for a week, some staying with Grammy and some, like us, renting cottages nearby.

Brian is the third oldest child in his Irish-Italian middle-class family. He and each of his four brothers hover around the six-foot mark. All of them are loud, garrulous, athletic, and emphatically heterosexual. Now that the siblings are in their thirties and forties, verbal jousting has replaced the physical competitiveness of youth. In the first few hours of the reunion weekend, it gets so loud that the sisters-in-law excuse ourselves and head for the beach to quiet our pounding heads.

When we're on the Cape, the only thing I need to worry about is keeping the kids out of the poison ivy that lines the dirt road leading to the beach. Our bayside beach is tailor-made for children. At high tide, waves lap just enough to thrill a three-year-old. At low tide, that three-year-old can run himself ragged over the flats before reaching water as high as his knees.

Sometimes after a beach day, we drive to Wellfleet to dip in Aunt Patty's secret pond in the woods across the street from her home. The brothers try to go on at least one fishing expedition together while the rest of us hit the craft fairs. At sundown, we gather on Grammy's deck to watch the sun melt into puddles of orange and cerise over the black water of the bay.

Earlier this year, Brian's parents decided to separate. Grammy, fed up with Bob's alcoholism, left the family home just outside of Boston and moved into the Cape house. Things between them must have improved because Grammy invited Bob to join the family on the Cape for reunion week and he accepted.

My family has never had a reunion. Even though each parent has found happiness with another partner, the tension between my parents still exists when they are in the same room. Fortunately, my brother lives an hour south of San Francisco and we see each other frequently.

At Brian's family reunions, I am struck by the difference between our fathers. Since I've known him, Bob has been a peripheral figure in the family. The first time I was invited for dinner, I was shocked when Bob carried his plate into the TV room and closed the door behind him. Although he is quick with a joke and a master at insinuating a story into conversation, a skill Brian has also mastered, Bob's alcoholism has caused much grief, worry, anger, and tension in the family. No one talks about it, but I sense ambivalence when he's around.

Our mothers have more in common. Finding themselves in unhappy marriages, both pursued education as the ticket to financial independence. When I express amazement to Grammy that she could earn both bachelor and master's degrees while raising seven children, she downplays her accomplishment.

Over the summers, I have grown to appreciate the way Brian and his siblings, all very different people, support and accept each other. Growing up, they invented their own language, played games, and suffered Bob's frequent surliness together. They learned to value stoicism, fairness, justice, and a good joke. They also learned to avoid feelings.

The morning after we arrive from California, Grammy and I stroll through her garden where she points to her favorite rose— Moonstone—a large flower with petals that are pale pink outside and satiny white inside.

"If I didn't have this garden to dig my troubles into," says Grammy, "I would have lost my mental health long ago!"

Besides Bob, two of her children are also alcoholics. She herself struggles with her own mother's curse, depression. Grammy steers me toward the small vegetable garden in the backyard where she grows tomatoes, basil, and zucchini. She picks a handful of basil for tonight's pasta with pesto sauce. When she plucks a zucchini from the vine, I'm reminded about the watermelons I grew when I was a kid. Our homegrown melons were much sweeter than the store bought ones, and in the heat of summer, my mother and I cooled off by devouring slice after refreshing slice, sometimes polishing off half of a melon by ourselves.

This summer, my good friend Jeanne from graduate school is also vacationing on the Cape. She arrives with her husband and two daughters, one a year older, the other a year younger than Corianne. Shortly after they arrive, the guys agree to watch the kids so we can walk and talk on the beach without distraction.

Jeanne eyes my protruding abdomen. "God love ya, Barkin. I couldn't do it. Two's enough for me, baby."

She pinches my cheeks and throws her arms around me. "How the fuck are you anyway, sugar?"

Jeanne, a second generation Italian-American, swears like a sailor and looks like an angel: tall and slender, big brown Bambi eyes, dark long lashes, and a soft girlish voice. It's impossible to reconcile her language with her appearance. The cruder she is, the harder I laugh.

When we first met in graduate school, Jeanne worked weekends at the Jewish Home for the Aged. I asked why she worked there instead of on a psych unit where she could make more money.

"Honey, geriatric nursing IS psychiatric nursing. Old people need to talk about their lives, their families, their fears, their regrets before they go. But, there's another reason I work there. I miss grabbing old ass!"

I had just met Jeanne so I didn't know what kind of person she is. I looked at her skeptically and she explained: "An old person's circulation isn't so good. Their skin gets dry and papery and breaks down around the pressure points. So, I glob on the lotion and massage their butts like crazy to prevent pressure ulcers. While I'm massaging they tell me about their lives. Jesus, Laur, it's such a fuckin' kick! It's like I'm taking care of my own grandparents!"

I hope that when my parents become infirm, they will be fortunate enough to be cared for by a nurse like Jeanne.

At low tide, Jeanne and I walk on the squishy wet beach sand chatting about her work with Alzheimer's patients. She crabs about cuts in staffing and having to work every other weekend, but for the most part, she loves her job. As usual, she is full of funny stories about her patients and their families.

"Now tell me about your job," she says when she's finished her latest tale.

I could entertain her with my own humorous stories—there are a few—but instead I tell her about the young African-American men shot on the streets, the 101 California Street massacre, people who survived torture in other countries, and the shocking percentage of my patients who were exposed to serious trauma during childhood.

Jeanne cringes. "So, honeybabe, how can you stand to listen to these stories day in and day out? Doesn't it get under your skin?"

I want to be macho and deny it but I'm talking to Jeanne who would see right through me if I were less than honest. "Some of the stories stay with you. I've had a few nightmares. I can't do much to change a screwed up childhood. But I can make things better for people when they're in the hospital."

"Do you have a place at work to talk about this stuff?" she asks.

"As in an old-fashioned process group? Are you kidding? Psychiatry in San Francisco has gone biological. No one processes shit." (I tend to curse more when I'm around Jeanne) "But Janice, Antionette, and I talk about our patients over lunch a few times a week, which helps."

"I've got news for you, sweetheart. Things are changing here too, just more slowly. Forget feelings. It's all about pills and quick fixes. The supervisors don't want to hear how staff feel when a patient attempts suicide on the unit or when someone is assaulted. Hey, it's just a job. Take it or leave it. That's the attitude. Pretty shortsighted when you figure that women like us are leaving nursing in droves."

She's right. Jeanne and I have been in nursing long enough to see the pattern of nursing shortages followed by a decrease in entry-level standards for nursing school. It doesn't bode well for our profession.

"Listen sugar," she says on our way back to the cottage. "How are you going to manage working with two young kids and a new baby? I don't mean the babysitter stuff. I mean the emotional stuff."

"I'll be taking six months off. After that, I don't know. Aren't we supposed to be able to handle it all?"

"Do you buy that bullshit? Sometimes I think I should hang it up and stay home with my kids. If I didn't have such a great job right now, I would be tempted."

Jeanne and her family stay for Shabbat dinner, which Brian and I host on Friday night of reunion week. Just before sundown, all thirty-two members of the family and guests gather in the backyard of our cottage and hold hands around a table draped with a white sheet and topped with two braided loaves of challah, an old bronze candelabrum, a bouquet of flowers, a bottle of wine, and nine wine glasses, one for each family. We hold hands and say prayers over the challah and the wine and bless our children after which a representative from each family expresses appreciation for something that has happened since our last Shabbat together or offers a prayer for someone they know who is ill, troubled, or grieving a loss. The children, even the shyer ones, relish the opportunity to say what's on their minds. We end by singing, "Shabbat Shalom!" or "Welcome, Sabbath!" Although bedlam breaks out as soon as the ceremony has ended with everyone diving for the trays of food we've spent most of the day preparing, Shabbat provides our families with a rare moment to speak from the heart or to journey inward.

Seven weeks after our return home from Cape Cod, my water breaks. When labor is in full swing and my girlfriend arrives, Brian and I drive to the hospital. My obstetrician had wanted me to schedule a C-section with this baby because of my history: a four-day labor with Corianne and a two-day labor with Danny, both of which ended in C-sections for "failure to progress." After many hours, labor again fails to progress; I consent to another C-section.

I am still a little woozy when the nurse hands me a swathed bundle of baby boy who seems to react to my voice and soon figures out how to latch onto my nipple.

Once again, I marvel that everything is as it should be. My arm bends at the elbow at exactly the right angle to support Ben's head and to cuddle him as he nurses. My hips are a shelf for easy portability. The only improvement I would suggest is a pouch to free up my hands. Those marsupials have a good thing going for them.

The obstetrical nurses call Ben, Jean-Luc Picard after the bald captain in Star Trek. They were very sweet to give me the Golden Gate room with a view of the bridge. We know each other from my days as a consultant on their unit. In fact, one of the issues we struggled with back then had to do with a new mother who demanded to have this same Golden Gate room and used her connections to the CEO to get it. Most of the nurses come from middle class backgrounds and they're peeved when entitled patients are rewarded for whining.

I hold Benny in my arms and tell him about our family. His brother, Danny, will be two years old in six weeks; we can expect some loud protests from him when we get home; his five-year-old sister, Corianne, will like him better than she does Danny, as long as he stays out of her stuff. He seems to respond to my voice, the one he has heard for months muffled by membrane and fluid. I feel the swelling tide of motherhood rise in my heart. I am in love again.

My mother spends the first week with us. I have heard horror stories of grandparents who come to help but expect the new mother to wait on them as well. My mother is not one of them. She sits on the floor and plays games with Danny and Corianne. She reads to them, straightens the house, cooks, and cleans the dishes. She brushes the cats, clips their nails, and wipes away the layers of dust on each leaf of the Ficus plant. She organizes my linen closet and arranges my spice rack alphabetically. She also follows my housecleaner around, pointing out areas he's missed, and places he's never thought to look.

"After all, Warren dear," she tells him, "Four eyes are better than two. And when WAS the last time you pulled out the sofa bed?"

Warren seems to take it in his stride but I give him combat pay anyway. He and I have an understanding. He doesn't bug me about the stacks of papers and books I leave around the house and I don't bug him about details like dusty Ficus leaves.

My father arrives the day after my mother's departure. Like most men his age, he requires a certain amount of tending to, but unlike many men, his joy is holding babies, especially my babies. Each morning after I breastfeed Ben, my father cuddles him and coos to him while I take a long, hot shower. I know that when Dad leaves, shower time evaporates.

Benny is a most agreeable little guy, especially in contrast to our two-year-old raging bull who locks his knees, scrunches his face, and screams at the world. With Benny, I have perfected the art of breastfeeding in my sleep. At night, I lay him down in a bassinet next to our bed. When he starts to snuffle at two or three in the morning, I bring him into our bed where he stays for the rest of the night.

Three weeks after his birth, when my parents have left, when I've dropped Corianne at kindergarten, when my babysitter has taken Danny to the park for a few hours, I finally have him all to myself.

While I feed Ben, I look at the hospital through our living room windows and think about all I've seen and heard in my year at The General. With the distance afforded by maternity leave, I see the hospital as a huge and chaotic family run by well-intentioned but overwhelmed adults who can't control their children or provide safety for the people they employ to care for them. Earlier this year, three E.R. doctors were shot at Los Angeles County Hospital by a patient with a gun. It could easily happen at The General. There are a number of ways to enter the hospital and none of them has metal detectors or security guards. If his assailant's friends were packing a gun when they entered the ICU disguised as medical residents, Greg Herrold could have been shot again.

When I gaze at the hospital and think about the sad stories within those concrete towers, the towers seem to sway. I imagine their windows bursting open, and keening, wailing voices flowing over the ledges, oozing down over the city. Emotion needs its release. So exactly how is it, I wonder, that our department of psychiatry—full of highly educated people who understand emotions, their role in stress and disease and the benefits of talk therapy—can so easily fail to take its own medicine? How can caretakers be expected to contain our very human feelings and reactions when our patients tell us about the trauma, neglect, and depravity they have endured throughout their lives?

These thoughts gnaw at me until Ben nods off in my arms.

This year, Christmas Day falls on Friday, the same day of the week that we celebrate Shabbat. Luckily, the eight-day Chanukah holiday ended last week. Otherwise, in addition to the challah—the braided egg bread that I bake each week for Shabbat—and the tortellini we make each year for Christmas dinner, we'd also be making potato latkes and spinning dreidels.

Brian began hosting Christmas at our house three years ago when, as a new partner at his law firm, he invited young lawyers without families in the area to join us for the holiday. We also began making homemade tortellini in his family's tradition. His Italian mother gave him the recipe for the dumplings they call "tootling" in the dialect of her family's village in the Po valley.

The phone rings as we are making tortellini on Christmas Eve. It is our next-door neighbor Phillip, who tells us he had to take Jean-Michel—his dear friend and housemate—to the hospital the previous night. The diagnosis is pneumocystis pneumonia, an AIDS-related infection of the lungs. The prognosis stinks. I pack up a container of fresh tortellini con brodo and drive to Davies Hospital.

Although he has made a living as a master cabinetmaker in the city, Jean-Michel has poured his passion into the cabin he built in Guerneville, a gay enclave ninety minutes north of San Francisco. A few years ago, he told Brian and me that he had just hung ten-foot wide sliding glass doors in his bedroom.

"Now I have a view of the redwood grove from my bed. You must come up sometime with the children."

He smiled as if he were already there. "You know, redwoods are the tallest trees on earth but they have shallow roots. So, to keep from falling over during storms they weave their roots together. I love this about them. It is like they are holding hands underground!"

This is how Jean-Michel feels in Guerneville, surrounded by friends who gather there with him each weekend.

At the hospital, Jean-Michel opens his eyes as soon as I enter and smiles despite being in great pain. His face looks wan and tired but he squeezes my hand. Soon after, his eyelids close as morphine transports him to a gentler place. Leaving the TV on, I whisper goodbye and close the door behind me.

Before leaving the unit, I find Jean-Michel's nurse. Since I'm not a family member, Tim is reluctant to talk to me, but his demeanor changes when I mention I'm a nurse at The General.

"Jean-Michel doesn't have much longer."

He rattles off some lab values that I pretend to understand but have not committed to memory. With a familiar, well-worn look of professional sympathy, he adds, "You know how fast they go at this point."

A week later on Saturday morning, Brian and I decide that Benny and I will represent the family at the memorial service on Cemetery Hill—a ridge high above Jean-Michel's cabin. When we arrive in Guerneville, it's pouring rain and my head aches. Since we are too late to attend the service, I follow the directions to Jean-Michel's cabin. Although hunger will awaken him soon enough, Benny snoozes as only fat babies and old, overfed cats can. While we wait for the others to arrive, raindrops drum the roof of the van like thousands of fingers tapping a desktop. Water flows over the windshield in a drapery of gray silk. In the dim light, my thoughts turn toward the night before Jean-Michel died when I visited him at Davies Hospital.

Brian and I had a neighborly relationship with Jean-Michel—sharing seeds, plants, and even a few dinners—but we were more cordial than close. When I visited him in the hospital, I refrained from asking him questions that I would normally ask a terminal patient: Would you like to talk about what is happening to you? Have you spoken with your family? Do you feel at peace or in conflict? Is there someone I can call for you? Instead, I freshened his water, massaged his neck and shoulders, and contained my feelings under an invisible nurse's cap, avoiding the intimacy of his dying.

At home, I handed the car keys to Brian who took his turn visiting Jean-Michel. An hour later, he returned and trudged up the stairs.

"Hold me," he said. We stood like that for a long time. Brian had never before sat with a dying person. "I felt so helpless," he said. "All I could do was hold his hand and pat his arm."

"That was the best thing you could do," I said, noting the irony that my husband, more intellectual than emotional, could feel so much about Jean-Michel's dying whereas I felt muffled.

Maybe my job has gotten to me. Maybe I've begun to turn off my feelings the way I've seen other nurses do.

The mourners begin to arrive. During a break in the rain, I unfasten Benny's car seat and transport him to the front door. Phillip greets me at the entrance.

"Let me show you a quiet place for the baby." I place my sleeping babe on his bed and take advantage of the privacy to speak with Phillip alone.

Phillip tells me about Jean-Michel's last few hours; how they signed him out against medical advice, how Phillip and Jean-Michel's other friends tried to keep him alert and comfortable during the journey, how they settled him down on a pile of blankets and pillows where he died minutes later looking up into his beloved redwoods.

I hug him and tell him he did right by his friend.

Phillip wipes his eyes, then leads me into the kitchen where Jean-Michel's love of artisanship shines in every inch of the room. Phillip, an architect and designer, points to the counters that Jean-Michel fashioned from "pink-hued hemlock," the armoire he made of oak, the cabinet handles he fashioned from madrone, and how the kitchen cabinetry matches the wood-paneled walls in the living room. I wish now that we had visited Jean-Michel here when he was healthy. I would have enjoyed seeing the pleasure he must have taken from showing off his work.

I sit on the couch with a plate of food and watch Jean-Michel's friends as they support each other through yet another loss. A few weeks ago at Jean-Michel and Phillip's annual Christmas party, I danced with some of them to Gloria Gaynor singing, "I Will Survive!" Now they stand with their arms braided around each other recounting tales of happier times.

With my ear to the bedroom door, I hear the beginning of Benny's hungry sounds. Seeing me, he wriggles and smiles a true smile, not the kind accompanied by gas. While he waits for my breast, his eyes light up, and his tongue laps against his lips. Once we are situated in the leather chair, he wastes no time.

"You greedy thing," I say, feeling the smooth squishiness of his supple body against mine. Ten minutes later when I unlatch him to switch breasts, he bristles. "How dare you!" he seems to say. After a smooching session, I carry him into the living room.

"Could I hold the baby?" asks a sweet-faced man.

"At your own risk. He's a prodigious spitter-upper."

The man lays the cloth diaper over his shoulder and holds Benny to his chest, supporting his head with an expert hand. Whispers of "baby" sweep the room. When Benny burps, the sweet-faced man calmly mops it with the diaper. Others ask to hold him and soon Benny is passed around like a ladle of water among people thirsting to remember that life gives as it takes away. Later, as the mourners are leaving, they thank me for bringing the baby. Although I didn't plan it this way, I too am glad.

With only a handful of people left in the house, I carry Benny back into Jean-Michel's bedroom closing the door behind us. Once again, we sit in the leather chair where I sing to him until his eyes close. Looking out at the redwood grove, I picture Jean-Michel laid out on the blankets, smiling up at his beloved trees. Then other faces appear: Alice, who gripped my hand though a difficult night on a ventilator; Jack, who died waiting for a heart transplant; Stuart, a schizophrenic boy who hung himself behind his parent's home. I feel a swelling in my chest and tears fall on the blanket I've wrapped around Ben.

It feels good to cry but now I wonder—will Benny absorb my sadness? Will the combination of crying and breastfeeding deplete me? *No, I don't think so.* Emotions are like a nursing mother's breasts: the more they are tapped, the more they replenish themselves.

On the way home, I imagine Jean-Michel's community of friends —their arms braiding themselves into strong cord, weaving themselves into a fireman's net, a blanket, or perhaps a trampoline—and I think, this is what we need, those of us who open our hearts to our patients' traumas: a blanket for comfort, a fireman's net for safety, a trampoline for resilience. Maybe instead of standing like lone pines, we could become a grove of redwoods, our roots entwined, holding hands together underground.

11

Support needed

O n the morning I am scheduled to return to work, Chandra, our new baby sitter, arrives early. She's come over a few times in the last couple of weeks and the kids seem to like her. My house-cleaner, Warren, knows her mother, a devout Hari Krishna like himself. When he learned that Chandra was looking for a child-care job and that Graciella had decided to go back to Bolivia, he arranged an introduction.

All of us took an immediate liking to Chandra, who is barely twenty. She grew up in an ashram outside of Los Angeles where she learned to cook fantastic vegetarian meals. She does not smoke, watch TV, or drive, and loves to do art projects with kids. When I saw how she convinced Danny to walk with her to the park — squatting down to his eye level, holding out her hand, beckoning with her eyes and voice — I knew she'd do just fine.

While Chandra holds Benny and helps Danny with breakfast, I get ready for work. For the last month, I've been weaning Benny down to just two breast feedings with the rest of his calories obtained from bottle feedings.

I'm ready to go back to work, maybe not as ready as I was after the other two, but almost. The truth is there's no way I would let this job go. So many hospitals are merging, downsizing, and cutting "non-essential" nursing positions like mine that it would be unlikely I'd find another psych consultation gig in the area. No matter how ready I am to go back to work, I falter when it's time to walk out the door. Knowing there is no easy way to do it, I quickly kiss the boys goodbye and fly down the stairs with Corianne, tasting freedom, and feeling pulled at the same time.

This morning, I enter the hospital grounds from Potrero Avenue, the main entrance to the hospital. After walking up the concrete path that bisects a wide lawn, I cross the service road and step onto the slab of concrete that fronts the hospital lobby. There, Mr. Reeves of the putrid foot and Mr. Gerard, Antionette's perennial problem patient, sit in their wheelchairs smoking cigarettes. I can almost hear these two one-upping each other with stories of past sexual conquests and current lawsuits against the city or boasting about the number of nurses they've reduced to tears. Mr. Reeves, I see, had both feet amputated. The stumps are freshly wrapped in white bandages. Both men nod at me as I walk past them.

After a six-month hiatus, I find myself noticing the hospital's concrete rectangular entryway. Couldn't the architects have put a little more thought into it? Other hospitals feature statues, sculptures, plaques, fountains or Latin or Hebrew words carved into arched vestibules as reminders to visitors that the space inside belongs to the ill and injured and those who care for them. Why not here? Even worse, the lobby doors open into a space as dark as the mouth of a whale.

On the way to my office, Benny's little face appears in my mind and I choke up. Maybe this transition will be harder than I had anticipated. I will myself into thinking about the pink camellias that blossomed in February and the fat lilac buds that are going to burst open any minute. I smile thinking about the sweet peas and how their delicate tendrils grasp the trellis as tightly as Benny's tiny hands close around my fingers.

Thinking about tendrils and trellises, I remember the idea of forming a support group for trauma patients. That's the least that any world-renowned trauma program such as ours should offer its patients. Now that I'm back, I resolve to make this a priority. And, despite my department's resistance to staff "process" groups, I will resume my campaign to encourage those as well. My plan is to gently steer the discussion in that direction whenever the opportunity presents itself.

Antionette and Janice are in the office when I arrive. They've set out mugs, a plate of muffins, and a thermos full of hot water for tea. Their warm greetings melt some of my ambivalence about returning. Barry, a psychiatrist on our team, knocks on our open door and joins us.

After hugs and pictures, Janice says, "You'd better sit down. A few things have happened since you've been gone."

"Don't tell me, our star psychiatrist has decided to go back to Yale?"

"Not exactly. But Miranda has applied for Dylan's position!"

"What? Dylan's leaving?" Dylan is also a psychiatrist on our team.

"No, but his position is being searched."

Janice gestures toward Barry. "You can best explain to Laurie what that means."

Since Barry just popped a muffin into his mouth, Antionette fills in for him. "At staff meeting last week Miranda said that since Dylan's position had to be searched, she was going to vie for it. No one could believe it."

Barry finishes swallowing and takes a sip of tea. "Many of us university docs were hired while there was only an acting chief of psychiatry. We were told when we were hired that our positions could be searched when a permanent chief came on board and that we could lose our jobs if people who are more qualified applied, especially if the applicants are women or minorities. Now that there is a permanent chief, a number of us have had our positions searched. Ads have been run in national journals. Unless one of us is really awful, or someone outside is truly outstanding, there's been no need to lose sleep over it. No one's lost their job yet."

He pauses and lowers his voice. "What Miranda is doing is unprecedented. She was hired as a substitute doc for a year. When she heard that Dylan's job was being searched, she figured it was fair game."

"That girl's got a lot of chutzpah."

I refuse to consider the idea that Miranda could wrest Dylan's position from him. "But Dylan shouldn't have anything to worry about. He's a better clinician by far."

"That's for sure," says Janice, "but this is UCSF and those Ivy League credentials of hers along with the psychopharm text she edited look pretty impressive."

"Not to mention that *Science* magazine recently published an article criticizing UCSF med school for being an "old boys' club," says Barry.

Antionette looks pensive. "So they must be feeling pressure to hire more women and people of color. Rejecting a woman from Yale would be tough."

I'm feeling a boot on my chest. Miranda as the anti-sexism poster child? I bet that girl has manipulated her way around every closed door or glass ceiling she's ever encountered.

The phone rings on Janice's desk. "This is she," she says, rolling her eyes. Her normally soft voice sounds strident and pointed. "I told you; my patient is suicidal. I don't know how else to make that clear to you. If you don't want to hospitalize him, I will need your agency to approve more psychotherapy sessions. Two won't cut it."

"Damn managed care!" she sputters after slamming down the phone. "How does a kid right out of high school get off telling me how many sessions I can have for a suicidal patient?"

"I know what you mean," says Barry. "But managed care is the wave of the future whether we like it or not."

Janice and Barry both have small private practices. While they complain about the latest professional indignities, Antionette and I say goodbye and head to our clinical areas.

On the trauma unit, the nurses want to see pictures of the baby. When I show them the latest photos, my breasts ache and my eyes tear. *It's just the hormones.* I take a deep breath and ready myself to see patients.

The nurses have warned me that Stephanie Young is refusing to speak with anyone from psychiatry and becomes hostile every time the subject is broached by her physicians. She's sad, not hostile when I approach her, a white woman with dark, reddened, and soulful eyes.

"I miss my kids," she says. "I need to see them."

Her story unfolds easily. "Me and my husband and the kids were living in a room downtown. My husband, he just got out of prison. He kept bothering me to cop some dope for him. I didn't want to do it. I'm on methadone, trying to stay clean. I told him we needed the money to feed the kids. Then we argued. I could see where it was going so I took the kids downstairs to my girlfriend's room so they wouldn't get hurt but I forgot to give her their shoes. Later, when my husband was starting to get really pissed, I told him I needed to take the shoes downstairs for the kids. That's when he really lost it, said he was going to kill me, blocked the door to the hall. I looked out the window."

She shudders at the memory and moistens her lips. "I saw an open window across the way and down a bit. I thought I could make it but I missed the ledge and landed between two buildings, got wedged in there real tight. By the time they lifted me out, I got, what's it called—department syndrome?"

"I think you mean compartment syndrome."

"That's it. So they had to amputate my leg." She shows me the bandaged stump.

Stephanie's story cuts and scrapes me from the inside.

Wow, have I grown soft! What happened to my emotional calluses?

I tamp down my physical discomfort and force myself to keep listening.

"They found my husband and hauled his ass back to jail for carrying a gun. My kids, they're in foster care." Then Stephanie yells, "That bitch of a foster mother won't bring them here! I told her I need to see my boys. I HAVE to see them. I'll go crazy if I can't touch them. I need to know that they're OK!"

Stephanie thrashes on her bed like a fish pulled from the sea and thrown on deck.

I understand completely. My breasts throb. They've grown hard and full and I feel them leaking through my cotton knit shirt. I grab a couple of Stephanie's tissues and turn around. "Excuse me for a second." I stuff the tissues into my bra.

"Are you alright?" asks Stephanie.

"Just leaking. I have a baby at home and I'm still nursing a little."

"So you know how I'm feeling."

Do I know what it's like to fear my husband so much that I would jump out of a window? I don't think so!

"I have an idea how hard it is for you to be separated from your kids," I reply. At that, Stephanie bursts out sobbing. I do everything I can not to cry too. Although I manage to maintain control, my breasts leak milk as if they are crying for me.

I hand Stephanie the box of tissues and tell her I'll be right back. Holding my book bag to my chest, I run to the bathroom where I express some milk into the sink and blot the wet spots on my shirt with paper towels. Then, with my book bag still shielding my wet shirt, I page Stephanie's social worker. When I explain the situation, she offers to call the foster mother later in the afternoon when she has time.

"In that case," I tell her, "I'll make the call myself."

"Mrs. Johnson?" I say when an older female voice answers. "I'm calling from the trauma unit at General Hospital. Yes, I know it's difficult to bring the kids here but it's a doctor's order. She needs to see those kids today!"

When Mrs. Johnson begins to make excuses, I cut her off. "If you can't bring them here, I'll pick them up right now myself. Shall I do that?"

Mrs. Johnson changes her tune and assures me she'll bring the kids within the hour. I return to Stephanie and tell her we'll hope for the best. Then I ask Trudy for some absorbent bandages to replace the soaked tissues in my bra.

"Welcome back," says a familiar voice from across the counter in the nurses' station. Ruby, the trauma nurse practitioner, closes the chart in front of her and opens another.

"Were you really going to pick up her kids?"

I shrug. "Stephanie was so desperate that I needed to do something."

"Well, I'm desperate for a cup of coffee. Can you come with me? I wanted to run a patient by you."

"Great. I want to talk to you too."

Over coffee, Ruby tells me about a patient named Pauline Holloway. "I was working in the emergency room this weekend when an older woman came in with a knife wound to the throat. There was a lot of bleeding but luckily, the guy who did this to her missed her major vessels. If there had been a social worker on duty, she could have been discharged to a women's shelter. The social worker called in sick and all we could do was sew her up and discharge her home, in this case, to the projects where it happened. I felt so bad having to do that."

Ruby makes a fist and presses it into the table.

"Sometimes you feel so helpless."

"What do you want me to do?"

"I was wondering if you could follow up. I'm worried about her state of mind. I know she's not an inpatient but she needs follow-up."

"That's a coincidence because she's exactly the kind of patient I wanted to talk to you about, people who need psychological support after a trauma. Now that I'm back, I've decided to start a trauma support group."

"Your predecessor tried to get one going," says Ruby. "I was going to co-lead it with her but we couldn't get the nod from the chief of surgery or the chief of psychiatry."

"You're kidding! You'd think they'd be happy to have a support group for their patients."

Ruby explains there was an issue about which department would take ownership for the group, surgery or psychiatry. "At least that's what it seemed to be about. In any case, we knew it wouldn't work if we didn't have approval from both chiefs. Long story short, it never got off the ground."

This sounds like a totally lame excuse to me. "Well I'm going to discuss it with Donald. If he's fine with the idea of a group, would you co-lead it with me?"

Ruby tucks her long arms and legs close to her body, drops her head into her hands, and hunches over the table. She lifts her head to meet my questioning eyes.

"Sorry, Laurie. I need to tell you that I'm out of here as soon as they can find a replacement for me."

She waits for my shock to subside. "It's been five years and I need a break from this craziness. I work in the trauma clinic every afternoon and there's no protection there. I'm tired of worrying about being caught in the crossfire between gangs."

She rubs her face and wipes her eyes while I remain speechless.

"The other reason is that my compassion has been questioned. I've said what I feel, which is that patients who shoot drugs, get loaded, sell drugs, and bash other people in the hospital should be thrown out and barred from coming back. You know how it is here. They look at me as if I'm crazy. Maybe I am burned out. In any case, I need a break."

I don't know what to say. Ruby can't be replaced. She has worked in the worst inner-city hospitals in the country. She knows our patients and what they are up against. She is a passionate and committed teacher.

"Ruby," I lament looking at her face and noticing the dark circles under her eyes, "You have to do what's best for you."

Ruby reaches across the table and grasps my hand. "Thanks for that. I went back and forth and I finally figured out that if I don't look out for myself, no one else here will. The support group would have been fun. I hope it works out."

Before we head back to the trauma unit, Ruby gives me Pauline Holloway's phone number. When I call, I get her voice message. I leave my phone number with an explanation about what I do and offer to meet with her for emotional support.

At the end of the day, I knock on the door to Donald's office. "Do you have a minute?" I ask.

"Sure. What's on your mind?" Donald's office is small and lined with bookshelves topped with framed photos of both of his teenage daughters. Donald and his former wife, a nurse, divorced a few years ago.

"I've been thinking that I'd like to start a trauma support group for my patients. I've called a number of them and more than a few are having a hard time. They can't sleep; they feel paranoid when they go out and scenes of the trauma keep flashing in their minds. I think we need to offer them something."

When I finish, Donald leans back in his chair and smiles thoughtfully.

"It's a good idea, but it's something that should have a research component to it. Someone needs to write a grant to get some money so that we could have a control group and really do this thing right."

Research? I don't want to do research. I want to help my patients now.

"But that would take so long," I protest.

"In the meantime, you could always refer them to a community mental health clinic."

He's got to be kidding. Donald knows that it's nearly impossible to get a medical-surgical patient without a history of major mental illness into those clinics. Psychotic patients, suicidal patients, and those recently released from General's psychiatric wards have priority. Why would he stonewall this idea?

The more I think about it, the more pissed I become. I know that most physicians at SFGH are employed by the university, and, for that reason, feel pressure to do research and publish. I'm all for research. But, when there is a pressing need for treatment, shouldn't the patients' needs come first?

On my way out of the hospital for the day, I pass Stephanie Young in a wheelchair with a blanket over her lap hiding her stump. Two young boys walk next to her. Beaming, she introduces me to her sons who glance downward at first, then wave goodbye when Stephanie begins to wheel herself back to the lobby. Instead of feeling frustrated about the trauma group, I decide to end the day by letting myself feel some satisfaction for uniting Stephanie with her boys.

The next morning, forty minutes into a staff meeting, Donald asks for other agenda items. I raise my hand. "Could we take some time to discuss the situation between Dylan and Miranda?"

Before Donald can answer, one of the neuropsychologists asks for time to address the quality assurance project he is conducting. Donald gives him the floor first. When he finishes, we have twelve minutes to talk about the Dylan/Miranda battle for the same position.

"Maybe we can end a little early," says Donald looking up at the clock.

"What about my agenda item?"

"Ah, yes. Go right ahead."

No one except Janice looks at me. Even Barry is doodling in his weekly planner. Since Dylan and Miranda are sitting on opposite ends of the same side of the oblong table—out of each other's vision—I look at one, then the other.

"I'm wondering how it's going for the two of you. This is an unusual situation that affects all of us. It would be good if we could talk about it openly."

An uncomfortable silence settles upon the room before Janice comes to the rescue.

"Yes, I was wondering the same thing myself. How has it been for the two of you to work together while you're competing for the same job?"

Miranda rises to the challenge. "It's fine. It really is," she says, flashing her broad, toothpaste-commercial grin. "I think we're handling this really well. It's felt totally comfortable between us, hasn't it, Dylan?"

Dylan blushes and fiddles with his gold earring. In response to Miranda's question, he nods his head once and makes a vaguely affirmative, 'if you say so' grimace accompanied by a slight "mmmm" sound.

I dive in again. "It's hard to believe things are as good as you say, Miranda. The fact is that someone is going to win and someone is going to lose. A lot is at stake. Feelings will be hurt. That doesn't feel like a very comfortable situation."

"I have to agree," chimes Barry. "And if it feels awkward to me,

I imagine it must feel more awkward to both of you."

Nice try Barry, but neither of them is biting.

After a silence Donald says, "It's time to stop." He pauses and looks at me. "If people are still feeling uncomfortable and awkward next week, we can resume this conversation then."

Right. I'm sure it will be number one on the agenda.

Once inside the privacy of our office, Antionette pats me on the back. "You get credit for trying."

"Yes, but there's almost no point," says Janice. "Leadership here has never set an example for open sharing of feelings. Without their support, it's an uphill battle."

I try once again to call Mrs. Holloway, the patient that Ruby wanted me to follow. After the eighteenth ring, she finally answers. When she speaks, her voice is colorless and flat, her speech slow and halting. She tells me she is afraid to leave her home in the projects.

"The people here, they're friends of his," she says, meaning her assailant, the man who slit her throat. She is reluctant to stay on the phone but after I describe the symptoms of an acute stress response, she says she will think about coming to the hospital to see me.

A week later when I come to work, the flashing light on our message machine indicates that someone called at 3:49 a.m.

"I've been thinking about your offer," says the tired voice on the other end of the line. "Would you have time to see me sometime this morning? I'm not doing too well."

This time when I call Mrs. Holloway, she answers on the first ring. We arrange to meet in the cafeteria later in the morning. She will page me when she arrives.

I wish I could offer Mrs. Holloway a van service. I see them around the city emblazoned with the logos of private hospitals, delivering patients to their appointments. Although there is a city van that picks up alcoholics off the street and delivers them to our emergency department, the city does not pay a van service to pick up patients from their homes and deliver them to their appointments. Ruby often spoke of no-shows for follow-up appointments, noting that our patients can't afford taxis and are in too much pain to hobble to a bus stop.

"No one tracks that," she said. "We give great trauma care during the crisis but drop the ball on follow-up."

I think about other trauma patients who, like Ms. Holloway, are terrified to step outside their apartments. After my conversation with Donald, I have all but decided to start the group even without his approval. I make a note to myself to beg the social work department for taxi vouchers to get our trauma patients to and from the group.

Barry is at the nurses' station on the trauma unit stroking his red beard while writing in a patient's chart.

I tease: "What is it with you psychiatrists and your beards?"

"Displaced masturbatory urges, " he laughs.

The unit assistant, a middle-aged black woman, narrows her eyes, "I don't know about you psych people."

"Yeah, the surgeons consider us the lowest form of life until a homicidal paranoid schizophrenic turns up on their case list," says Barry. "Then we're golden."

He closes the chart. When the unit assistant answers the phone, Barry whispers, "Have you seen Dylan?"

"Not today and not much last week. Maybe this Miranda thing is getting to him."

Barry makes a face at the mention of her name and strokes the hair on his face.

"Between you and me, she's a disaster. She agreed from the beginning to help me prepare classes for the medical students but she's never once followed through with anything I've asked her to do."

"That's interesting, Barry. You mention Miranda and you start stroking your beard again. I'm wondering what that's about."

Barry laughs. "Save it, Process Queen. Hey, what's happening with the trauma group?"

"Didn't I tell you? Donald nixed it unless I write a grant proposal to fund a research project to study the group. I might start it on my own anyway."

"I've been thinking that observing a support group would be a great teaching tool for med students. They would learn about the psychological aspects of post-trauma recovery. Even if they don't go into psychiatry, it would be a great learning experience."

"Let me get it off the ground first. Then we'll talk about having students observe."

Although we forgot to exchange descriptions of each other, I recognize Mrs. Holloway as soon as she enters the cafeteria. When we shake hands, I feel the delicate bones in her fingers and have an urge to warm her cold hands in mine. Even though few people are in the cafeteria at this hour, I lead her to a corner table. Mrs. Holloway wears a navy turtleneck under a green and blue plaid wool suit that must have been elegant in its time. Now, however, the shoulders droop and the piping has frayed. Her hair, black but for a few silver strands at the temples, is pulled straight back and twisted into a chignon. Prominent dark circles under her eyes mar a smooth ebony complexion.

"Do you drink coffee or tea?" I ask. I leave for a moment and return with tea, coffee, an almond biscotto, and a banana.

"Pick your poison."

I am hoping she'll take the banana because I bet she hasn't eaten much for days but she makes no move toward the food. Instead, she slowly tears off the top of each of two sugar packets, squeezes the juice of a lemon slice, and stirs the tea, making small concentric circles. Not a grain of sugar spills onto the table. She sits back, compact and erect as an alert cat. I am suddenly aware of the tension in my own body and force my shoulders and neck to relax.

"I'm glad you came in. I know it wasn't easy. I'm going to ask you to describe exactly what happened to you. Just talking helps a lot of people but you should only say what you feel comfortable saying."

Although I support the idea of survivors telling their story as the first step in healing, people need to feel that they are in control of this decision. A few people choose not to talk or simply can't, and I try to respect this.

Mrs. Holloway looks at me full on for the first time.

I will try to take each step with you so you are not alone.

She closes her eyes, then opens them and begins. "For 19 years, I worked for a large company here in San Francisco. When they moved the operation to the Central Valley, I didn't want to follow. After that, my mother died and everything went downhill fast. I got sick with a woman's problem, my husband left me, and I was forced to move into the projects. That's where this happened."

Her hand touches the bandage underneath her turtleneck. "It's hard to talk about this but I think I'll go crazy if I don't."

I watch as she makes a fist, puts it to her mouth, and shuts her eyes tightly. We sit in silence until she draws deeply from an inner reservoir. Then her face muscles relax and she lowers her hand. The impression of her front teeth remains on her knuckle. After Mrs. Holloway takes a sip of tea, she locks her teary eyes onto mine. When I hand her a napkin she sobs softly.

"I'm never like this," she says sounding both apologetic and angry at the same time. "I'm not one to carry on about things. But this shouldn't have happened to me."

She clenches her jaw and forces the words out. "I don't belong there."

"Where?"

"Where I have to live now in the projects. With people who speak badly, behave badly. And I have to live with them."

There's bitterness in her voice. "Most of them have never worked. Their parents have never worked. No one there brings home a paycheck or opens a savings account."

"You feel like an outsider there."

"Yes, and most of the time, I keep to myself."

"So how did this happen to you?"

Mrs. Holloway stares at the cup of tea nested between her hands. "A man I knew there told me I was looking unhappy. He suggested that I smoke crack with him. He said that it would make me feel better. I was desperate so I did."

She presses her lips together, and then sighs forcefully. "He was right. I did feel better right away. I smoked with him a couple of times after that. When this happened, we were in my apartment. He told me he wanted me to—to have sex with him."

Mrs. Holloway lowers her eyes and sips her tea. "He got mad when I said no. He took out a knife."

She closes her eyes. The muscles in her face quiver until she regains control. "I didn't feel it, didn't feel anything, except the blood."

She touches her throat, lowers her chin, and stares into her teacup. When she speaks again, her voice seems separate from her body. "I was lying on the floor, bleeding, pretending to be dead. I could hear him rustling through my closet, taking things out. I felt the blood dripping down my neck. I knew I didn't have much time but I was afraid if I said anything he'd kill me for sure."

Ms. Holloway's voice has become almost inaudible. "I don't know how long it was—it felt like hours—but I felt myself getting weaker and I knew that I had to let someone know I was there. When I couldn't hear him anymore, I decided to take a chance. I pulled myself up and yelled out the window for someone to call

911. Only when he didn't kill me did I know for sure he was gone."

Suddenly aware that I have been holding my breath throughout the story, I exhale loudly. My neck and shoulders feel like concrete. My body slumps, exhausted.

"The ambulance arrived quickly," she says. "The emergency room doctors gave me blood and sewed me up. Then they sent me home—exactly where I didn't want to go."

I remember Ruby telling me that had a social worker been there on that day, Mrs. Holloway would have been sent to a women's shelter or encouraged to stay with a friend.

Since being home, Mrs. Holloway has slept poorly and eaten very little. She has remained in a state of frozen terror, expecting any moment for her assailant to knock on her door. Panic attacks have left her gasping for breath. When she dozes off, she is startled awake by nightmares. Yet when I mention the idea of living with friends or family, she flatly refuses.

"I am the big sister who took care of my brothers. I'm the one who cared for my mother when she was ill. Now my mother is dead and my brothers have their own families. I won't impose."

At the end of our session, I call Barry who meets us shortly afterward. I summarize Mrs. Holloway's story and symptoms. Barry asks a few questions, after which he prescribes medication to help Mrs. Holloway sleep and to take the edge off her extreme anxiety. She and I will meet again tomorrow morning. When we shake hands goodbye, Mrs. Holloway covers my cold hand with hers.

Barry knocks on my office door when I arrive the next morning. "The group's on," he says. "Donald says it's a go."

Did I hear that right?

"What?"

"I told him it would be a good experience for the medical students and that I'd like to co-lead it with you."

"That's it? He didn't say anything about a research component?"

"No. He just said it sounds like a great idea."

"Well, how about that."

"I thought you'd be happy. Let's talk later. Gotta run."

Maybe I'll be happy later but right now, I'm irritated.

Why was it so easy for Barry to get the OK? Is it because he's a doc?

Thanks to the medication, Mrs. Holloway got a few good hours of sleep last night. This morning she talks about losing her mother, an invalid, two years ago. Mrs. Holloway had taken her mother in and cared for her for ten years. She cries as she describes her mother's wisdom and generosity; she says how much she misses her. Although the sleeping medication Barry prescribed has an antidepressant effect, it will take a while for it to kick in. For the next few weeks, I will meet with Mrs. Holloway frequently to monitor her symptoms, help her grieve her loss, and work through the trauma she survived. I will also be doing what I can to get a support group up and running. To recover and get on with her life, Mrs. Holloway will need all the help she can get.

12

The bully

O ver lunch, Barry and I talk about the trauma group. Each of us will meet with different departments in the hospital to chat it up and clarify the referral process. We agree to hold the group in the reading room of the medical staff library, a cozy, wood-paneled room with a fireplace, chandelier, and comfortable chairs.

Groups work because people who share similar problems benefit from hearing about how others cope. Even when there is no good solution, knowing that others are also struggling ameliorates the feeling of being alone in the world. The primary goal of the group leaders is to make the group feel safe so that people can speak freely.

I learned to lead psychotherapy groups when I worked at McLean Hospital. Each week for six months, my co-therapist and I submitted a verbatim of the group to a senior therapist who analyzed our interventions and suggested how we could improve our skills. Since McLean, I've led or co-led many other kinds of groups: community meetings, women's groups, a family dynamics group, medication groups, a singing group for chronically mentally ill patients, and a sibling group for their healthy brothers and sisters. It's one of my favorite things to do as a psychiatric nurse.

As Barry and I leave the cafeteria, my beeper goes off. "Laurie? It's Miranda. You cover trauma patients, right? Could you take a look at a lady who's trying to leave against medical orders on 4D? She was stabbed in the abdomen by her boyfriend a few days ago. Her name is Gwendolyn Baylor."

"Sure, Miranda. I can see her. Is she…?"

Before I can finish my question, Miranda hangs up.

For the first time that I can recall, the double doors at the entrance to 4D are closed. Through small windows, I can see the back of Trudy's head blocking the door. A patient stands in front of her. I enter the unit from the set of double doors on the other side of the unit and cross over. Seeing me, Trudy says, "Here is someone I want you to speak with before you go anywhere, Ms. Baylor."

I introduce myself to the patient, a slender, young African-American woman wearing a flimsy blue bathrobe and no shoes.

"I know you want to leave, Ms. Baylor, but your doctors want you to stay a little longer. Could we go back to your room to talk about it?"

Sensing her internal chaos, I speak in my most gentle voice. She stares at me for a few long seconds. "Come," I urge. "Let's talk in your room."

The double doors behind me suddenly burst open nearly knocking both of us into each other. A flood of medical trainees funnels around us. Ms. Baylor gives in to the current and sweeps down the hall with them, turning off into her room with me in tow. She walks past her bed to the window and gazes outside.

I position myself at the other end of the window, leaving about five feet between us. This way we have something in common to look at, and enough space between us for her to feel comfortable. At least, I hope it's enough space for her. I can't tell if she is watching the scene in the parking lot between an attendant and an angry person, or observing the traffic backed up on Highway 101. She may be too internally preoccupied to notice anything outside herself.

Searching for a way to begin, I say, "I'm glad I'm missing that traffic."

Silence.

"Are you watching what's going on in the parking lot?"

Ms. Baylor's face remains blank. No light sparks her eyes. Maybe she's one of those people who goes numb after a trauma.

"Ms. Baylor, could you tell me how you're feeling?"

In the silence that persists, I remember that I had recently asked Corianne where she hurt herself when she fell. "Over there," she said in between tearful heaves, pointing to the spot in the family room where she had slipped on a piece of paper.

"No, honey, I mean where on your body does it hurt?"

Children and people with schizophrenia think in concrete terms. Maybe I need to rephrase the question.

"Ms. Baylor, tell me what you are thinking right now."

"Safe. I feel safe here."

"And where are you right now?"

No time like the present to assess her orientation to person, place, time, date, and situation.

"I'm in the hospital. Next time, I won't use a butcher knife," she says in a flat tone.

"What?"

"It hurts too much with a butcher knife."

"Oh!"

Didn't Miranda say her boyfriend...

"Are you saying you hurt yourself with a knife?"

"I had to or they would hurt me worse."

"You mean your boyfriend?"

"No, not him. The others."

Her high, childlike voice floats in the air between us. Devoid of energy, resonance, and emotion, disconnected from her body, her voice almost gets lost in the air currents. A few seconds elapse before I can reconfigure my patient from a victim of interpersonal violence to a psychotic person who has made a suicide attempt. Although I haven't interviewed a person with hallucinations and delusions for a long time, the clinical questions boomerang back.

"Are you in any danger right now?"

"Not here. But I need to get a gun to protect myself."

"You don't have one at home?"

"Not yet, but I aim to get one."

"Have you been hearing voices lately when no one else was in the room?"

"Yes."

"What do the voices tell you?"

"That it's my turn to die."

"What do you do when you hear these voices?"

"I tried a glass of wine but it didn't work."

"Do voices talk to you from the radio or TV?

"No. But someone out there with ESP can read my mind."

"Are you hearing voices besides mine and yours right now?"

"No."

"If you do, could you tell your nurse right away?"

"Yes."

I have little faith in her response but maybe my question will give her the idea that others are here to help.

I spend a few more minutes trying to put some of the puzzle pieces together. Ms. Baylor recently lost her job as a word processor and broke up with her boyfriend. Shortly afterward, she began hearing voices telling her to hurt herself.

This is not just a nurse's case after all; Ms. Baylor is going to need anti-psychotic medications. I page Miranda. When she calls, I will inform her that a psychiatrist needs to evaluate Ms. Baylor for a legal hold, make a recommendation for anti-psychotic medication, and begin the process of negotiating with the psychiatric inpatient units for a transfer once she is medically cleared. Because I can't trust Ms. Baylor not to harm herself while she's here, I let Trudy know that she will need a sitter to be with her until we can negotiate a transfer to the medical psych unit. God only knows when those voices will decide this isn't a safe place after all.

I wait a few minutes for Miranda to answer my page. Then I page her again.

"Ms. Baylor is psychotic," I say to Trudy who is on hold with the nursing office about the sitter. "She needs to be seen by a doc. Miranda is on call but she's not answering my page."

"You know, I told Miranda that this lady seemed a little nutsy to me but she said a psych nurse could handle it. You nurses don't usually evaluate the really crazy ones do you?"

"Not in this hospital because most of the time they need medication and a hearing to determine competency. You all keep us busy enough with the trauma patients and the character disorders."

"You might try paging Dylan. He just left here a few seconds ago," says Trudy. "By the way, I heard that Miranda is trying to steal his job. That would be a real shame. He's a gem."

As if to prove her point, Dylan answers his page promptly.

"Hey Dr. Donahue, long time no see." I give him a rundown on Ms. Baylor and tell him what I think she needs.

"Isn't Miranda supposed to be on call?"

"She is but she's not answering her page."

"That's interesting," he replies. "I'll be right over."

Dylan's small gold earring peeks through his shaggy dark hair. I tell him what I know about Ms. Baylor.

"Why don't you come in with me and we'll see her together," he says. "It sounds like she trusts you."

I introduce Dylan to Ms. Baylor who regards him without expression. He too respects her physical space and gives her time to answer his questions. His approach is unhurried, gentle, concerned. However, at the end of the interview, when Ms. Baylor is unable to agree to stay in the hospital another day, Dylan informs her that he must place her on a seventy-two-hour psychiatric hold because of the seriousness of her actions. He tells her he will prescribe medication to help shut the voices out of her mind, and order a sitter to ensure her safety. As we leave the room, a heavy-set woman that I recognize as a sitter for other patients, smiles at me and drags a chair into Ms. Baylor's room. I don't know how well she works with psychotic patients, but she looks like she could block the door and summon help if necessary.

At the nurses' station, Dylan calls Psychiatric Emergency to obtain more information about Ms. Baylor but they've never heard of her. He calls her mother and when there is no response, he leaves a message. Both of us are wondering if this episode could be Ms. Baylor's first psychotic break.

"You once told me how you used to diagnose patients at that day-treatment center you worked at in Cambridge. What words did you use?"

"Mishuggah and Mishuggah auf toit."

"That's right. Yiddish for crazy and what's 'auf toit' again?"

"From the deep."

"That's it. I'd say right now that she's mishuggah. Let's hope we can head off the auf toit part."

While Dylan makes more phone calls, I follow up with a couple of my patients. I return to the nurses' station as he is finishing his note on Ms. Baylor.

"I placed Ms. Baylor on a hold," he says without looking up. "We're going to transfer her to med psych as soon as a bed opens there. I've also suggested an antipsychotic for her. You might want to review the side effects with the nursing staff."

Dylan sounds uncharacteristically businesslike.

"How's drumming?" I ask.

"What?"

"Are you still playing with two bands? I always thought that was how you kept so cool, beating those drums seven nights a week."

"Yeah, I'm still with them."

Dylan signs his name and closes the chart.

OK, Laurie, it's now or never.

"So, how are you doing with this Miranda thing?"

Dylan scowls. "She's a strong candidate," he says returning the chart to its home and selecting another.

"Aren't you generous!"

"It's a clinical skill," he replies with deadpan delivery.

"All I know is that I feel like smacking her."

"That's funny, Laurie. I wouldn't have taken you for having a violent streak. Maybe my clinical skills aren't so good after all."

"They're excellent, much better than hers. No one can believe she's challenging your position!"

"She is perfectly within her rights to do that. Who knows, if our roles were switched I might do the same."

Dylan's voice is soft and steady as usual, but detecting the slight inflection of a prim schoolmaster, I roll my eyes.

"Dylan, the problem is that you are pathologically nice. It may be her right to challenge your position but it's not collegial. In fact, it's downright rotten. I bet no one has ever said 'no' to this girl. She is spoiled, entitled, and..."

Dylan cuts me off.

"It's not all about her," he says quietly. "Surely Donald has some input in this decision as does the chief of psychiatry. Listen, I've logged more hours than any psychiatrist on the team has. My assessments are timely and thorough. Their lack of support makes the decision crystal clear to me. I intend to go through the entire process knowing it will be a sham."

Dylan slams the chart shut. "By the way, it sounds to me like you have your own issues with Miranda that have nothing to do with me."

Without waiting for my response, Dylan walks down the hall to his next patient's room.

Whoa! I didn't expect any of that, especially his last comment. He's right though. Something about her gets under my skin.

On Saturday morning, I put all thoughts of work aside in favor of pondering what to do with the plum shrub that I should have had removed when we landscaped the backyard. If I'm going to dig it out, the time is now before the ground dries up.

The plum shrub looks like a tall birdcage for a big bird. From its short but stout trunk, six vertical branches bow slightly outward before growing straight up. Although it's only about five feet high, its roots are tough and deep. Once again, I chastise myself for insisting that we preserve it even though it grows in the middle of what we've planned as a small swath of lawn. According to a gardener friend, if I relocate it to a sunnier spot it may flower and bear fruit. For this reason, and because it is the most substantial plant in my young garden, I will move it to a more favorable location.

The day is bright and clear with a cool ocean breeze. Within minutes of shoveling the clay soil from around the trunk, I break into a sweat. It takes another half-hour of hard work to uncover six thick roots—one for each branch—that plunge downward out of sight. Taking a break, I lean on my spade and gulp down a glass of water that Brian has brought me.

Even though my neck and shoulders ache, I like the physical nature of the work. Most of the time when I'm pushing my body hard, all other concerns fall away. Today, while I stretch my tired muscles, Dylan's words surface and turn over in my mind.

"You have your own issues with Miranda that have nothing to do with me."

I grab the spade and jump on it with renewed vigor hoping to eradicate hospital politics from my mind but failing.

Maybe you're jealous of her. She's a doc, Ivy League, and accomplished.

That could be it, but I've gotten along well with other female doctors.

How is she different?

She's like a pit bull. When she wants something, nothing stops her.

Sounds like a pit bully.

That's it! She's a bully.

So what are you going to do? Ram Miranda in the gut with your head?

I have to admit to a certain satisfaction at the thought. But no, I can see this is Dylan's battle, not mine.

Satisfied with that kernel of truth, I let go of Miranda and reapply myself to the task. After digging a basin around the plum shrub that is four feet in diameter and eighteen inches deep, I push against the shrub and hear the satisfying crack of rootlets beginning to give way. Remembering my neighbor's advice to keep the roots wet, I pull the hose over to the basin. While the water sinks in, I begin digging a new hole for the plum shrub in a sunnier part of the garden. Almost immediately, the spade crunches against a deposit of buried glass. Like a surgeon picking out shrapnel from a soldier's body, I sift through each spadeful looking for shards. Although tedious, the work is unexpectedly satisfying.

If only we psych people could remove shards of schizophrenia or slivers of trauma from our patients' brains!

By the time I've dug a hole large enough to accommodate the

root ball, it's time for lunch. Before taking a break, I fill the hole with water.

When I resume working, the saturated soil makes each spadeful of dirt doubly heavy. Even though lifting and carrying children has given me a strong back and impressive deltoid muscles, by the time I've removed enough mud to feel the roots ease their underground grip, my energy is nearly spent. In a last surge of strength, I pry the remaining roots from the soil, lift the shrub, and carry it to its new home. Holding it straight and steady, I fill the space around it with the excavated soil, give it a thorough soaking, and call it quits for the day. Sweaty and filthy but exhilarated, I strip out of my clothes and boots and leave them in a heap on the deck outside the kitchen door.

The kids make fun of my mud-streaked face. After I've showered, Brian hands the kids over to me and leaves for the office. Although my body feels tired, for the rest of the day I feel buoyant and peaceful, as if I had buried all of my worries and concerns in the earth. At night, while reading a story aloud to the boys, my eyelids slam shut mid-sentence. Corianne is annoyed when I ask her to finish reading to them, but it's all I can do to brush my teeth and slip into bed.

In early June during staff meeting, Donald announces the Department of Psychiatry is going to develop an outpatient mental-health clinic, which will include an outpatient trauma clinic.

"You mean we'll have a place to refer our trauma patients for psych counseling?" I ask.

"Eventually, yes."

"Fantastic!" I add, even though I am not sure what this means for the trauma support group which is scheduled to begin next month.

As if reading my mind Donald adds, "Of course it will take a while to organize the clinic, hire new staff, and write policies and procedures. Dr. Patricia Clematti, presently chief of neuropsychology, has been selected to run the new department.

"For those of you who don't know her," says one of the neuro-psychologists, "She's smart, energetic, and committed to our patients."

Everyone is excited by the idea of a mental health clinic on the SFGH campus. We spend the rest of the meeting discussing what kinds of services would most benefit our patient population, how the clinic will be funded, who will staff it, and how referrals will be made. Sometime during the discussion, I notice that neither Dylan nor Miranda is present.

Before the meeting ends, Donald clears his voice. "One more thing." Donald fiddles with his pen until we come to attention. "It was decided that Miranda will be relieving Dylan of his position. Dylan had the option of staying on for a month but decided to leave as of today."

With our office door closed, the bosom-beating begins. "Oy-oy-oy," I groan in a culturally-ingrained Yiddish inflection.

"Oh my God," repeats Janice shaking her head back and forth.

Antionette cups her hands over her eyes, "How can this be true?"

A sharp rap on the door interrupts our moaning. It's Barry.

"May I join you?"

Safe inside our office, Barry tells us what he knows.

"Donald and the chief of psychiatry made the decision. Basically, it comes down to the fact that she's published and he's not. She's from Yale and he went to a state medical school. That's what they value around here."

"I wonder how Dylan is," says Janice.

Antionette frowns, "It doesn't feel right for him to leave without seeing us again. We need to say goodbye."

"We could have a farewell party at my house," I offer. "We could even use the first hour for a good old-fashioned process meeting and pop champagne after that."

Everyone favors the idea.

"Barry," says Janice, "You might want to tip off Miranda about the process group part so she doesn't come."

"Sure," replies Barry, "even though she'd steer clear of it anyway."

The next day, I call Dylan and run the idea by him. He sounds reluctant at first but agrees to attend when I tell him that the party is as much for us as it is for him.

On party day, Janice and Antionette leave work early to help me with preparations. Everyone else arrives at the appointed time except Donald, who told me earlier he had a prior commitment, and Molly, one of the neuropsychologists, who warned me that her presence was iffy.

Four people share the couch in our living room. Dylan sits in one of our two comfortable upholstered chairs. When I'm ready to take my place in the circle, the others have already seated themselves in the stacking metal chairs, thoughtfully leaving the second comfortable chair for me. No sooner have I sat down and prepared myself mentally to begin the group, when the doorbell rings. Instead of running downstairs to let Molly in, I step out onto the deck off the living room and call down to her, "It's open. Come on in and walk all the way up."

Half a minute later when Miranda's long, lithe form appears instead of Molly's short squat one, adrenaline squirts into my system electrifying every nerve ending in my body.

I shoot a look at Barry who raises his shoulders and shakes his head with an expression of incredulity on his face, which I take to mean that he spoke to her and she just blew him off. This girl has nerve.

Miranda enters and greets everyone as if nothing is out of the ordinary. She seats herself in the comfortable chair without concerning herself where I will sit. While I walk down to the basement to retrieve a stacking chair for myself, I decide to proceed as planned despite Miranda's presence, in the hope that everyone will express themselves as if she weren't here because Lord knows, if she possessed even a shred of sensitivity, she wouldn't be.

I don't betray the fact that my heart is beating like a boxer's fists against a punching bag. Instead, I open the meeting the way I've been trained to do. "We're here to honor Dylan's three years on our service. Who would like to begin?"

People jump right in. Several of the physicians and psychologists testify to Dylan's superb clinical skills, his willingness to work long hours, his commitment to his patients, his thorough reports, his modesty, and honesty. Antionette testifies to Dylan's respectful relationships with all members of the treatment team, especially the nurses. Forced to listen, Dylan's pale Irish skin defies all efforts to be cool, turning maraschino-cherry red during the litany of praise heaped upon him.

Then Janice speaks. "Dylan, you and I have dealt with some really difficult situations over the last few years, especially on pediatrics."

Dylan smiles and nods as if the memories are still fresh in his mind.

"I could always count on you to be there when I needed you, to keep your cool, and to keep the patient's best interest in mind."

Janice hesitates, seeming to organize her thoughts before proceeding. When she does, her honeyed voice turns hard like rock candy. "I need to say that I feel uncomfortable with the circumstances that have led to your leaving."

She straightens up in her chair and looks directly at Miranda. "Frankly, I think it was bad form for someone inside the department to challenge a colleague's position. That's all I have to say."

Throughout the testimony, I've been watching Miranda's face closely. Either she's trained herself to betray nothing or she truly feels nothing. Although the big smile has disappeared, her expression remains pleasant in a plastic kind of way that make my blood boil. Janice shrugs and looks my way.

In the silence that follows Janice's comments, I force down my feelings about Miranda. I tell Dylan how sad I am that we must say goodbye to him as a colleague. I acknowledge that everything everyone has said about him is true, that it has been a pleasure to work with someone who is consistently ethical, humble, and patient-centered. I need to say something more.

"Like Janice, I have had trouble with how and why you were bumped out of the department."

I glance at Miranda. Her eyes are glazed over as if she is unaware of my confrontation.

Is she even paying attention?

Another wave surges in my body.

OK, honey, here goes.

"What I'm saying, Miranda, is that you may have had every right to challenge Dylan's position but it was a really rotten thing to do. I'm pissed that he had to lose his job and that we have lost him because of you."

Miranda looks up at the mention of her name. When our eyes meet, a flash of lighter-fluid fury cannonballs toward me. My stomach lurches but I hold fast and regard her with the most professionally detached, neutral gaze I can muster. Then a startling image appears in my mind: I see myself lowering my head and pounding it into her stomach repeatedly. No matter how many times I ram into her, she does not flinch or cry.

I refuse to avert my gaze from hers. A few uncomfortable seconds of silence slink by before Miranda begins to speak.

"Clearly Dylan, yours are hard shoes to fill." Miranda's voice sounds husky. She wets her lips and looks down before continuing.

The bully

Good. Maybe she finally gets it! Maybe now she understands that bullying her way into Dylan's position will backfire on her.

Miranda looks up. For a fleeing moment, her chin juts forward, her lips forming a fist. Then she tames that expression into the same posture of poise and confidence she displayed the first time she was introduced to us.

"It's been great working with you, Dylan," she says in a virtuoso imitation of cheerful sincerity. "And I wish you all the best."

Then she simply stops talking. A pleasant smile remains frozen on her face.

Dylan frowns while he figures out what to say in the ensuing silence. "Thanks Laurie, for hosting the party, and to all of you for coming. Uhhh, can we eat dinner now?"

Everyone jumps out of the chairs at the same time. Antionette, Janice, and I pull food from the oven and refrigerator, and place it on the dining room table. While people mill around chattering, out of the corner of my eye I glimpse Miranda quietly slipping down the stairs to the safety of the street. I say nothing. It doesn't take long before everyone else notices that she's gone.

13

Boundary violations

Today like most mornings, people in wheelchairs and on crutches crowd around the hospital's main entrance on their way to clinic appointments and physical therapy sessions.

Should I invite all of them to this afternoon's trauma support group?

That would be one way of getting patients to come since none turned up two weeks ago at the group's debut. On closer inspection, when it becomes clear that one of my possible candidates is hallucinating and another is hawking the stuffed bears given as gifts to patients on the AIDS unit, I remember why it's a good idea to screen patients first. At this late date, all I can do is hope that the hours I've spent calling patients and staff members to remind them about today's group will pay off.

Stepping off the elevator, I run smack into the line of prisoners in orange jumpsuits and their guards in khaki uniforms. They are on their way to the jail unit. Bringing up the rear this morning is a gurney surrounded by four guards. Passing them, I notice that the prisoner on the gurney is in four-point leather restraints.

Although the guards and prisoners usually banter back and forth during their march to the medical jail unit, today the guards look straight ahead, their facial muscles pulled taut. My curiosity piqued, I catch a glimpse of the patient in the gurney. Although his pale face and longish dark hair look familiar, I can't place him. Probably a criminal whose picture I recognize from the newspaper, or maybe a former patient. Many of them have spent time in jail.

Inside our office, I check the message machine for new trauma consults. There is none. Nor are there new trauma consults noted in our referral log. When was the last time that happened?

On 4D, Trudy shakes her head. "I don't know what's going on but things seem awfully quiet out there. Except for a patient who should be arriving soon from the ER, we haven't had any new trauma patients for two days."

Then she scrutinizes the dry erase board.

"Maybe you should stop in to see Maria Sousa in 12-1. She was hit by a car over the weekend. Her left leg is badly fractured. She seemed fine until this morning when I walked by and she was crying but she didn't want to talk about it. Maybe she'll talk to you."

Maria, a blond-haired woman in her fifties, lies on her back with her leg elevated on pillows. A bouquet of irises, calla lilies, and roses dwarfs her bedside table. Crumpled tissues lay on her abdomen. Maria dabs her eyes while I explain my presence.

Then I ask, "Are you in pain?"

"This?" she asks pointing to her leg. "Of course."

Glancing at the flowers and pressing her hand to her bosom, she adds, "But this is where it hurts the most."

Reflexively, I take her wrist to feel her pulse. "Have you had problems with your heart before?"

"Not since I was a young girl," she replies. "Back then my heart was broken every week."

After I clarify with Maria that I was asking about cardiac problems, she laughs.

"No darling, not that kind of problem! But, I almost had a heart attack last night when the love of my life called. I haven't seen him since I was nineteen."

Maria starts crying. "Look at me! I don't want him to see me like this but he insisted. His plane arrives this afternoon!"

Blue-purple bruises and scabbed over-abrasions discolor Maria's left eye and cheek. Wisps of blond hair splay from her pillow on both sides like a clown's wig.

"I'm sure he'll look beyond your abrasions," I say, trying to soothe her fears.

"No darling, that's not what I'm talking about," chides Maria. "The last time I saw him, I weighed 112 pounds. After high school, he wanted us to marry and live in Maine where we grew up. I was a dancer and I had to try to make it in New York. For a while I did but I don't look anything like a dancer now. I'd rather die than let him see me like this!"

After blowing her nose and collecting herself, Maria tells me that Sal had recently attended their fortieth high school reunion with the hope of seeing her. When she didn't show up, he convinced one of Maria's friends to send him her phone number and address.

Short of emergency liposuction, there's not much to be done for Maria before Sal arrives. As long as I'm speaking with her, I decide to conduct a trauma interview. When I ask about the circumstances leading to her injury, she tells me that on the day of the accident, she was so astounded to have received a letter from Sal that she ran out of her house and across the street just as a car was passing.

"Darling," she interrupts when I question her about signs and symptoms of an acute stress reaction. "Could you hand me my compact and my lipstick? Right about now, I need a girlfriend more than

I need a psychiatric nurse."

Although Maria is very good at making me feel completely incompetent, she's right. This is a time for marshalling cosmetic defenses, not assessing psychological ones. I'm no make-up artist but I might be able to find someone who can help.

"Maria, would you like me to call the hairdresser? She shampoos and styles and she may even do make-up."

Maria's eyes light up. I make the call.

Helga, a seventy-five-year-old volunteer, answers the page right away. When I explain the situation, Helga agrees to see Maria as soon as she finishes cutting another patient's hair. Maria is overjoyed. So am I for finally doing something right by her.

I return to the nurses' station and tell Trudy about my nursing intervention. "Sometimes Helga is the best medicine," she laughs. "But our new lady could really use you after her nurse completes the admission process."

Trudy tells me that the patient, a victim of domestic violence, arrived from the ER a few minutes ago. "In the meantime, can you join me for a quick cup of coffee?" she asks.

Being able to shoot the breeze with Trudy is a rare treat. As the epicenter of the trauma unit, the charge nurse routinely juggles dozens of balls at once. When I ask, Trudy tells me that she has worked on 4D for eighteen years and has been day-shift charge nurse here for the last eight.

"Have you ever worked at a private hospital?" I ask.

Trudy breaks into a smile. "As a matter of fact, many years ago, I did. This place was driving me nuts so I left and signed on at my local community hospital. I lasted two months. The most exciting thing that happened was when a little old lady lost her dentures. Everyone was frantic. All I could think was 'Get a grip.' They had no idea. I couldn't stand it so I came back here."

"Back to the front lines?"

"Back to real life," she replies. "I like the action but mostly I love our patients. Yesterday I helped the sweetest Arabic woman in room five. She must be eighty if she's a day and just had surgery for bladder cancer. Doesn't speak a word of English. We used hand signals, and somehow, we understood each other. When I said goodbye at the end of the day, she grabbed my hand and kissed it. This morning she was overjoyed to see me again."

Trudy's blue eyes shine and her face crinkles in laughter. "I mean my husband loves me, but not like that!"

SFGH is full of employees like Trudy who would be bored working anywhere else. One of the other nurses told me that working here for her is like traveling the world, learning about other people's cultures, and being paid for it.

The admitting nurse tells me that the new patient, Alyssa Darnell, is tearful but that she has agreed to meet with me. According to the ER record she is "a thirty-nine-year-old African-American woman admitted with a neck/chest wall abscess and mild symptoms of neck compression. She has a long history of asthma and chronic obstructive pulmonary disease (COPD) with multiple hospital admissions and courses of steroidal therapy. She smokes a pack a day and drinks a bottle of brandy every two days. For the last three days, she has had a fever, chills, night sweats, and has been coughing up green sputum."

Even though her mother is at her bedside, Alyssa gets right to the point. Her injuries were caused by her husband's fists. She is petrified that he will visit her in the hospital and hurt her again. Five times before, she has tried to leave him. Each time, he has beaten her and threatened to hurt the children if she leaves. She is not their biological mother but she adores them and is proud of her ability to mother them.

"I make good meals and I work with them on their homework every night. I didn't do too good in school 'cause I had dyslexia. But my kids, they doin' real good."

Alyssa smiles a bright toothy smile. I am glad there is a small ray of light in her life. She tells me her husband has been out of work for almost a year.

"Sometime he gone for days. I know he sellin' crack. Sometime he even bring women home. He watch me all the time. Even if he be away, his friends be watchin' me. I feel like a prisoner only I haven't done nothin' wrong!"

She cries hard as she says this repeatedly. The idea of violence toward women sickens me as much as violence directed at children. As she sobs, I fantasize about being a female Clint Eastwood, which only makes me more upset. I practice a relaxation technique. Inhaling deeply and slowly I say to myself, "Re---" and then, exhaling, "---lax."

After Alyssa stops sobbing, we are both ready to make a plan. We agree that if her husband enters her hospital room at any time, she will scream bloody murder to alert the nurses. She gives me a description of him that I will pass on to the nursing staff and to the institutional police. Lucky for us he's easy to spot: short, walks with a limp, and has a gold tooth.

"Tell them security officers to be careful," she warns. "He got a gun."

In the nurses' station, I asterisk a note in red ink on the nursing rand, a movable file containing a synopsis of each patient's nursing care requirements. After alerting Trudy about Alyssa's plan to scream if she sees her husband, I call the institutional police to give them a heads up and a description. Although I think the probability of a patient's abuser coming to the unit where she is hospitalized as a result of his brutality is unlikely, I need to do what I can to make

Alyssa feel a little more secure. I also leave messages for Alyssa's social worker and call in a referral to a substance-abuse counselor.

When my pager goes off, I recognize the number as Janice's. A few minutes later, before I've had a chance to call her back, Antionette walks into the 4D nurses' station. I rarely see her here on a surgical unit since the medical units keep her so busy.

"Hey, stranger. Welcome to my home."

"You haven't spoken to Janice yet, have you?" asks Antionette.

"No, but I was just going to return her page."

"Don't bother. She wants us to meet her in the office as soon as possible. I have no idea what it's about but going by her voice, it's serious."

"Have either of you heard?" whispers Janice after we sit down in the office. She searches our faces. "I guess not."

Janice shakes her head and runs her hands through her hair. Two deep furrows appear between her eyebrows. After sighing deeply she becomes businesslike.

"Over the past few months, a bipolar patient has been coming to psych emergency services saying that he's been having an affair with Dr. Gluznick who used to work there. Do either of you know who he is?"

"By sight only," says Antionette.

I shake my head no.

"Gluznick is a psychiatrist on staff. He left psych emergency services a few months ago to become the chief of 6B."

Since 6B is one of the psychiatric inpatient units at SFGH and we spend our time on the medical-surgical side of the hospital, Dr. Gluznick is not someone we would have contact with during the course of our day.

"When I was head nurse on psych emergency, patients would occasionally say such things about their therapists. But this time, it turns out to be true."

"Oy," I groan.

Antionette frowns, "Jesus have mercy."

"It gets worse," says Janice. "Last night someone heard scream-ing from a house and called the police. When the cops arrived, Dr. Gluznick and his lover—the bipolar patient—were naked and cov-ered with blood. Apparently, both of them were high on metham-phetamine. It seems that Dr. Gluznick attacked the patient with a camping ax."

Janice grimaces and stops for a moment.

"The upshot is that the patient is in the ICU. They're not sure he's going to make it."

I curse under my breath. Antionette gasps and cups her mouth, her eyes wide with disbelief.

"Where is Gluznick now?" I ask.

"He's here, on the jail unit. I don't know how much Patricia is going to say about it at staff meeting but I thought you should know ahead of time."

Ding, ding, ding. The prisoner on the gurney this morning was Dr. Gluznick.

On our way back to our units, Antionette and I stop in the caf-eteria for tea. At the hot water canister, we run into a licensed psych tech that Antionette knows.

"I suppose you've heard about Gluznick?" he asks.

"Not until a few minutes ago," she replies.

"Well, I worked with the guy on psych emergency and on 6B. It's about time he got caught. Too bad he had to take someone down with him."

"What do you mean, 'It's time he got caught?'" I ask.

"Everyone knew he was on something. His pupils were always dilated and he acted strange. Psych emergency staff couldn't stand him so they transferred him to 6B. He used to visit male patients late at night in their rooms with the door closed. Come on! I never could figure out why he wasn't canned earlier."

While Antionette and I stand there not knowing what to say, the psych tech gives his tea a stir and leaves. Over his shoulder he calls out, "It's gonna be a wild ride on psychiatry today!"

Antionette and I walk to the elevators where we wait in silence. After boarding, we remain speechless until the doors open onto the fourth floor.

"See you at staff meeting," she whispers just before the doors close and the elevator whisks her to the fifth floor.

On 4D, before I have a chance to tell Trudy about Gluznick, high-pitched screams pierce the unit. A blur of a masculine figure streaks past me toward the entry doors. Allysa stands in her bathrobe in the hallway outside her door, shoulders raised, and fists pressed to her chest, fighting for breath.

"That was him," she wheezes as I approach her. "He started to hurt me. I screamed. Just like we said."

With my arm around Alyssa's waist, I catch Trudy's eye as she comes toward us.

"Call security and get her nurse," I say as calmly as I can. She nods and heads back toward the nursing station. Alyssa's mother appears and the two of us help her into a chair.

"You did it," I tell her. "You stood up to him, Alyssa. Trudy is notifying security. Maybe they'll find him and turn him over to the police."

My words do not soothe her. Alyssa is still struggling to breathe. I stay with her until her nurse arrives with medication for her asthma attack. When I return to the nursing station, Trudy slams down the phone.

"He's gone!" she says through her teeth. "Whoever answered the phone in security didn't know anything about the call you made to them earlier. Sometimes I could just scream!"

Alone in our office ten minutes before staff meeting begins, I can still hear Alyssa's screams and feel her trembling body. Damn her husband! He uses the one positive thing in her life, her love for his children, to extort her loyalty and her silence. I hope that this time she will find the strength to stand up to his sadistic manipulation. If she doesn't, she may not survive the next beating.

When my colleagues arrive, we three nurses trudge toward the seventh floor conference room for staff meeting. Taking my seat, I notice the potted Norfolk Pine in the corner of the room. After hitting the ceiling some time ago, it bent at a right angle and has continued to grow horizontally toward the window. Although I must have seen it before, I don't recall noticing how awkward it looks.

While I muse about the plant, Patricia, our new boss, and Donald, our department's head psychiatrist, enter and take their seats. After everyone has arrived, Patricia clears her throat and begins the meeting.

"Some of you might have heard that Dr. Gluznick, the chief psychiatrist on 6B, is currently hospitalized on the jail unit."

From the lack of audible gasps, I'd say that news has traveled at the speed of nerve impulses from the body to the brain.

Patricia continues. "He was arrested early this morning in connection with an attempted murder of a psych emergency patient. There is speculation that he was sexually involved with the patient who has survived but is in the ICU unconscious and in critical condition. I'd like to avoid sending a psychiatrist from our department to evaluate the patient. To that end, would one of you nurses take the case? Laurie, don't you usually cover the adult trauma cases?"

A wave of nausea funnels up my throat. "I do."

Please God, spare me.

This is going to be a sticky, sleazy case with legal and political complications. However, in this moment I can't come up with a reason not to sign on. "Sure I'll see him, but given his mental status, it doesn't sound like I'll be able to interview him any time soon."

"Thanks," says Donald. "I hear it's not at all clear that he will pull through this. I understand that his father is on his way here from the East Coast. It might be a good idea to check in with him. By the way, his father is a physician."

Now I feel even ickier. By sending me as the department emissary, the physicians can avoid the father, a fellow physician, with whom they would bond under normal conditions. How could they explain that one of their own attempted to murder his son? How can I explain that?

Patricia shuffles some papers in preparation for her next topic.

"Wait," I say. "This is a really big deal with serious repercussions. Can we spend some time talking about it?"

"No," says Patricia firmly. "We've got to move on."

What? Did she really say no?

Suddenly I feel like the Norfolk Pine, cramped and uncomfortable.

Why can't we talk about it? Does it feel too dangerous? Does she think someone will get hurt?

I tune out the rest of the meeting. All I can think about is how much I want to escape the confines of the hospital. I feel like driving to Ocean Beach right now, throwing off my shoes, and running along the edge of the water. Short of that, when the meeting is over I take the elevator to the lobby and quickly walk to The Comfort Garden.

Outside, the fog has cleared and the day has blossomed into petals of sunshine. While roses bloom in their own rarified air in a corner of the garden, the rest of the plants tumble over themselves in kaleidoscopic frenzy. On the garden path, my breathing slows. I pick a wand of lavender, crush its flower head, and inhale its spicy sweet fragrance. Moving through the garden, I pull my hand through sprays of Breath of Heaven, a small shrub with star-shaped pink flowers and tiny spring-green leaves that release the scent of nutmeg when you crush them. I continue down the path feeling textures, sniffing, even tasting the lemon balm growing in a shady knoll, until I am calm enough to gather my thoughts.

All psychiatric trainees are taught about "boundary violations." These include accepting gifts from patients, socializing with patients and, of course, sex with patients. I heard a lecture once by a psychiatrist who works with therapists who've had sexual relations with their patients. He spoke about how each major violation begins with a small transgression like extending the time of a session. Next might come sharing personal information with a patient, a meal together, then a casual date. His final remarks were humorous but wise: "If you're thinking of having sex with a patient, don't do it. You can't possibly measure up to the patient's fantasy of you which means that he or she will only be disappointed by your performance!"

Drug use, a real hazard for doctors and nurses—people who have access to pharmaceuticals—is another form of boundary violation. As a physician working in psychiatric emergency services, Dr. Gluznick must have seen plenty of cases of methamphetamine-induced psychosis. I know that denial is as powerful as addiction. Still, the whole thing shocks me: a speed-freak physician who had sex with his mentally ill patient, then attacked him with an ax. I hope they take away his license and put him behind bars for attempted murder, but I doubt that will happen. I've seen how reluctant physicians are to implicate one of their own, even when the charges are serious.

Nurses, in contrast, respond to each other's errors in the opposite way. In a flash, one nurse will write up her colleague for giving a patient an extra dose of Tylenol or missing a dressing change. Nurses judge each other to the point where some say we eat our young. Our problem is excessive criticism, not denial, not collusion.

Patricia's response really bothers me. Janice had warned me against expecting that Patricia would support process time for staff. "She's a neuropsychologist, Laurie. They are trained to interpret psychological testing, not to process feelings."

Still, I had hoped.

A bee with bad boundaries alights on my head. I force myself to freeze but the darn thing is caught in my unmanageable frizz. I want to whack my head with my purse but I don't want to look crazy or get stung.

"Hold still," says a familiar voice behind me. Antoine, the gardener, pokes something into my hair and frees the angry insect. "He was probably attracted to your flowered shirt."

"Thanks, Antoine."

"Hey, how's your bindweed problem?"

"I pinch it back as soon as I see it, just like you suggested. That seems to keep it in check."

Antoine smiles. "It should be so easy with some of your psychiatric patients."

"What do you mean?"

"You know the atrium on the seventh floor? A few of the psych patients keep destroying whatever we plant there. Isn't somebody supposed to be keeping the patients in check?"

"They should. But these days psychiatry seems to have trouble just keeping itself in check."

Antoine goes back to work without asking me what I meant by that. I'm glad. He wouldn't have believed me anyway.

My beeper goes off. I jump when I recognize Barry's number in the display. During the events of the day, I had almost forgotten about today's support group. I run back across campus and race up to 4D to gather the juice boxes that Trudy said I could have for group. From there I run out of the main hospital to the medical library, located in one of the hospital's original brick buildings across the service road.

Arriving fifteen minutes before group begins, I sign out the key from the librarian and open the door. With its paneled walls, built-in bookshelves, marbled fireplace, brass chandelier, and upholstered-red, faux-leather chairs, the small room reminds me of a study in an old Victorian home. It even has a musty smell. As I open windows and pull six red chairs into a circle, Barry arrives. Lo and behold, so does Mrs. Holloway, looking well, and wearing a buttoned-up blouse that hides the knife scar on her neck. I am so excited that she's come that I have to restrain myself from throwing my arms around her. She extends her hand to me and thanks Barry for the anti-depressant medication he has been prescribing for her since the assault three months ago. I saw her frequently for a month afterward but, of late, we've spoken only by phone.

After three other patients have arrived—a man and a woman I recognize from the trauma unit and another woman I don't recognize—we begin the group. I review the purpose of a support group and ask the participants to introduce themselves.

The patients I recognize from the trauma unit relate the details of their accidents. One was a pedestrian who was crossing a busy street with his girlfriend when a driver ran the red light and plowed into them. His girlfriend was killed immediately. He suffered a broken femur. The other patient, a young woman from Scotland, was a passenger on her boyfriend's motorcycle when they were sideswiped by a truck eight months ago. Since then, she has undergone four surgeries and spent months on a rehabilitation unit. With the help of braces and crutches, she has just begun to take her first steps toward independence.

The patient I didn't recognize was referred by Janice. She tells the group that she was jogging in a neighborhood park when a deranged young man appeared from nowhere and stabbed her multiple times in the upper body and abdomen. She describes the emotional toll this has taken on her, her husband, and especially her young daughter.

Mrs. Holloway tells the group that she too was attacked with a knife and that for months afterward, she was paranoid and unable to sleep. Although aided by medication and the knowledge that her assailant is in custody, she worries that his buddies blame her for his incarceration. Since they live in the same housing project, she can't avoid seeing them when she leaves her apartment.

Barry and I focus on the experience of trauma and the meaning it has for each person. We encourage participants to talk about their strengths as well as their vulnerabilities, listening carefully to those aspects of character, such as determination, optimism, courage, and flexibility that will help them through each stage of recovery. We also try to help people set realistic goals for themselves.

With little prodding from us, the participants talk about coping with pain and disfigurement, living with scars and symptoms of post-traumatic-stress, grieving losses, and the insensitivity of others to these issues. Toward the end of group, the jogger points out the obvious differences between people who are victims of violent crime versus those who are victims of unintended trauma.

"Would it be possible to have two different groups?" she asks. It make sense but given how much time and effort it took to get four people to show up this time, it's not going to happen in the near future. Nevertheless, I encourage her to return to trauma group because there seems to be enough overlap of issues for her to reap some benefit.

When everyone has left, Barry stays long enough to say he thought the group went well. "Maybe we can talk about it tomorrow," he says as he rushes out the door. "I've got to see a patient on med psych before I leave. Hey, have you seen Gluznick's lover yet?"

I shake my head. "I've saved the worst for last."

Before I go to the ICU, I need to return the unused juice boxes to 4D. After placing the boxes back in the unit refrigerator and walking toward the nurses' station to tell Trudy about the group, a man pushing a wheelchair with Maria in it whizzes by in a blur.

"Come with me, baby. I'll take you places you've never been!" he says in a gravelly voice.

"Sal, slow down!" Maria squeals. With a head full of newly coiffed yellow curls framing her rouged face, she looks as regal as an operatic Viking queen. In their wake, a mist of perfume settles over the nurses' station where Trudy stands with phone to ear. I wave at the fumes.

"I guess that beats most of the odors around here."

"I haven't smelled Old Spice that strong since a reunion of my father's navy buddies," says Trudy after hanging up. "So what's the story with this guy Sal?"

"A long lost boyfriend. Until today she hadn't seen him for forty years." I repeat the story of how Maria was so flustered after receiving Sal's letter that she ran out of her house and into traffic.

"And they say that love is blind," says Trudy.

"I guess you could also say she was head over heels in love."

Trudy elbows me in the ribs. "Jeez Laurie, you're sicker than me!"

The penultimate thing I want to do before I leave for the day is to see the victim of Dr. Gluznick's methamphetamine-induced rage. The absolute last thing I want to do is to meet with his father. I pray he has not yet arrived.

I enter the door marked "ICU: Authorized Personnel Only" and tiptoe down a hallway past a few beds occupied by lifeless bodies strung with tubes and surrounded by monitors, intravenous solutions, harsh lights, medical residents, and nurses. Finally, I reach the nurses' station where a large, dry-erase board indicates that my patient is in bed #10.

I can barely see him for all the bandages and tubes. His eyes are closed. He breathes with the assistance of a ventilator. There is nothing soft, nothing colorful, nothing alive in this room except my patient, who is barely so. Even if he did open his eyes, what would spark a memory of beauty in this world? I imagine an ICU where wires and monitors are camouflaged by tropical vines and wild orchids, where ferns sprout from each corner and infuse the air with oxygen. Next time, I'll remember to bring a lavender wand from the garden for him to smell.

Although the ICU is technology at its best and aesthetics at its worst, the nurses here enjoy the most collegial relationships with physicians in the hospital. It's a relationship based on mutual respect and interdependence.

I do not try to wake the patient. According to his nurse, my patient has yet to open his eyes. When I turn around to leave, I am startled to see a small man in a suit and tie sitting hunched over in a plastic chair in the corner.

"You must be Mr. Rosano," I say softly.

He remains motionless. "Yes, I'm Dr. Rosano," he says in a nearly inaudible whisper.

"I'm sorry, Dr. Rosano. I *had* heard that you are a physician."

"An oncologist," he rasps before I have time to ask.

I wish he would make eye contact with me. Instead, he stares at the floor.

I introduce myself and briefly describe my role. "When your son is awake and alert, I will be the person who talks with him about what happened, what he remembers, and how he is coping."

Dr. Rosano does not respond. The only sounds in the room are the swishes and beeps of machines that maintain his son's life. I pull a chair alongside his in order to decrease his sense of my intrusion into his life.

"I'm so very sorry that this has happened," I say, breaking the silence. Although I speak softly, my voice seems to echo in the small space.

"Is there anything I can do for you? May I get you some coffee or tea? Something to eat?"

Still, no response.

Why should he talk to me? I'm part of the institution that did not protect his son. How could he trust me or anyone else here?

In the silence, I wonder when he last spoke with his son. Is he aware of his diagnosis of bipolar disorder? Does he know his son is gay? My questions will remain unanswered. Dr. Rosano is impassive and unreachable, as if in shock. Nothing I say elicits any kind of response. It is as though he has retreated somewhere deep into his being, leaving only a shadow behind. Perhaps for now, this is where he needs to be.

14

Absorbing trauma

"I don't... want... the... bus! Mommy! I can't go on the bus!"
Corianne gulps air in between crying jags. I hold her close while
her body shudders through her thick winter jacket.

*Is my child having an anxiety attack? She took the bus at
the beginning of this year without a problem. Why not now?*

Fred, the school bus driver, will pull up soon. When he does,
I will be in a bind. I can't be late to this morning's care conference.

"Mommy, I'm afraid. I don't want to go on."

She clings to me as if I were her last hope. The other children
at our bus stop look worried but maintain their distance. I keep my
voice low.

"Did something happen at school?"

"No."

"Is there a bully on the bus?"

"No."

"Then what's so frightening, honey?"

"I don't know. I'm just scared."

After a big heave of breath, her body relaxes a bit against mine.

"That's it, Cor. Let's just concentrate on breathing slowly. In and out to the count of three, do it with me... breathe in one... two... three, now out... one... two..."

She slows her breathing.

"OK, baby. Keep breathing just like this while I talk to you. Something is bothering you and we're going to figure out what it is but we can't do it right now. Fred will be here soon."

I feel her tighten her grip around my neck. "No, Mommy, no."

"Deep breath, honey."

She releases her grip a tiny bit.

"Will it help if you sit close to Fred?"

"Maybe," she sniffs.

"Good. After daddy gets home tonight, you and I will spend some special time together, OK?"

She knows that I will be busy with her little brothers until Brian comes home.

Fred's big yellow school bus pulls up to our corner. He opens the door and two kids climb in. Fred looks at me and raises his eyebrows as if to say, *What's going on?*

I shake my head. I have no idea.

"Miss Corianne," he says gently, "your coach awaits you."

"Go on, baby," I unclasp Corianne's arms and turn her toward the bus. "Fred, can Corianne sit right behind you? She's feeling a little uneasy this morning."

"Sure thing." He steps out of his seat and reaches toward her. "Come on sweetheart. Let me help you up the stairs."

Corianne's lower lip quivers and her eyes fill with water. "Go on, baby." I kiss her on the forehead. "I'll see you tonight."

She hesitates, then steps onto the bus.

"Don't you worry, Mom," says Fred. "I'll take good care of her."

I get into my car and cry hard. Maybe I should have taken her to school myself.

I arrive just as the care conference begins. It concerns a thirty-seven-year-old heroin addict with a history of necrotizing fasciitis that destroyed her thigh muscles. She has been grafted four times with healthy skin from her back and stomach. Each graft has failed because the patient refuses to stay immobile in bed for ten days so the graft can "take." The consequences of not being grafted would be a massive infection and probable death. If we continue to graft and she continues to violate the order for bed rest, the surgeons would eventually run out of available healthy skin at which point she would die of a massive infection. Does she understand these consequences? Will understanding them convince her to change her behavior? Most of us agree that in the face of a long-term addiction, behavior change is doubtful.

The representative from the surgical team states that they don't care one way or the other; they will continue to graft the patient if that's what the rest of the team wants. From their perspective, it's good practice for the trainees.

At the end of the meeting, the consensus is that a slim chance is better than no chance. Before the next graft, the surgical team will once again spell out to the patient that death is the ultimate consequence of violating the order for strict bed rest. Nurses, physical therapists, substance abuse counselors, and social workers will reinforce this notion.

Personally, I wrestle with the question of continuing to treat a non-compliant patient. The nurse part of me, who has seen a half a million dollars blown on one liver transplant for a sixty-eight-year-old alcoholic oil executive, declares that we must ration health-care money. The psych nurse part of me screams that we must set limits on destructive behavior: that we must sit down with the patient, clarify the number of times we are willing to graft her, spell out the consequences if she chooses to be non-compliant, and follow through with the limit we set. The "General Hospital" part of me whispers that these are our patients; they don't make good choices; they abuse the system. We disapprove of their lifestyles but they have nowhere to go and we cannot abandon them.

After the meeting, Barry calls to ask if I will work with the nurses caring for his patient, Kevin, a paranoid schizophrenic with a burned back. While Kevin's nurse is in his room assisting a team of surgeons, I chat with Kevin's parents who have flown in from Virginia. Both are recently retired: he, as a professor of comparative literature and she, as an administrator of a nonprofit environmental organization. True to stereotype, Joe—as he's asked me to call him—wears a Harris Tweed and gold corduroy pants. Kevin's mother, June, hasn't yet removed her grey raincoat.

We spend a few minutes talking about the failure of the local community mental health system to offer chronic mentally ill patients the social stability they need to stay out of the hospital. In the middle of our conversation, a voice screams, "They're raping me! HELP——ME——SOMEONE! Don't let them rape me!"

Trudy rushes to Kevin's door and cracks it open. The volume intensifies, then diminishes after she closes the door. I feel rattled. June and Joe grasp hands and wait out the crisis in silence.

"It's OK," says Trudy as she emerges from Kevin's room. "They're almost finished changing his dressing."

Kevin's parents tell me that twenty years ago while he was a student at Massachusetts Institute of Technology, Kevin heeded Harvard professor Tim Leary's advice to "tune in and drop out." After taking a hit of LSD, Kevin became paranoid and delusional. He has never recovered. Over the years, he has engineered ingenious ways to escape from the institutions that are supposed to contain and treat him. This time, after escaping from a locked psychiatric facility, he built a fire to stay warm at night, got too close, and burned his back.

"How do you cope?" I ask when their son's screams subside.

Kevin's father pulls out his wallet from a back pocket and unfolds a copy of a recent story in *The New York Times* about John Forbes Nash, Jr., a mathematician at Princeton University. In 1958, at age thirty, Dr. Nash was stricken with schizophrenia. With the support of his family and community, twenty years later, he became well enough to work again. Later he was awarded the Nobel Prize for work he had done in 1949.

"We have hope," his father says.

After the team of plastic surgeons, medical students, and nurses leave Kevin's room, Joe and June step inside. Although Joe extends his hand to his son and June kisses his cheek, Kevin barely acknowledges them. I drag a few blue plastic chairs into the room so they can visit there instead of leaving the unit. Kevin is not yet on a psychiatric hold and I don't want him to be tempted to run away. I leave them alone and check in with Kevin's nurse who looks drained by the dressing change ordeal.

Late in the day, an hour before I need to leave to pick up Corianne from school and relieve my babysitter at home, Patricia, our new boss, asks to speak with me about the trauma support group. She has been supportive of the group since she arrived. When Barry decided he was too busy to commit to the group, Patricia found a co-therapist for me, an Israeli psychologist who lost a leg in one of the Arab-Israeli wars. She has also enlisted the aid of a graduate student who is now helping me to contact trauma patients at home and encourage them to come to group.

We meet in my office where Patricia sets her petite self down in Antionette's swivel chair. Her long dark bangs hang just over her eyes. The rest of her hair falls into a neat pageboy. Patricia's age is hard to read but I would guess she's in her late forties. She is interested in how the group has been progressing and wants me to summarize the issues that trauma patients face after discharge from the hospital.

Patricia takes notes and seems pleased with what she hears. She cautions that in the new world of "managed care" we need to think about generating revenue. If we call it a "psychotherapy group," the department can bill for the service. This would require keeping records and charts on everyone who attends. Or, I can continue calling it a "support group," which would neither be remunerated nor require documentation. No paperwork sounds like a great idea to me.

In the last fifteen minutes of our meeting, Patricia mentions some concerns she has about possible legal situations that could arise. She asks, for example, how I would handle a person in group who reveals that he is acutely suicidal.

The phone rings. It's Miranda. Would I have time to see another case this afternoon, one referred to her that she deems more appropriate for a nurse than a psychiatrist?

"Sorry, Miranda. I'm in a meeting and have to leave the hospital in a few minutes. If it's an emergency, why don't you run it by me and..."

"If you don't have time, it doesn't make sense to tell you about the case."

She hangs up without waiting for my response.

Patricia and I resume talking about "what if" scenarios. By the end of our meeting, I think I've convinced her that I'm competent to handle crises should they arise.

After leaving the hospital, I see Kevin's parents near the lobby sitting on a bench, their heads bowed, bodies huddled together, braced against the wind.

Can they ever look at Kevin without feeling sad? Do they ever stop imagining the life he could have had?

I hug Corianne especially tight when I pick her up from school.

At night, she says, "Mommy, come cuddle."

I slide under the covers with her and hold her to my chest.

"How was school today, honey?"

"I hate Mr. Yamamuro! He benches kids for the stupidest things. Can't I get a different teacher? He's so mean."

I'm glad my girl is a talker. Without my needing to ask many questions, the story that explains this morning's anxiety attack unfolds. Apparently, Mr. Yamamuro has a short fuse. Any infraction of his strict classroom rules and kids must stay on the bench for the entire lunch period. Corianne has so far avoided being benched but she lives in fear of this disgrace. I tell her that I would not flip out if she were benched. Although it wouldn't be a pleasant experience for her, it seems she would be in good company seeing as everyone, except for a handful of kids, has been benched. I assure her that I will discuss the subject with Mr. Yamamuro during the upcoming parent-teacher conference.

In the meantime, she agrees to let me teach her progressive relaxation techniques so she can learn to use her breath to calm her mind and body. There are so many things I want to teach her—how to be safe, how to take care of her body, how to choose a good boyfriend—but now I take a tip from Maria in "The Sound of Music." After she has relaxed each muscle group in her body, I suggest that we think about our favorite things.

"Chocolate," she says, "and Po."

While she squeezes the polar bear that shares her pillow every night, I stroke her silky hair and she drifts into sleep.

On the heels of my arrival to work the next morning, Patricia taps on my door.

"We need to talk," she says stepping inside our office and closing the door behind her. "I must tell you that Donald received a complaint from Miranda yesterday that you were rude and uncooperative when she called you about a patient. Was that her on the phone yesterday toward the end of our meeting?"

I nod.

"Did you speak with her at any other time during the day?"

I shake my head.

"Good, because I told Donald I was in the room with you when you took the call and at no time were you rude or uncooperative."

I feel violence rise up in my body. It takes the shape of a boomerang that hooks Miranda around the neck, carries her over the city, and dumps her in the ocean. After some general flailing, shark fins appear. There is satisfying silence.

The fantasy helps me get through the morning, but when Miranda walks in late for our psych consult meeting, my anger rises once again.

Looking at Miranda, I do not see her as the very pregnant person she is. We've figured out that she must have known about her condition when she booted Dylan from his job. After finally acknowledging her pregnancy, Miranda insisted that she would take only a two-month maternity leave. She has since changed her tune and now wants to take a year off just like her predecessor who remains out on leave. Patricia does not support this plan. From the moment she assumed leadership of our psych consult service, Patricia has expressed disapproval that so many staff members work part-time. In the interest of continuity of care, she has deemed that any new hires must commit to full-time status. Rumor has it that Miranda is preparing for a fight.

By summoning the boomerang image again, I cool myself down while pretending to pay attention to the discussion about Troy Gerard, Antionette's recalcitrant patient who has been acting out his frustration with life by regularly mowing people down with his wheelchair.

When Donald asks for other cases, Miranda raises her hand. She describes a patient referred to her yesterday by a pulmonary specialist. "I did the initial work-up but I'm too swamped to do the follow-up." She presents the case of a woman in her mid-thirties who was admitted a few weeks ago with pneumonia and sarcoidosis, a disease characterized by lesions in affected organs. The patient herself asked the lung specialist to find her a psychiatrist.

"The patient's children were murdered ten years ago by her boy-friend while he was high on crack," says Miranda. "Right after the incident the patient left home and has been shooting heroin ever since."

Although Miranda relates this information without much emotion, some of us, particularly those of us who are parents, react viscerally.

"When I saw her briefly yesterday, she told me she's never spoken to anyone about what happened that day. Now she says she needs to talk about her kids. Any takers?"

Miranda flashes the big toothpaste-commercial smile, which strikes me as bizarre in this context.

No way, José.

I avoided pediatrics because I can't tolerate children in pain, children who have been abused, or children who are about to die of an untreatable disease. Now that I have my own kids, these feelings have only intensified.

Given the group's silence, I'm not the only one who wants to avoid the subject. Miranda tries again. "How about if we give the case to a medical student?"

A medical student? A twenty-five-year-old whose only experience with loss may be losing baby teeth? It's bad enough that they have to confront patients their own age dying of AIDS and bullet wounds.

For once, Miranda looks troubled. If no one takes the case, she might actually have to sit down and listen to a patient talk about her feelings. No medication will take away the story that needs to be told.

"I'll take the case," I hear myself say.

Am I am feeling protective of the medical students? Am I doing this to show Miranda a thing or two? Or, am I doing it for the patient's sake? Probably some of all three.

After the meeting, I locate the patient and step inside her room. Rosalina's skin is the color of cumin. She lies crumpled halfway down the length of the bed, unable to summon the strength to push her ninety-pound frame toward the pillow. I reposition her nasal prongs so that oxygen will fill her lungs. Then I tuck my arms under her back and shoulders, lifting and pulling until her head reaches the pillow. She needs a few moments to catch her breath. I ask if I should come back later when she feels stronger.

"No," she says, grasping my forearm with her cold bony hand and locking her eyes with mine. She does not take her hand off my arm, even after her breathing quiets.

"I am ready to talk about it now," she says in a low voice thick with regret. Her words stretch over the surface of a deep lake.

"I have to talk about it. I'm thirty-five. I've spent ten years running from it, city to city, shooting up, doing things I never would have done. Things it shames me to say, all because I couldn't face it. I've been clean for six months. Now I can see it's been killing me."

From her chart, I know that in addition to pneumonia and sarcoidosis, Rosalina has suffered from a long-standing sleep disturbance, chronic nightmares, loss of appetite, anhedonia (the inability to experience pleasure), abdominal discomfort, and fatigue. She has been estranged from her family and alone in the world since "it" happened. "It" has claimed her words, her feelings, her morals, her health, and her family. I steady myself and prepare to absorb a piece of her nightmare.

"My parents were both hooked on heroin," she says. "They were good parents. I know that sounds funny but they worked every day, kept the house clean, and kept us kids fed. They died in a car accident when the youngest was a baby."

She stops here and stares out the window at the billows of fog sweeping through the city like ghosts on a rampage. Her hand still grasps my arm. I worry that she will spill too much too fast. Heroin might have soothed her soul but it has deprived her of learning how to tame rage and sorrow. I fear she will run into its welcoming arms again instead of willing herself to go forward alone. A good therapist would spend months bolstering her fragile self, strengthening their relationship, and teaching her how to bear strong feelings before ever approaching "it"—the traumatic event. We don't have months. She has pushed open a stuck door. I need to support her as she peeks inside.

Her voice, when she finds it again, sounds flat. Although she stares straight ahead at the wall and seems not to breathe, Rosalina tightens her grip on my forearm.

"My daughter was just four, my son seven. One night when I wasn't home, my boyfriend came over, crazy high on crack. He took a knife to my kids. He slit their throats. I was told they didn't suffer long."

Her voice is calm and her face placid but her hand, which has found mine, grips my fingers together so hard that I can feel bone against bone. I make a fist with my other hand and squeeze, hoping that the pain of my own fingernails pressing into my palm will reroute the emotion rising in my chest. I cannot allow myself to think about my own young children at home or imagine how I would feel in her place. That will happen later. Right now, I must stay with her and help her to bear "it."

For a long minute, we sit in silence. Above the muffled voices in the hallway outside her room, a jackhammer pounds like a heart that has been scared witless.

"Afterward," she whispers, "they wouldn't let me listen to the radio or watch TV or see a newspaper. I did testify in court. He'll be in prison for a long time."

Her grip on my hand has eased although I continue to squeeze my fist. Rosalina tells me that in the courtroom, she had asked to see pictures of her children's injuries but no one would show them to her. She wonders if her daughter had been sexually molested.

"I need to know," she says. "I need to know what happened to them."

She rests with her eyes closed. I watch each shallow breath until a slight retraction of her grasp tells me she's asleep. I place her hand at her side on top of the white sheets. Her doctor's plan to discharge her tomorrow seems cruel and uncaring.

When Corianne and I arrive home, I look up at the house from the street and feel panic. No lights appear to be on. Neither of the boys is peering out of the window much less pounding on it, nor do I hear any other rambunctious boy sounds that usually greet our arrival. There are twenty-eight stairs to climb before we reach the front door. I am panting with terror. Turning the key, a mental image of carnage appears in my mind's eye. My throat goes dry with dread. When I hear my babysitter call, "Hey boys, Mommy's home," followed by the patter of light feet upstairs, I burst into tears of relief and yell, "I'll be right up!"

What is wrong with me? Am I going nuts?

In my bedroom, after stripping off my work clothes and pulling on my sweats, I use a trick I learned at a hypnotherapy conference designed to help therapists leave their work at the office. I close my eyes and imagine being with Rosalina, summarizing the work we did that day, and saying goodbye. She smiles back at me and waves. As I walk away, her image grows smaller and smaller. Maybe it will work. I open my eyes, take a few deep breaths, and run up the stairs where the boys clamor for my attention. Lying on the floor, I let them crawl all over me, our usual transition time activity, only instead of being a mother revitalized, I feel like an insect being devoured.

Later, when thirteen-month-old Benny starts drooping, I carry him to his crib. Before putting him down, I hold his squishy-soft body against mine and listen to the soothing sounds of his breathing. Nestled in the curve of my neck, his head feels warm and heavy. During moments like these, it is impossible to imagine a life that derails, a life that love cannot save.

Gently, I lower Benny into his crib. He begins to cry in protest of our separation. Usually I leave knowing that as soon as he finds his blanket he will settle in for the night and wake up tomorrow happy to see me. On this night, I hesitate. We are told that giving children the opportunity to fall asleep on their own teaches them to self-soothe. What if small traumas like nightly separations harm vulnerable children? What if my child is one of those vulnerable children?

Danny, now three, climbs into his bed. While cuddling with him, I suddenly feel overwhelmed with the responsibilities of parenthood.

How will I be able to protect my kids from all the bad things that happen in the world? Even if I am the best parent I know how to be, I won't be able to protect them from drugs and bad company.

Then I remember hearing Kevin scream, "They're raping me!" on 4D this morning while the medical team changed his dressing.

Kevin's parents couldn't prevent him from taking LSD or developing schizophrenia.

At one time Kevin's parents must have kissed and cuddled him, filled with hope and expectations for the future. Perhaps they tolerated his adolescence knowing that teenagers sulk and rage, experiment and test. Who among us could imagine hearing our child screaming in terror as a thirty-eight-year-old adult, inconsolable, and lost in a world of voices that accuse and persecute?

I kiss Danny goodnight. When Brian has finished telling Corianne the latest Athena story, he and I trade places.

"How did the bus ride go this morning?" I ask Corianne after I've settled myself into her loft.

"OK, but I still don't like Mr. Yamamuro."

She describes today's classroom events and admits that one of the boys who was benched deserved it. Then she gathers Po in her arms and drifts off. Borrowing some peacefulness from her sleep, I let go of my previous thoughts and kiss Corianne's cheek. More than anything, I hope that we will always be able to talk, even when she is angry or needing distance.

Later in my own bed, I keep hearing Kevin's voice yelling, "They're raping me! They're raping me!"

Unable to sleep, I trudge up to the attic to write. I write about the promise June and Joe must have felt when their son began his studies at MIT, the cruel turn of events, and the article that Kevin's father keeps in his wallet about the Princeton mathematician who recovered from schizophrenia. June and Joe have developed an admirable coping plan for themselves. They visit Kevin twice a year, staying a week each time. Immediately after their visits, they take a week "somewhere pleasurable" where they recover from the emotional toll of visiting their mentally ill son. It's a good strategy for those who can afford it. Being a parent of such a child can mean a lifetime of giving without receiving much in return.

When I am ready to put my journal away for the night, I am startled by a feeling of cold pressure on my hand.

Rosalina, I wanted to forget about you.

Before I can divert myself, the image of her children lying listless with their throats slashed takes hold. I shudder. Then I hold myself and rock in my chair.

Dear God, how can she bear it?.

15

Mismanaged care

In April, Antionette, Janice and I fly to San Diego to speak at our National Psychiatric Consultation-Liaison Nursing Conference. Our presentation, "From the Eye of the Storm: Violence in Inner City Hospitals," opens the second day of the three-day event. While fifty psych liaison nurses from all over the country find their places, I play a recording of Dianne Reeves singing a song she co-wrote, entitled "How Long?" in which she bemoans the violence that leaves a mother holding the lifeless body of her bullet-riddled son.

Dianne's robust alto grabs the attention of our audience. Listening to her words helps me to focus. It also helps that I wrote out my introductory paragraph.

"It feels like a war out there. In our inner cities, bullets hit innocent bystanders as well as the street soldiers of the drug trade for whom they are intended. Each day, we listen to their stories of hopelessness, helplessness, frustration, anger, and despair. We see how the white master has been replaced by a white powder that enslaves its users, obscuring human dignity and values, producing cravings so intense that a mother will endanger her children for the next high, however brief it is."

With my voice box warmed up, I relax and give an overview of our presentation. Janice follows with a description of our patient population demographics:

Last year, SFGH recorded over 70,000 visits to Emergency Services alone.

Of those, sixty-four perecent were male.

Of the trauma cases, seventy-seven percent were male.

Sixty-five percent of SFGH patients were under the age of forty.

Seventy-three percent of our trauma patients were under the age of forty.

Sixty-nine percent of our patients were ethnic minorities.

African-Americans and Hispanics who total twenty-four percent of the city's population, made up fifty-three percent of our patients.

Whites, who are forty percent of the city's population, are twenty-seven percent of our patients.

Asian/Pacific Islanders, who total twenty-nine percent of the city's population, were only fifteen percent of the hospital patient population.

Janice follows the statistics with a description of the role of the psychiatric consultation-liaison nurse at SFGH. Then she hones in on one of the most important aspects of our jobs: to identify and intervene proactively with potentially violent patients.

Antionette is on next with a description of the violence prevention workshops we have taught at the hospital including the one we did for the emergency department after the incident in Los Angeles where emergency room doctors were killed by a distraught patient. She talks about barriers to reducing violence such as institutional denial of danger and the attitude by many hospital employees that violence "comes with the territory," which results in under-reporting of violent incidents that do occur.

Mismanaged care

I wrap up the formal presentation with an overview of community approaches to countering inner city violence. I cite examples of grassroots organizations around the country: SOSAD (Save Our Sons and Daughters) in Detroit and MOMS (Mothers of Murdered Sons) in Atlanta that challenge the glamorization of guns and violence in our culture. I suggest that we educate kids about guns by bringing victims of violence—people with quadriplegia and ostomies—into the schools to describe what happens when a bullet lodges in your back or blows a hole through your intestines.

During the discussion, Antionette points out that age (young) and gender (male) are statistically significant for both victims and perpetrators of violence and that cultural differences may contribute to interpersonal difficulties between staff and patients. Janice reports that incidents of violence and aggression at SFGH have almost doubled in the last five years and that as many as 40% of physicians and 60% of nurses have been assaulted at some point in their careers. Since many assaults go unreported, the rates are probably higher.

Toward the end of our talk, we are asked how we cope on a daily basis with seeing the carnage of urban warfare. Antionette acknowledges the importance of having close working relationships with colleagues, exercising, spending time with friends outside of work, and shopping at Nordstrom's. Janice talks about her "Girls Night Out" group and their trips to Mexico to celebrate each other's birthdays.

I talk about the therapeutic benefits of gardening and how having young children commands my attention as soon as I come home from work, distracting me from my tendency to dwell on my patients' stories.

And what about the rest of it? Why don't you tell them about your nightmares or how your heart pounds on your way home from work wondering if the kids are safe and that you feel something close to panic just before you unlock the door?

No way! They'd think I'd lost it.

I've always thought of myself as being a strong person, someone who could handle the stress of a job like this. Over a 20-year career, I've heard lots of gut-wrenching stories that didn't shake me up or keep me awake at night. So why am I handling these stories differently now? Has something changed or have I been overestimating myself all along?

Maybe it's motherhood. I've noticed that since I've become a mother, a child's cry—any child's cry—pierces my heart to the point of causing physical discomfort. And lately when I listen to my patients' stories of painful childhoods, my boundaries seem to dissolve such that I imagine the horrible things that happened to them, happening to my own kids. Maybe motherhood and all its attendant hormonal shifts have fundamentally altered something in my brain.

Or maybe it's the proverbial loose screw?

At the end of our presentation, our audience rewards us with an enthusiastic critique. During a short break, we congratulate ourselves. Then we take our seats in the audience for the next presentation.

Upon returning to SFGH the following week, we feel re-energized, enthusiastic about our work, and inspired to expand our repertoire. It's easy to forget that what we do makes a difference. Because we try to prevent violence by making sure patients have adequate pain medication or by early detection and intervention, our work is often invisible. Administration must recognize that we are making a contribution or our positions would have been cut a long time ago.

We stroll into staff meeting where we expect to give a brief account of our success in San Diego. Patricia calls us to order. Once again, the meeting begins without Miranda who was due back weeks ago.

Patricia welcomes us back with a quick smile. "The psych nurses presented at their national conference over the weekend. I'm sure it went well."

She looks down at the stack of papers in front of her. "We have a lot to cover today so I'd like to get started."

Apparently, basking time is over. "Before getting to the business at hand, let me just say that Miranda Lowenthal will not be returning to our service as anticipated. She has decided that a full-time position is more than she would like at this time."

I glance at Barry who points to his watch. "Lunch?" he mouths. I nod. Barry will give us the real scoop, straight from Deep Throat, in the privacy of our office.

When Patricia tries to continue speaking, she erupts into a coughing fit. Then the coughs turn into wheezes. Those of us at the table exchange looks.

That sounded terrible. Is it asthma or bronchitis? Can we do something to help her?

"Excuse me," she says, regaining composure. She moves on. "You've all heard me talk about the state of hospital economics and that major changes are on the horizon. Well, that day is now. 'Managed care' has arrived at SFGH."

She lifts the thick stack of stapled papers. "These are billing forms. Each of you will be required to fill one out for every patient that you see. You must indicate a diagnosis and the time you spent on the consult. You must also differentiate between a "direct" visit and an "indirect" visit."

Patricia passes the stack of papers around the room.

My stomach tightens. For years, we've heard words like "downsizing," "restructuring," and "carve-outs," things I'd like to do to my body, not to the health care system. Now we have to deal with "capitation," which, I admit, sounds better than its alternative. We have to memorize a completely new vocabulary of acronyms like IPA (Independent Practice Association), PPO (Preferred Provider Organization), RAF (Referral Authorization Form), and FFS (Fee For Service). I'm having enough trouble remembering that these days, PCP stands for Primary Care Physician, not the chemical abbreviation for Angel Dust that made people crazy in the 70s and 80s. I see where this is going and, like a kid, I want to plug my ears when I hear bad things. Don't talk to me about your financial woes; just let me see patients and I'll be happy.

Line by excruciating line, Patricia reviews the forms, and how we must fill out each section. "Our department needs to show an increase in productivity," says Patricia. "The new computer system will measure each person's productivity on a monthly basis. Direct visits are productive visits. We can bill for these. Anything else is indirect care and though it may be important, it is non-billable."

In other words, teaching, writing policies and procedures, organizing care conferences, consulting with individual nurses, meeting with nurse managers, attending professional conferences, and committee work—all the things we do in addition to seeing our patients, will not be reimbursed. It is no longer valued. Suddenly, I feel sick. In fact, my head hurts so much that decapitation seems like a fine idea.

"They can't do this," says Barry in the privacy of our office. "We're a teaching hospital. We're not about profit centers. That's why a lot of us work here! How can I meet productivity expectations when so much of my job is about teaching psychiatry to medical students?"

"Can we not talk about that right now?" I ask. "I'm sure all of us would much rather hear an update on Mama Miranda than discuss mismanaged care."

But Barry isn't ready to let go. "Jeez, I didn't even think that, on top of it, we'll be down another shrink."

"Maybe they could rehire Dylan?" suggests Antionette.

"Fat chance. He's happy with his new job."

"Barry," says Janice, "Tell us about Mama Miranda."

Barry sips his tea and lowers his voice. "OK, but you didn't get this from me, right?"

The three of us scoot closer to hear the news. "My source in the oval office reports that Miranda threatened the department with a lawsuit because Patricia wouldn't let her go part-time. Donald hired Miranda before Patricia took over the department and Patricia wants her out. Before she left for maternity leave, Miranda had agreed in writing that she would come back full-time. Predictably, since being home with baby, she's changed her mind. But, Patricia is holding to her guns. So... "

"Uh oh, here it comes," says Janice.

"Miranda is out—but she got them to sign her letter of recommendation!"

"What do you mean 'her' letter of recommendation?" I ask. "And what could it possibly say?"

"She wrote her own letter of recommendation," says Barry, "which aside from detailing her virtues as a crackerjack psychiatrist, praises her leadership in redesigning my training program. You know, the one she never helped me with? And the big chief of psychiatry himself signed the letter."

"The same guy who chose her over Dylan?"

"The same one."

"So it's out with Mama Miranda and in with managed care," says Janice. "Around here it's always something."

The last thing any of us want is to be drawn into a horserace where we compete against each other to become Billable Hour Queen or King. As a professional group, everyone here values the good care we try to give to all of our patients. If the quantity of time billed is valued over the quality of care we provide, patient care will suffer.

There are many things the hospital could do to save money. For one, we could decide on a policy to deal with non-compliant patients like the one who refused to stay on bed rest long enough to permit her skin grafts to heal. Her case alone has cost taxpayers hundreds of thousands of dollars. Patricia is piloting an emergency department case management system to cut down on our "frequent flyers"—patients who abuse emergency room services. This would save a bundle. Isn't there another way to deal with heroin addicts who are hospitalized for six weeks of intravenous antibiotic treatment after skin popping—shooting themselves up with dirty needles to create a hospital-worthy infection that earns them a break from the streets? And then there was the high-level nurse administrator who was demoted and spent years working in laundry services at her former salary; the transporter who always stinks of alcohol; and the staff who spend more time smoking on the patio with patients than working. The bigger issue is the lack of community programs offering our most vulnerable patients a safe, stable living situation coupled with day treatment programs. I know from working in such programs elsewhere that providing this kind of structure and stability drastically reduces hospital days and emergency room visits.

On the way home, I have that awful feeling in my stomach, the same one I used to feel the moment a romance soured and I knew it had to end. I had hoped SFGH would be my professional life partner and that we would work together through good times and bad. Maybe all this will pass like the threats to cut our positions that surface during budget time but never materialize. I hope so. There's still no other place I would rather work.

16

Limit-setting will not be tolerated in San Francisco

Sometime after our presentation in San Diego, I decided that in order to thrive in my job under the ever-tightening chokehold of managed care, I had better bolster my coping strategies. From here on out, my goals are to spend more time with friends, to get my butt on the treadmill, and to bring more laughter into my life.

On Saturday morning, I leave the kids with Brian and drive to the first of three sessions with a personal trainer. Brian, bless him, never mentions the weight I've gained since our wedding day. But it's time for those pounds, all twenty-eight of them, to move along like little doggies.

Powerhouse Gym is the real thing. It smells of male sweat and antiperspirant. Stains of God-only-knows-what mar the worn carpeting. Metal contraptions litter the floor like Texas oil rigs. Pounding music distorted by a raging ventilation system bounces off the mirrors and high ceilings. Women here—a definite minority—wear oversized t-shirts and stretch pants instead of sexy workout attire.

My trainer's name is Louis. He's my height, soft-spoken and buff but not intimidating. When Louis smiles, his bright white teeth gleam against his black skin. He smiles easily and frequently throughout our conversation. His expressive brown eyes remain fixed on mine. While he takes my height and weight, Louis asks me about my job and my family.

"Five feet five inches, 164 pounds. Not bad," he says.

"You lie, but that's OK. I need encouragement."

I've avoided the scale since Benny was born. Now I cringe.

"What's your goal?" asks Louis, poised with pen in hand to fill in the blank on my workout card.

"Marrying a plastic surgeon who does liposuction but I blew that already."

"Be serious now," he admonishes. "I mean your goal weight."

"I hate diets so how about just stretching me five inches? Can't one of these big machines do that?"

Louis taps the blank space with his pen and waits.

"Honestly, if I could lose twenty-four pounds, I'd sell my children to the devil."

"That's one pound for every year of my life." He smiles as he fills the space with '24 POUND WEIGHT LOSS' in capital letters.

"Louis, up until that last comment I was very impressed with your social skills."

I like making Louis laugh until he positions me on my hands and knees and asks me to extend my left leg and right arm. I collapse trying.

"Louis, I'm liking you less and less," I say between embarrassing grunts as I struggle to maintain my balance in this pose.

"Sorry, but you're paying me for this."

"That's the crazy thing," I gasp.

I fare better on the upper body exercises. Then he makes me

do fancy sit-ups with my back resting on a giant balloon. Again, my abdominal muscles fail me. After three pregnancies, they are as flaccid as breast tissue.

Louis tells me we need to improve my "core strength."

Pointing to a cartoonish bevy of muscled men in the free weight area, he says, "See those guys? They just want to look big. But they can't do any of the core exercises you're going to be able to do."

Louis shows me the layout of the gym and seats me at a contraption that looks like a giant insect with multiple appendages growing out of the floor.

"How old are your kids?" he asks as my lattissimus dorsi muscles contract to pull seventy pounds.

"Seven, three, and one."

"No wonder you've got such good upper body strength. Kids will give you that."

"You married?" I ask.

"No, but I've got three kids. My oldest is seven, too."

Quickly, I do the math. "You were a father at seventeen?"

"Yeah," he says. "That wasn't unusual where I grew up."

I detect a little discomfort, maybe embarrassment in his voice.

"So what do you do at The General?" he asks.

In between sets, I tell him about my work on the trauma unit.

"Sounds like you've met some of my old homies," he says. "I grew up in the projects near Japantown."

We go from machine to machine with Louis showing me how to customize each contraption for my height and strength. He notes the weight I can pull or push on my workout card. In between three sets of twelve on each machine, he tells me his story. His dad was a cop who left the family because his mom was crazy. In sixth grade, Louis came home one day to find that she had purposefully overdosed on something. He called 911 and stayed with his mom until the paramedics came. She survived that attempt but after the next one, she was institutionalized. Louis moved in with his grandmother who lived nearby and worked in Japantown. After school each day he watched the Taiko drumming classes, discovered martial arts, and learned to eat Japanese food. At sixteen, he got a janitorial job at the Japan Cultural Center. At seventeen, he dropped out of school and moved into the projects with his girlfriend who was pregnant.

"What was it like for you to move into the projects?" I ask.

Over my protestation that saddlebags are built-in weight enough, Louis has me doing lunges while holding ten-pound weights.

"It was a high-energy place. Everyone's door was always open. Guns were going off at night." Louis whistles air in a gesture that conveys both relief and disbelief. "No one had any secrets. Music was blasting constantly. Everyone was smoking weed. It was crazy, man."

"It must have been about 1988, the height of the crack epidemic."

Louis shakes his head.

"'Playin' the crack game,' we called it. With the money they were makin' there was so much energy on the streets! Those guys were playin' with fire and they knew it."

"You seem different from the young men I see on the unit," I say.

"I played basketball and smoked weed with those guys ever since we were little," he says. "But I also talked to Japanese people and hung out in the Japanese bookstore. It gave me a more balanced view of the world than they had."

As he talks, I jog on the treadmill, working up a sweat.

"When I was eighteen, I got a job with a bank. To tell you the truth, I got a big rush suiting up and working downtown then coming back to the hood to be a nigga again. I knew how to conduct myself in both worlds. Then the pressure got to be too much. I wanted to come home to relax but I had to duck down in front of my own windows."

After the session, we sit in Louis's cubicle and review the

workout routine. Since his next appointment cancelled, he has some free time. "Do you want to go next door and get some coffee?" he asks.

Over steaming cups of soy chai lattes, we continue our conversation.

"You must see a lot of guys shot up in your job," he says.

"Too many. And there's no end in sight."

"Yeah," he says. "What I don't understand is why we do this to each other. No one else does anything to us. Nobody white ever robbed me but I was held up twice at gunpoint."

"It's good you made it out."

"My grandma made me get my GED. I'm at City College now to be a teacher. This year I worked as a teacher's aide in a tough school."

Louis' face darkens. "Every day the kids would ask me, 'Are you coming back tomorrow?' because most of the black men they see hanging out on the corner are selling drugs. I must have hugged 200 kids a day."

"It must feel good to make such a difference in kids' lives."

"Good and bad," he says. "Like you, it's good to help but it's bad to see so many people needing it."

Louis walks me to my car. "It's been really nice talking with you. It helps to let off a little steam. I always wondered if I should talk to someone sometime."

"Well, if you ever decide to do it, I can help you find a good therapist," I offer.

I don't think I've ever spoken to anyone like Louis outside of the hospital. It's good to know that there are resilient people like him who leave the ghetto and make a go of a different life.

I've had patients from meager beginnings who've pursued and achieved the American dream and I bet some folks on staff have also brought themselves up through equally tough circumstances. But so many of my patients are high school dropouts who scoff at the idea of working a minimum wage job. I know it drives Antionette crazy when she hears young African-American guys say that doing well in school is acting "white." When I told her what my patient Anthony said—that working in a fast food restaurant was beneath him—she marched up to his room and gave him a piece of her mind.

Before I know it, the weekend is gone and I'm back on 4D. My muscles still ache from Saturday's workout, but overall I feel good.

At the nurses' station, Trudy squares off with a new trauma resident. "I'm sorry but you cannot send Mr. Hong home with an oxygen tank. He's only three days post-op. If he still needs oxygen, he needs to stay here!"

The resident protests. "We've got to start cutting costs around here. My senior wants me to discharge him today with an oxygen tank. I've already written the order."

"Well then, you're a flunky," states Trudy. "Around here you need to do what's right, not just what you're told to do."

The resident glares at her before striding off the unit.

"And a happy managed care morning to you!" I say.

"God give me patience," says Trudy. "These guys are taking this managed care thing to extremes. I know we've got to tighten up but let's be safe about it."

Barry walks onto the unit. "What happened? I just saw a resident punch the wall on his way out of here."

Trudy explains about Mr. Hong's orders.

"Yet another case of managed uncaring," says Barry.

"I wish I could find something funny about it," I say, thinking about my vow to use humor as a coping strategy.

"If you want something to laugh about," says Trudy, "turn around and look at the urology team."

A group of trainees stands around the chief of urology outside a patient's room.

"Yes, I see them but what's so funny?"

"Here's a hint. They're discussing Jack Whitman."

"Don't know him."

"Young guy. Cute like Brad Pitt in "Thelma and Louise." Anyway, he's been back and forth between here and the ICU but I guess you've missed him."

"Does it have anything to do with the fact that all the males are clasping their hands in front of their penises?" asks Barry.

"Yes, for $500!" laughs Trudy. "Mr. Whitman's penis was amputated in a construction accident."

"Ow," says Barry, reaching for his crotch. "Just kidding."

Trudy tsk tsks and eyes Barry as if he were a precocious but naughty child.

"The first surgery to reattach it didn't work. He's just out of the ICU from the second surgery. Laurie, after the team leaves, you might want to add Jack to your list."

"Maybe I should evaluate how the men on the team are coping first. They all look so... "

"Scared stiff?" offers Barry.

I punch his shoulder. "More like worried, as if a penile amputation were something you could catch."

I save Jack for later in the day when the crowds will have dispersed. In the meantime, I have plenty of follow-ups to do. Before lunch, I check on a young support group patient who is back in the hospital for yet another surgery to her pelvis. In group, she's been weighing the pros and cons of moving back home with her mom in southern California to recuperate. Toward the end of our discussion, my beeper goes off.

When I dial the number, Patricia answers. "We've been interviewing a candidate for medical director of the new trauma outpatient clinic. Her name is Tamara Shapiro. She graduated from Harvard Med and just completed a trauma fellowship with Judith

Herman at Cambridge Hospital. I'd like your opinion about her. Could you meet with her sometime today?"

"Sure, I can meet her for lunch."

As soon as I hang up, I regret committing my lunchtime to someone who already reminds me of Miranda. At least if she gets the job, we won't overlap much. She'll be spending most of her time in the new clinic.

Tamara and I agree to meet at the local Thai restaurant. When I arrive, it is nearly full with hospital staff. I'm supposed to recognize Tamara by her dark, short curly hair. I scan the crowd but no one by that description pops out at me.

The waiter seats me at a small table for two against the green wall. He motions another woman to take the table behind me.

"Laurie?" she asks, catching my eye. I must look startled because she says, "I wish I could say it was my uncanny intuition but your ID is the giveaway."

Tamara is slender with a small build and bright blue eyes that rival Janice's in intensity. She smiles broadly and extends a delicate hand. Then she closes her eyes and inhales the aroma of red curry with Thai fish sauce and coconut cream served to a person seated nearby.

"I'm starving!" she says. "Is the food as great as it smells?"

"Better." I say.

The waiter takes our orders and brings us small white bowls of steaming rice soup.

"It's so nice to meet you," she says. "I hear you're a Cambridge Hospital alum. We probably know a lot of the same people."

"Maybe. But it's been ten years since I left. I heard you did a trauma fellowship there with Judith Herman. How was that?"

In the '70s, Judith Herman did pioneering work with incest survivors. She has continued to be a trailblazer in the field of psychological trauma.

"Awesome," she says. Tamara describes the workings of the trauma clinic, its treatment philosophy, and the patients. She also mentions that on Fridays, time was put aside for staff to talk about how they were coping with the week's trauma stories. It almost sounds too good to be true.

Tamara's spicy eggplant curry arrives and is quickly followed by my order of spicy chicken with cashews. By this time, I'm starving too. After a few minutes of serious eating and ecstatic groaning, I ask Tamara why she wants to move three thousand miles away from her friends and family to take this job.

"You mean the real reason aside from the obvious fact that it gives me the chance to run my own trauma recovery program?"

"Sure. Let's have it."

"My boyfriend lives here."

"Don't feel bad. I did the same thing."

Then Tamara sets her mouth in a way that signals a serious discussion. "Can I ask you a few questions?"

From her tone and stance, I know she's asking me if I will level with her and if I can keep our conversation confidential.

"Of course."

Tamara lowers her voice. "Patricia said something that worries me. She told me that she wants to treat victims of domestic violence and their perpetrators in the same clinic. To tell you the truth, I was shocked to hear her say that. I'm concerned that she doesn't understand how murderous some of these guys are. The clinic needs to be a safe place for these women and their children. Otherwise, they won't come."

Tamara searches my face. I like many things about her including that she is strongly grounded in psychodynamic theory and equally knowledgeable about medications, a rare combination these days. If she's already butting heads with Patricia, I don't have much hope she'll be hired. Nevertheless, I level with her the best I can.

"San Francisco is a tolerant town, tolerant of anonymous sex in the bathhouses, tolerant of psychosis in the streets. You name it, it flies in SF."

I tell her about the borderline patient with necrotizing fasciitis whom we grafted until there was nothing more to graft because she refused to stay on bed rest. "Patricia's take on that patient was, 'Poor baby, she's had a tough life. Therefore, we can't read her the riot act.'"

Worry lines appear on Tamara's forehead. "So it will be like starting from scratch."

"Yup. You and I learned that setting limits on a person's self-destructive behavior is an act of compassion. People here don't see it that way. In San Francisco, individual rights trump common sense. I heard about a competency hearing where a psych patient on an involuntary hold convinced the DA that he could take care of himself by eating out of the dumpster at Stars restaurant."

Tamara looks miserable. Perhaps I've gone too far. By now, I sense that I would really like to work with her. She asked me for the truth and I owe it to her.

"The other thing you should know about psychiatry here as compared with Boston is that the phrase 'to process' does not exist in the local lingo. Staff support is paltry to non-existent and forget about supervision."

As far as I know, the Cambridge Hospital Department of Psychiatry still holds sacrosanct the weekly individual supervision hour with senior staff. While I worked at the day treatment center associated with the hospital, I was given two hours of individual supervision a week, one with a senior nurse and one with a psychiatrist at my agency.

Tamara purses her lips. "I don't think I can hear any more. How can you even think about running a trauma program without supporting your staff?"

"I'm beginning to wonder about that myself."

"So about Patricia and this perpetrator thing," she says gingerly. "Is it clinical naïveté—I know she's a neuropsychologist and that they're into Rorschachs and MMPI's—or is it denial, or maybe a rescue fantasy thing, or all of the above?"

"I don't know about her clinical skills but I can tell you that this whole institution is heavy into denial about safety issues. Sometimes patients from rival gangs are on the same unit and we don't even have metal detectors in the lobby or in the ER. Not to mention the unsecured back doors that open into the hospital."

Tamara's eyes grow big.

I begin backpedaling fast. "But you'd love living here. The city is gorgeous, the food is sublime, and you can count on me to help you bring a little bit of Cambridge Hospital to the Department of Psychiatry."

After we part ways, I feel as though a lifeline were cut. Tamara said she hoped we'd see each other again soon. From her expression, I'm not so sure we will.

On 4D, I knock on Jack Whitman's door across from the nurses' station and open it a crack. "Is this a good time to stop by?" I ask.

"Well I'm getting sucked off, but sure, come on in."

I hesitate. I've heard these stories from the nurses and I'm not sure that I want to stumble in on a love fest of any kind.

"Really," he calls. "Come on in and join us!"

"Trudy?" I try to get her attention but she's on the phone. As she listens to the person at the other end, she sweeps her hand toward Mr. Whitman's door and mouths, "This is a good time."

That's what I'm afraid of—that I'll be walking in on a good time.

I open the door centimeter-by-centimeter, ready to close it at the sound of giggling. I don't hear any female sounds, giggling or otherwise, but I do hear the same welcoming voice, apparently on the phone. "Hey Uncle George, you should see my dick. These girls are doing a great job!"

Oh my God!

I close the door and look at Trudy who is still on the phone. I am the daughter of a sex therapist and it takes a lot to make me blush. When other fathers talked about the stock market or politics at the dinner table, my father told us about premature ejaculation, priapism, and coitus interruptus. But now, my face feels like it's burning. I look to Trudy for direction but she just waves me toward Mr. Whitman's room again.

I will be stern. I will set limits. I will keep my cool.

After a steadying breath, I re-open the door and walk in. Mr. Whitman is still on the phone. "Bye Uncle George and remember what I said. It's a bet!"

"Hi!" he says in an enthusiastic voice. "So do you want to see the little suckers?"

Jack Whitman looks like a young cowboy, deeply tanned and rough around the edges. His mane of hair is streaked with natural blond highlights and his smile is worthy of Hollywood. Before I can register a response, he whips off his bed linens. Although his penis is splinted to a contraption that holds it straight up, all I can see are fat dark red worms squiggling on it. I stifle the urge to gag.

"Leeches!" Mr. Whitman announces, his voice awash in wonder. "Can you believe it's 1995 and they're still using leeches?"

My jaw drops. All I can do to match his wonderment is shake my head back and forth. "And they're doing a great job of keeping the swelling down, aren't you girls?"

"You, you seem to be dealing with this quite well," I stammer.

"Hey, I'm happy to have my dick back but I'll be happier when I know that it works the way it's supposed to."

"When do you expect to know?"

"Tonight I hope," he says, winking at me. "I got a date with myself."

Before I can nip it in the bud, laughter ripples out of me.

"I gotta hand it to you, Mr. Whitman."

"Ooh, you're good," he interrupts.

It takes me a second to catch his joke. I was going to tell him that I've never seen anyone cope so well under such dire circumstances, but I think I'll quit while I'm ahead.

On Wednesday, Patricia tells me that she has decided to offer Tamara the job as medical director of the new outpatient trauma clinic. She hopes to hear back from Tamara within the week. I am surprised and excited and pissed off at myself for painting such a dismal portrait of SFGH psychiatry. Nevertheless, I practically skip through the rest of the day fantasizing about the state-of-the-art trauma treatment program we could have, one that includes staff support and education.

I enter the medical library reading room where support group will meet in a few minutes.

"You're as lit up as a Christmas tree," says Ilan, my Israeli co-therapist. "What's up?"

I tell him about Tamara and my newfound hope for change in the department. Then I confess how I might have frightened her away from moving here.

"Have faith in love," says Ilan, "or in her boyfriend's skill in the bedroom!"

Although I don't know him well enough to ask, I find myself wondering how Ilan's sex life must have changed when he lost his entire leg during an Arab-Israeli war. Along the same theme, I remember that I need to follow up on Mr. Whitman after group. Too bad he lives a hundred miles away or I would encourage him to come to support group after his discharge from the hospital.

Six people show up for today's group. Mrs. Holloway is among them, the third time she's come to group, and the first time I've seen her wear something that reveals the five-inch scar on her neck.

For most of the group, Mrs. Holloway remains quiet and barely moves. When we go around the circle to "check in," she says, "I think I'll pass." Although I listen while two new members tell their stories, I watch Mrs. Holloway's eyes become distant. In the last fifteen minutes of group, I ask her to tell us what's going on.

The silence in the room lingers before she answers in a voice wrung of all emotion.

"My assailant has been released from police custody."

Mrs. Holloway pulls her skirt over her knees. She folds her left arm across her chest and balls her hand into a fist. Her right hand gently strokes her scar on her throat. "Apparently," she continues in a voice hard as steel, "he was not charged with attempted murder, only with possession of drugs."

She tells us that he has returned to the projects where he has always lived, where she is an interloper. "How will you stay safe?" I ask. Maybe this time she will ask her family for shelter.

"I'll do what I need to do."

Alarms go off in my mind. In the distance, I hear Ilan say that it's time for group to end.

"Mrs. Holloway?" I ask as people start to get out of their chairs. "May I speak with you a moment?"

If anyone else felt alarmed, they should know I intend to follow up with her. Ilan says he will call me later to review the group, then hops away on his crutches.

Mrs. Holloway sits ramrod straight, looking neither at me, nor away. I bring my chair close and match her posture. "Mrs. Holloway, I'm concerned about what you said in group. I need to know if you have a gun."

Although her body appears frozen, Mrs. Holloway's eyes dart in all directions. "I'm afraid I can't answer you," she says.

I feel like I'm looking down a long dark tunnel. Although it is risky, I put my hand over hers. She neither repels me nor warms to me.

"You and I have spent some time together. I know how terrified you must feel but messing with a gun could make a bad situation worse. There are other ways to deal with this."

"I don't want you to call the police," she says.

I can almost taste the bitterness in her mouth.

"They made matters worse for me."

"I understand. If we can come up with a way that feels safe to both of us, I agree not to call the police."

I feel my own fear rise.

What if she bolts? What if she has a gun in her purse?

"Would you agree to walk over to psych emergency services with me?"

"No." she says. "I am not the problem. He is the problem."

"That's true but I sense that you're as scared now as you were the day he hurt you. I'm asking you right now not to let your emotions cloud your better judgment. You need to be somewhere safe. That's why I think we should go to psych emergency. They can find a safe place for you."

"I don't want to go there."

We sit together in silence for a long few minutes. Then she places my hand in hers and squeezes it.

"I know you want what's best for me."

She could still bolt and I will be forced to call the institutional police, but her touch tells me we are working together.

"Please, Mrs. Holloway. Don't go back there."

"It's my home. I won't let him force me out of my home."

Even as she says that, I feel her resolve falter. Then a tear splatters on my hand.

"Maybe it's time to call your family. Would you do that?"

I count up to twelve-Mississippi before she answers.

"Alright. I'll call my brother in Fresno. I can stay with my cousin tonight."

"Is that a promise?"

"Yes," she says meeting my gaze. "You have my word."

No one is in the office. I put my head down on my desk as if it were a shoulder. I have not yet emerged from Mrs. Holloway's darkness. I feel the depth of her loneliness and the fangs of her rage. I also feel the place where we met, the soft spot where she opened to me and took what I had to offer. To calm myself, I focus on breathing in and out slowly. All kinds of random thoughts and images fly in and out of my consciousness until one image, my father's cocktail tree—a grapefruit tree grafted with tangerines, oranges, and tangelos—seems to lodge there. Maybe it's because I've been reading about grafting lately in one of my gardening books. It strikes me now that therapy is a kind of grafting; a therapist extends a sturdy root structure and healthy tissue toward her patient. In the process of severing the diseased parts, the patient binds herself to the therapist's tree, borrowing healthy tissue for re-growth.

Before leaving for the day, I head back up to 4D. The unit is quiet until I open the door to the nurses' lounge. Flowers and a cake are on the table. Nurses stand on chairs hanging decorations and a sign that says, "Happy Birthday, Trudy!" Apparently, the birthday girl is in the cafeteria on her break, unaware that she will be feted upon her return. I will join the festivities after I check in with Mr. Whitman and his leeches.

Mr. Whitman, or Jack, as he's asked me to call him, is alone in his single room. He greets me as if I were his long lost sister. "Hey, long time no see! How have you been?"

"From the sound of your voice I'd guess that everything's in working order with you," I say. "Am I right?"

"You bet. I had two hard-ons last night and three so far today. I was so happy, I even showed my mother!"

Imagining his mother's reaction, I burst out laughing. Jack seems pleased that he has me in stitches.

I return to the nurses' lounge in time to hear the staff singing the last line of 'Happy Birthday.'

"Listen up, everyone," I say when the song ends and someone has started to cut the cake.

"Mr. Whitman has had five erections since his surgery."

The nurses break into titters and applause.

"Although I don't want to know exactly what you did for him, let me just say—do we have a terrific nursing staff here or what!"

17

Survivor guilt

While I'm reviewing a patient's chart on 4D, Janice emerges from a room across from the nurses' station and throws her arm over my shoulders.

"Hey, you might have a new trauma group member tomorrow. His name is Brett Watanabe, a firefighter. Remember that Diamond Heights fire where Georgette was injured? She and Brett and another firefighter were trapped in the garage together."

"Was Brett injured too?"

"He was burned on the hands and neck. They put him in the ICU with Georgette for a couple of days before transferring him to St. Francis. After he was discharged, he came back here and has visited her almost every day for the last three months. You've probably seen him—young, Japanese-American, cute but so sad."

I recollect seeing someone like that on the unit. "So what's going on with him?"

"Mostly a bad case of survivor guilt. I've spent a fair bit of time talking with him and encouraging him to go to your group but he wasn't ready until now. Let me know if he shows up today."

Janice writes a note in Georgette's chart and departs for another consult on the pediatric unit.

Survivor guilt?

That's a tough one. Early in my career I worked with an elderly Holocaust survivor who had been a violinist in the orchestra at Auschwitz that played "welcome" music for each new group of prisoners. After three decades of maintaining silence about his experience, he broke. He was hospitalized after trying to commit suicide. He told me he could never forgive himself for living while so many others perished in the gas chambers.

To my surprise, Tamara took the job as medical director of our new trauma outpatient clinic and has already begun working. Over lunch at the Thai restaurant, and after we've chatted up Cape Cod and adjusting to cold summers, Tamara tells me that she will facilitate a department-wide trauma study group. She has already contacted staff at the rape crisis clinic, the refugee clinic, and the child and adolescent sexual abuse research center, all of whom jumped at the chance to meet with others who do trauma work. She wants me to begin the series by summarizing and discussing the first chapter of Judith Herman's book, *Trauma and Recovery*. I'm happy to do so, excited that it's already beginning to feel like East Coast psychiatry all over again.

I pick up a copy of the book that evening. After the kids are tucked in, I immediately become engrossed by Herman's history of trauma treatment. She describes how our culture represses and even denies the fact of psychological trauma because it flies in the face of our idealized self-image. Only a tsunamic convergence of social movements has the power to lift this veil of secrecy and even then, the effect is temporary. This happened during the 1960s when the collective turbulence of the civil rights movement, the women's movement, and the student anti-war movement generated enough energy to expose the psychological trauma suffered by Vietnam veterans, the ugliness of racism, and the abuse of women and children in their own homes.

I wonder now if those painful images have sunk back down into the still, murky waters of yesterday's news. Sometimes, I wish I could enjoy life blissfully unaware of others' pain. It seems, however, that I never developed the capacity for denial. Every day I see the damage done to abused children who are now damaged adults. Each story I hear about a childhood filled with terror, exploitation, and neglect causes my own anger to rise anew. I read well past the time Brian has turned off his own reading light.

I take the book with me to work the next day. Twenty minutes before it's time for support group, I leave the trauma unit and head over to the medical library to read in peaceful stillness before my patients arrive.

I love our cozy group room in the medical library. Tall, narrow windows circle the room and frame the sky and tops of trees. Below them, oak bookshelves bulge with bound volumes of medical journals like *Virology, Nucleic Acid Research, and Analytic Biochemistry*. To the left of the door is a collection of books on medical ethics: *Medical Malpractice, Society and Love, Pain Profit*, and *Which Babies Shall Live?* I arrange the red chairs in a circle on the brown carpet and sit in one closest to the black and white marbled fireplace facing the door.

Fifteen minutes later, a metal clink and a thud of rubber on linoleum signals Ilan's arrival. He greets me and sets his braces on a table. Then he pivots himself into a chair. "I was thinking last time that we've finally developed a core membership in this group."

"Yes, I think so despite the fact that so many things conspire against it."

"It's true. Mobility issues, pain, medical appointments not to mention that once people have recovered enough to go back to work, it's hard for them to attend a mid-afternoon meeting."

"And other people won't come if we hold it later because they don't like being out after dark, especially in this neighborhood."

"And yet," says Ilan, "we've managed to hold steady at four or five people each week. Good going!"

The door to the library slowly opens. A middle-aged, Chinese-American female crossing guard who was run over by a car limps in, followed by the young Scottish woman in a wheelchair who barely survived a motorcycle accident. Another regular, the psychology professor, pushes his walker through the door. This time his wife does not accompany him.

When I express surprise, he tells me she's meeting with a person in accounting to discuss their bill. "I'm becoming too dependent on her anyway," he says. "I need to start pushing myself to get out on my own."

Our punk hairdresser with a pink Mohawk walks in with a cane and a huge smile. "The doctor says no more surgeries!"

"That's something to celebrate!" I say, offering her the first pick from a box of candy.

When we are seated, it occurs to me that everyone in this room has been a victim of trauma except me.

What am I doing here? I've never been seriously injured. Can I ever really understand what it's like to be disabled, to be disfigured, or in constant pain? Doesn't that create a distance between them and me?

When it's time to begin, I peek down the hallway before closing the door. No sign of Brett, the firefighter. Too bad. But lots of people say they're going to come and never show up. I'll give him a call after group to extend a personal invitation.

The psychology professor begins by talking about how being struck by a van and thrown into the air has gotten him thinking about "jumping tracks" in life and retiring early. As he speaks, his wife enters and closes the door quietly behind her.

"The body at sixty is not what it was at thirty," he says wistfully.

"Thank God for my better half. She's taken over the business of bills and legal issues so I can concentrate on recovery."

He squeezes her knee. I notice that his wife's smile is tight and short-lived.

The tall Scotswoman, three decades younger than the professor and a former competitive skier, announces that she took her first steps without crutches in physical therapy the day before. Everyone claps and she beams. Recovery has been a long and painful process involving multiple surgeries. "They didn't expect that I would ever be able to walk on my own," she says, "but they didn't know me. Now they do!"

The Chinese-American woman tells the group that she "got rid" of her husband and his Rottweiler dog. "After the accident I could barely move. I had a cast on my leg and one on my arm. The dog kept humping me and my husband kept pestering me for sex. I had no use for either one of them. Last week I threw them both out!"

No one quite knows how to respond.

"Clap for me too!" she commands. "I am much happier now!"

The group claps.

A face presses into the door's small window. A young Asian man opens the door and asks, "Is this the support group?"

"You're in the right place," says Ilan. "Come join us."

Brett Watanabe could pass for a college kid. He settles his toned and compact body into a chair, clasps his hands, and presses his lips together. I notice that he wears tight fitting, flesh colored gloves.

"I've never done anything like this before so—what do you want me to say?" he asks after introductions have been made.

"The idea is to tell us your story, what happened to you," I tell Brett.

"I don't get how that's going to help with anything."

He squirms in his chair.

"It may not," I answer, "but sometimes just telling your story, especially to others who've also been injured, helps."

"OK. I'm not sure I get it, but here goes."

Brett blushes and hesitates. He bites his lip and works his fist into his palm.

"Well, I'm a firefighter. There was this fire in Diamond Heights. It was windy that night. They say seventy-mile-an-hour winds. Houses up there have a garage at street level and the living areas are on the floors below."

He looks around the room. Everyone is rapt. He clears his throat before continuing. "So, there were three of us. Me and Georgette, George, we call her—and Olivetti, our captain."

Brett stops and shakes his head. "Are you sure this is going to help? I'm not used to this therapy stuff."

"You're doing just fine," says Ilan. "If you get too uncomfortable, you can stop anytime."

Brett smiles briefly and takes a deep breath. "Most firefighters would rather throw back a few beers than talk about the stuff we see everyday."

When no one smiles, he gets back down to business. "OK, so we got there before anyone else. The three of us walked into the garage and for some reason no one can figure out, it slammed shut behind us." He swallows hard. "Am I still doing OK?"

I assure him that he is.

"Then we realize the garage is locked. We can't get it open. It's also dark. The fire is coming up the hill. It's getting really hot and smoky. We're trapped."

Brett stops and pinches his tear ducts with his thumb and forefinger.

"Take whatever time you need," I say softly, noting the change in verb tense from past to present. When I look around the room, I see tension in everyone's face.

"Sometimes it's tough to hear other people's stories. How is everyone doing right now?"

"It's hard to listen but I know it helps me," says the professor. "When I feel sorry for myself I think about what all of you have gone through. That gives me strength."

"What about the rest of you?" I ask.

Everyone indicates readiness for Brett to continue. He rubs his face vigorously and hunches forward with his elbows resting on his knees and his hands clasped under his chin.

"OK. So I heard George and Olivetti talking. I assumed they were all right. Then George's vibe alert went off. That meant she had 90 seconds of air left. I thought she was close to me so I figured we could buddy-breathe. Turns out she wasn't. She was closer to Olivetti who was on the opposite side of the garage from me. Anyway, it was getting really hot in there."

When he pauses I ask, "Did you think you were going to die?"

It's a hard question to put to him, but a survivor who thought he would die during a traumatic event is more likely to develop PTSD than one who thought he would live.

"No, I knew I'd make it out OK. I was shielded from some of the heat by the car in the garage. I knew I had to preserve air so I kept calm and got down to the floor."

Something in Brett's face changes; his eyes get that faraway look of someone reliving something horrible.

"Go on, Brett," says Ilan.

"At this point, it's getting really smoky—it's the smoke that kills you, not the fire—but somehow I find an air vent and push my hand through it so when the other crew arrives they'll know we're here, I mean—in there."

Brett's black eyes are shiny, fighting tears. "They must have seen my hand because the next thing I know they're cutting through the door."

Brett stops here and squeezes his eyes shut. The rest of us are silent, worried about what's to come.

"It might help to take some deep breaths," I suggest. "All of us, not just Brett."

Everyone breathes in and out slowly. After a few cycles, I have to say what comes to mind. "It sounds like a Lamaze class in here!"

Ilan smiles. "You could say we're in the middle of a difficult delivery."

Sighs and nervous chuckles help dispel the tension.

"I'm OK," says Brett. "Should I go on?"

Everyone is as ready as can be without knowing the ending to this story.

"Well, I didn't know it at the time but Olivetti had already expired. They say he had a heart attack and died in the garage. By the time they pulled George out, she had stopped breathing. They bagged her twice. In the ambulance, they told me to keep her talking. Just before we got to the hospital, she lost consciousness. Then they intubated her. She stayed like that in the ICU for three months. They told me that because she breathed in so much smoke, it affected the vision area of her brain and now she's legally blind."

Everyone in the room reacts. Burns are bad enough but most of us would take burns over blindness. Brett stares down at the brown carpet, his rounded posture conveying the burden he bears. I fight the urge to throw a comforting arm around him.

"What about you?" asks the professor. "Weren't you hurt too?"

"My hand was throbbing; my neck was fried. I was on the ICU for a few days with a fever and a tube down my throat. Then they sent me to St. Francis where I was grafted. That's why I have to wear this stuff on my hands and my neck."

Brett displays the flesh-colored sleeves on his hands. "But the thing for me is, I can't stop thinking that I could have done something more. I should have been able to…"

He chokes on the words and hangs his head. "I should have been able to save all of us."

No one, it seems, can respond until Ilan says softly, "Sometimes the guilt is more painful than the injury."

"No kidding," says the crossing guard. "My husband blamed the accident on me. He said, 'You stupid woman. You should have seen that car coming.' Now I realize I'm not going to take the blame for a senile man who didn't stop for people in a crosswalk. He should have had his license revoked twenty years ago!"

Another silence. Then the professor's wife addresses Brett. "But didn't you just tell us how you found the vent and stuck your hand through it?"

"Yes, but it was too late. Olivetti is dead and George is blind. I should have been able to do something earlier."

Oh, the tyranny of the "shoulds." Here's a guy who has pulled people out of burning apartments and restarted their hearts and lungs, and he feels like shit. But no one can talk him out of his guilt anymore than I could talk myself out of feeling guilty about my family's problems.

"Many of us who have survived trauma—when others have not—wrestle with guilt for the rest of our lives," says Ilan.

I should have been more understanding.

I should have been nicer.

I should have been more protective.

Brett's voice refocuses me on the present. "I try to visit George every day and every day I feel so bad about what happened. That's why I want to go back to work as soon as possible. I just put in for the busiest station in the city."

I feel Ilan's eyes on mine. It's time for me to say something but I can't formulate the words. I look up and shake my head ever so slightly to let him know that I'm stuck.

Ilan nods and asks, "What about this idea of guilt that Brett is struggling with? Does it weigh on other people here as well?"

Our punk hairdresser talks about feeling awful that she has had to move in with her mother and her mother's new husband, albeit temporarily. Then the quietest member of the group raises her hand.

"Ah yes," she says in her soft Scottish accent, "I knew I shouldn't have been riding motorcycles in the city. My mother was a nurse and I grew up hearing about all of the accidents, you know?"

The crossing guard comes to life again. "I feel bad when I'm out because we don't have enough subs. What if someone gets hurt because I'm not there?"

If guilt were gold, we'd all be able to retire.

"I saw Olivetti's wife at the funeral," says Brett. "She told me he was six months away from retirement. They were building their dream house and their daughter was expecting the first grandchild. I didn't know what to say to her. What could I have said?"

No one rushes in with an answer. By this time I've recovered enough from my lapse to respond. "Nothing you could have said would have made you or her feel better. Your presence honored her husband and provided support to his family. Maybe nothing we can say here will make you feel better, but we are here to support you so I hope you keep coming back."

Brett sighs deeply, visibly relieved that it's time for group to end.

When everyone has limped, shuffled, or wheeled out of the room, Ilan and I remain behind. "So," he teases, although I feel the seriousness underneath, "Do you want to talk about it? I've heard that talking helps."

I laugh even though I know it sounds forced. "I've heard that too but I'll take a pass for now. Thanks for asking though."

With Brian in New York for a court hearing, I spend more time than usual tonight putting each child to bed. When all of them have been cuddled and tucked in, I trudge upstairs and pour myself a vodka tonic. Since today's support group, I have felt the distant rumble of pounding hooves in my chest. It's an old but familiar sensation, one I used to feel with some frequency before I got married and had a family. Tonight, without Brian—my built-in antidepressant—to distract me, the pounding hooves grow louder.

I remember now about guilt, how it pounces on you every night like an overweight cat. How it sandpapers your face and kneads you with sharp claws before settling its dead weight onto your chest for the night.

Early in therapy, I focused on my poor relationship with my mother and my sister and my overly close relationship with my father. Although suppression has worked most of the time, guilt has never totally abandoned me. I can always sense its hulking presence in the shadow of my being.

Today in group, listening to Brett Watanabe talk about feeling guilty because he survived the tragedy that killed one colleague and blinded another has pushed my own guilt front and center. It's as if my brain is a library with my emotional history preserved on tape, archived, and accessed by empathic resonance. Will these old feelings always haunt me? Can't I shake them loose into the wind like cremated ashes? Even after years of therapy, guilt persists like a bad habit. In a perverse way, it has comforted me like an old friend and filled in the empty spaces of my life. I have counted on it to show up whenever I've needed a spiritual dunking. For the most part though, my work as a nurse has helped to keep the guilt hounds at bay. Marrying and raising a family has also allowed me to shift focus from my inadequacies to my strengths.

Over the weekend, sitting on our backyard deck with a cup of strong coffee, I think about how many of us caregivers and rescuers prefer feeling guilty to feeling helpless or powerless. We've convinced ourselves that we should have been able to save the people we love and serve from pain, distress, and ridicule, from their own demons, and even from death. Because we have failed, we conclude that we are worthless screw-ups. Perhaps we could have done better, but it was the best we could do at the time.

18

Holding up
the weight of the world

Over the weekend, I got a heads up about today's patients. On Saturday night after we had tucked the kids into their beds, Brian and I folded laundry and watched the 10 p.m. news with Dennis Richmond, our favorite TV news anchor. Maintaining his cool demeanor, Dennis reported, "This just in. A third floor deck in San Francisco's Pacific Heights district collapsed during a party this evening. One young woman was killed and thirteen others were sent to the hospital, one in critical condition. More on this as information becomes available."

On Sunday, we learned that the victims are in their twenties. Most work in the insurance business and all had gathered to attend a roommate's farewell party. An investigation has begun to determine if criminal negligence played a part in the deck's collapse.

On my way to work, I imagine the victims' families receiving the phone call every parent dreads. When they arrive, some after a tense drive or a long flight, they will learn the facts of their adult child's injuries. They will hang onto the doctors' words listening for hope in each pause. They will re-inhabit recently shed skins of parent as protector and provider. On the unit, they will meet the parents of other victims. Together they will wait.

The trauma unit buzzes with media people, families, friends, doctors, and administrators. As I enter 4D, Mr. Reeves, our perennial patient, wheels himself out, his white hair greasy and uncombed as usual.

"Damn zoo in there. Just like 101 California," he says referring to the last time there were so many television cameras on the unit. I recall that incident and what an African-American patient told me at the time: "Bunch of white people get hurt and it's news. Black people get shot and it's business as usual."

Mr. Reeves wheels away from me, stops, then calls over his shoulder, "Hey, sister, spare a quarter for the paper?"

Trudy rolls her eyes when she spies me. "Someone needs to tell these people that we have trauma patients here every day of the year."

She briefs me on the status of the six survivors who were brought here. Two have been released. Five are being treated at University Hospital. With so many involved, it makes sense to bring survivors, witnesses, and family members together for a debriefing. I run this idea by Janice who agrees and offers to co-lead it with me. We divvy up the tasks of organizing it for tomorrow afternoon. In the interim, I will try to check in with the patients and their families and see my other patients as well.

The next morning, Janice and I sketch out an agenda for the meeting. She's reserved a room large enough to contain all twenty-seven of us, including two hospital beds for patients in traction. With so many people, we will need to keep the group structured.

Fifteen minutes before group is scheduled to begin, a dietary aide arrives with tea, coffee, and cookies. The young people and their parents start to congregate. When everyone has been seated and we've positioned the hospital beds such that the patients in traction can participate, the meeting begins. A partygoer who witnessed the scene but was not injured is first to describe her experience. She speaks of her concern for her friend, a young woman on the ICU with severe head injuries, and of her grief for another young woman who died under the collapsed deck.

A young man tells of seeing the third floor deck bounce off the second floor deck, flip over, and crash in the backyard. "Just before it broke loose, the girls were talking on the third floor deck. Most of the guys were inside. We ran downstairs and saw what had happened. We tried to lift the deck off of them."

He stops and squeezes his eyes shut, then wipes his face before continuing. "It was so heavy; we could barely hold it up. The girls were crying and moaning underneath."

His eyes brim with emotion. "We could hear them, but we couldn't help them because we had to hold up the deck." He stops talking and stares into his lap.

The girls in traction describe their recollections. Both heard a terrible groaning sound, experienced darkness, and awoke to the sensation of pain. One of them recalls being placed on a gurney by paramedics, then nothing.

One by one, the other young men share their experiences. All of them describe hearing the girls' cries and feeling frustrated by their inability to pull them to safety.

"Maybe it was only ten minutes before the paramedics arrived, but it felt like forever," says one of the boys.

"Afterward, my muscles were killing me," says another. "Like they'd been frozen."

As they speak, their eyes shine, threatening tears; their voices crack. When one cannot continue, another puts an arm around him and says, "It's alright, man. It's OK."

After ninety minutes when everyone who wants to has spoken, Janice and I review symptoms of Acute Stress Reaction. We pass out brochures that list symptoms of ASR and PTSD, explaining that while most people experience a significant decrease in symptoms four to six weeks after the trauma, a small percentage may develop post-traumatic stress disorder. We encourage them to seek counseling and to continue to be each other's support network in the weeks and months to come.

When everyone has left the room, Janice and I embrace in a prolonged hug. During the meeting, we had to suppress our own emotions in order to pay close attention to the group's process. Now they bubble up and we sag under the weight.

"I felt for those parents," says Janice. Her girls are teenagers now, wanting more time away from the nest but not quite ready to fly.

"It's so hard to let go of your kids knowing that something like this can happen. Even the ones who weren't hurt will be affected. Life won't feel safe anymore."

I tell Janice about a young woman in my trauma group. "Just before her accident she was thinking life was good. She had a new man, a new job. She was in her car at the time, a couple of blocks from her home when, unexpectedly, someone plowed into her. Now every time she starts to feel good, she has this feeling of dread."

Janice sighs and sets her jaw. "All I know is that no one is going on our third floor deck until I get the inspector out. My daughters think I'm crazy but just looking at it makes me anxious."

"When is your next Girls' Night Out?"

"Tonight, thank God. I think this one will be worth a couple of margaritas! How about you? Can you take some time for yourself? I know it's hard with young kids."

"We're going up to Lake Tahoe for the weekend. Let's hope the cabin we're renting doesn't have a deck."

We try to get up to the snow at least once a year. We build

snowmen and snow forts and take the kids sledding. This time we'll try ski lessons for Corianne and Danny.

On Friday before we leave, I take the kids to "the bear store" where we rent snow clothes. The kids call it "the bear store" because of the stuffed Kodiak bear that stands on his hind legs in a perpetual snarl that displays his sharp white teeth. Between Corianne fretting about the color of her snowsuit and the sales clerk fretting about the boys playing in and out of camping tents on the showroom floor, by the time we leave the store I am on the same wave length as that bear.

After three hours on the road, Brian asks, "Who will be the first one to see snow?"

Both of us see the snow-capped Sierra in the distance, but the kids watch the sides of the road for drifts. As we gain altitude and the vegetation changes from chaparral plants to pines, my spirits lift. Being among the pines makes me nostalgic for our backpacking days. In just a couple more years, Benny will be five, old enough to go on a family backpack trip.

"I see snow! I saw it first!" yells Corianne. "Can we stop and feel it?"

"OK, but just for a minute. No rolling in the snow until we have our snowsuits on."

Brian pulls over at the first place with enough snow to make it worthwhile. The kids jump out. Benny scoops up a fistful, and then looks surprised when the ice bites his fingers. Corianne throws a snowball at Danny who blasts one back in her face.

"Hey, no fair!" she yells.

I can see where this is going. "OK everyone, back in the car. We'll be there soon enough."

Brian misses fall foliage, snow, and wearing tee shirts on sultry, East-Coast summer evenings. I miss them too with the exception of winter, which in Boston bullies its way into April, for God's sake. Still, I'm happy to visit the cold country once a year.

In the mountains, we pass an area where fire has left pines standing like an army of silver-gray skeletons. A fine mist lurks in the spaces between them as if the embers had just died down. We explain to the kids that although fire is a bad thing in the city, natural fires keep forests healthy by opening the forest floor to light. Fire also scars the seed coats of the giant sequoias so that water can enter them and germination can occur.

"But what about the animals? Do they die?"

"No. They're smart enough to run away," I reply.

Unlike the two little boys who recently died in a house fire. Their charred bodies were found in their bedroom closet.

This year we've rented a cozy cabin not far from the lake. After we stuff them into their snow clothes, the kids run outside to play on the white, snowplowed banks of the parking lot. Benny strips off his gloves and scoops snow into his hands. His face registers delight, then shock followed by displeasure when, once again, the cold begins to sting his small pink fingers. With angry tears streaking his face, he lumbers back to the cabin. I blow on his hands and rub them warm. We replace his gloves and he joins the other two who dig foxholes in the snow. Later, we find a place nearby to sled.

In the morning, we bundle up and drive to Squaw Valley Ski resort, home of the 1960 Winter Olympics. We enroll Danny and Corianne in ski school. Benny, at three, is too young. He will stay in day care and hang out with me later in the day after my lesson. Having grown up in the desert, I never skied as a kid. In fact, I've only skied downhill twice in my life. Maybe that's why I'm a wuss when it comes to going fast.

After my lesson, while I am standing in line at the green circle that signifies a beginner's run, a ski instructor asks me if I would escort a little boy onto the lift.

"Could you just make sure that he gets off safely?"

I feel a tad uncomfortable since this guy doesn't know me or how I ski, but I can handle the task. He introduces me to Albert, a 6-year-old Korean-American child, who waits in front of me. It's almost our turn to embark when I hear a woman yell at the lift operator.

"I told you this was ski school! You need to slow down so we can get the kids on the chairs safely."

Before I can register alarm, it's our turn. Although the operator still has not attempted to slow down, I manage to situate Albert and myself on the seat a millisecond before we are whisked into the air. At thirty feet aloft, I am acutely aware of the absence of a restraining device.

"How are you doing, Albert? Are you comfortable?" I ask, making sure he's sitting as far back in his seat as possible. Just as I check his position, the lift stops abruptly.

"Yeah, I'm OK," says Albert. "But why does it always stop?"

Aware that people are yelling behind us, I ask, "How many times have you been on a ski lift?"

"This is my third time," says Albert, a chatty child. "We came here last year when I was five and the year before when I was four."

I glance behind us and see a little girl dangling from the lift by one arm. Her skis have dropped to the ground, landing upright but crisscrossed in the snow.

"Yeah," says Albert. "It happens every time. As soon as it starts, all of a sudden it stops!"

He doesn't seem to notice the commotion going on behind us. I glance again. The little girl is about ten. The girl with her, perhaps a friend, is screaming. A crowd of employees gathers below them. Albert still hasn't noticed. Before he does, I do my best to distract him.

"Yeah well, these things happen," I say, drawing out each word as if I'm feeling dreamy. "But sometimes it's kind of nice because when you're not moving you can notice how beautifully the snow sits on the limbs of the pines and how blue the sky is against the white snow and the dark green Douglas firs."

Albert looks where I point. "It IS beautiful and I never knew the sky was SO blue!"

I love this about young children; how easily they become enraptured by nature. While I continue to point out a bird flying overhead and a large cloud in the distance, I steal another glance at the horrifying scene behind us.

A group of ten staff has positioned their hands to form a human trampoline. They yell to the girl, "Let go. Let go!"

"I can't," she screams. "I'm too scared!"

Suspecting that Albert has tired of serenity, I switch gears fast. "Wow," I say, "Look how fast that guy is skiing down the mountain! How fast do you think he's going, Albert?"

"Wow," he says. "Faster than anything. Maybe he's going 4,873!"

I have to think about that for a second. "Yup, Albert, I think you're right."

I look behind us just as the girl lets go of her grip. She falls safely onto the human net. Right away, even before we witnesses can let out a sigh of relief, the lift resumes operating.

"I hope we don't have to stop again," says Albert.

"Me too," I say.

Once down the mountain, I stop by the medical hut to inquire about the little girl who fell. When I tell the nurse that I work on the trauma unit at SFGH, she reports that the girl dislocated her shoulder. Of course, I don't tell her I'm a psych nurse—nurses like her don't think psych nurses are real nurses—but I do confess to being new at the sport.

"Does that kind of thing happen very often?" I ask the nurse.

"Slipping off the lift? No, but we see plenty of action here: collisions, concussions, broken bones."

"About how many injuries do you see in a week?" I ask.

She eyes me with suspicion. "If you came here to ask me that, maybe this isn't going to be your kind of sport."

I think I agree with her.

This time, on our way home when we pass the skeletons of burnt pines, I notice wreaths of new green growth at the base of the charred trees. I point to them and say to the kids. "See? The forest is already growing back."

Just like my patients.

As we wind through the mountains, I think about how trauma changes a person's internal landscape. Nothing is as it was. People feel lost and confused. Roles change in the face of pain and disability. In group, Ilan and I dig around our patients' lives for some evidence of roots like those of chaparral plants that can bear devastation and support the creation of new life. We listen for the echo of a deep well of faith, optimism, or hope. Hearing those life-giving gurgles gives me confidence that my trauma patients will survive the journey ahead.

When our trauma support group last met, we talked about the idea of trauma as a transformative experience in a person's life. Despite our culture's penchant for these stories, I fear this is the exception and not the rule. However, I know of at least a couple of patients who have transformed their lives by dedicating themselves to helping others. Yvonne, the young wife whose husband shielded her from a gunman's bullet in the law firm, has quit her job and now works for an anti-gun lobby. The young Scottish woman, a former ski champion who was badly injured in a motorcycle accident, is working with injured children. Like new green growth at the base of charred trees, transformation after trauma may occur more commonly than I know.

Having left the mountains, we enter the urban landscape of Sacramento where I think about the defective deck for the first time all weekend. My mind replays the look on the boys' faces as they recounted lifting and holding up the deck, hearing the girls' cries of pain while feeling impotent to help them, and all the while wondering when the paramedics would arrive.

Sometimes I feel like that's what we do at the hospital. We hold up the weight of the world. And, in doing so, we hear screams and witness the suffering that sometimes becomes our screams and our suffering, only we choke it back and continue bearing the weight without complaining and without acknowledging that we too need relief.

19

It has a name!

It's dark. My children and I are running away from someone
or something. They hang on my arms, ride my back, and hold
onto the hem of my long skirt. Hearing the thudding of steps
behind us, we scramble over a short fence to get to a tall tree. I
whisper to them, "Climb the tree!"

Somehow, we all climb the tree, and hide in the branches.
Just when I think we are safe, shots are fired, then silence. When
I look for my kids, I see them dangling lifeless from the tree like
overripe fruit. I scream.

It's 3:07 a.m. I lay frozen in bed, aware of my heart beating
like the wings of a frightened bird. It was only a dream, only a
dream, only a dream. Brian turns toward me, mumbles, and places
a warm hand on my forearm. The cat lies pressed against my other
side. Then I hear noises. Could the gunshots in the dream be real?
A man down the street was murdered while walking home from the
subway station. Cars have been stolen. Someone tried to break into
my neighbor's home through her window. I sit up in bed and listen
to the sound of something clicking. I grab my glasses and tiptoe

toward the boys' bedroom. In front of me, the bathroom door is half closed. Behind the door, the figure of Rosalina is bent over her children's bodies.

After catching my breath, I refocus my eyes to find nothing amiss. Silently, I turn the doorknob to the boys' bedroom and push the door open. Both of them lay breathing and untouched.

Thank you, God.

In the next room, Corianne is curled into a tight ball clutching the ever-present Po, who like me, is wide-awake. I kiss Corianne and Po and go upstairs to scan the street. All is quiet. I slip back into bed and listen to my heart, hoping it will slow down enough to lull me to sleep.

The week fills with the usual assortment of cases: an 84-year-old woman beaten by a home intruder; a skin-popping prostitute with AIDS; a young woman hit by a stray bullet meant for a gang member; a recently married construction worker with a crushed pelvis; a speed freak with a stab wound and a bad attitude; two more young African-American boys riddled with bullets.

Although only four people appear for trauma support group, this week's meeting is particularly poignant. A graduate psychology student describes how he was waiting at a bus stop when a car full of young rowdies stopped in front of him and screamed, "Die, faggot!"

A second later, they jumped out of the car wielding baseball bats. The student says that, during the beating, he deliberately covered the left side of his head with his arms "so that no matter what else they did to me, I would be able to talk about it later."

After group, when the last person has left, I stay inside our cozy refuge and cry.

In early November, I attend two days of the five-day International Society for Traumatic Stress Studies conference at a downtown hotel. It's a large conference with close to a thousand participants. This is the twelfth annual meeting and the first time I've participated.

I attend the opening plenary session entitled, "Prevention of Interpersonal Violence: Criminal Justice vs. Public Health Approaches" during which a police chief talks about responding to domestic violence with mandatory arrests, community policing, anti-stalking laws, and penalties for repeat offenders. A physician from the Centers for Disease Control (CDC) talks about preventing youth violence, violence against women, and whether drug offenders and sexual predators should be given mental health treatment or longer prison terms. After that, the morning's choices are overwhelming. In one time slot, there are forty-four different presentations from which to choose. Subjects range from studies of Vietnam vets to children of Holocaust survivors to survivors of childhood trauma, and issues related to critical-incident debriefing.

I decide to go to a talk called, "Beyond Conflict Resolution: School-based Treatment of Children Exposed to Violence." The talk attracts me because the chair, Robert Pynoos, takes a community psychiatry approach in his work screening and treating at-risk kids in Los Angeles. After years of picking up the pieces of adults who were abused and neglected as children, I'm interested in early intervention.

The discussant, Lenore Terr, a San Francisco psychiatrist who has done pioneering research and treatment with traumatized children, ends the session by stating that providing eighteen months of individualized therapy for every child victim of violence would be far less expensive to society in the long run than waiting until those kids are grown up. It makes good sense. What if Keith had been treated by a child therapist after his mother's suicide? What if we could rescue and treat child victims of sexual abuse? Maybe then, abused children would have a chance to grow up without feeling compelled to obliterate their memories with alcohol or heroin. Maybe they could feel their lives had value instead of living from one suicide attempt to another.

During the break for lunch, I leave the hotel and walk down Market Street to Stacy's Books where I pick up a copy of *Emotional Intelligence* by Daniel Goleman, a book I've been wanting to read. Slipping into a nearby Japanese restaurant, I leaf through it in between mouthfuls of sashimi and seaweed salad.

At the beginning of his book, Goleman, a psychologist who writes for *The New York Times,* acknowledges that "the place of feeling in mental life has been surprisingly slighted by research."

He defines emotional intelligence as the ability to control one's impulses, to empathize, to read emotions in others, to self-motivate, and to navigate interpersonal relationships. *Now I'm listening.* He describes how scientists are collecting neurobiological data through recent advances in brain imagery.

The hard science of feelings? What's next? A little respect for psychiatry?

Flipping through the book, mindful that I have to get back to the conference, I see a heading that stirs my heart: "Emotional Relearning and Recovery from Trauma" in which he talks about how important it is to retell and reconstruct the trauma story. *Yes! This is what we do!* When I see another title, "Psychotherapy as an Emotional Tutorial," I'm ready to lay down my life for Daniel Goleman.

Apparently, I've been starved for a little professional validation.

I go back to the conference and attend another couple of sessions, hear horrible stories, listen to sad statistics, and feel myself droop under the weight of it all. That night after we put the kids to bed, I dive back into the book. In page after page, Dr. Goleman describes why emotional intelligence is more highly correlated with success than intellectual brilliance. He cites studies that demonstrate how emotional support for medical and surgical patients boosts their immune systems and hastens recovery. I can't wait to tell Janice and Antionette about it. All of us could use a lift, especially after the most recent announcement that more budget cuts must be made and that to survive, we must improve our productivity numbers.

The next day's program offers a surprising array of presentations on "Occupational Trauma." Each one seems to use a different name to describe the stress experienced by caregivers and crisis workers: "PTSD" among the police; "traumatic stress" in emergency medical personnel; "secondary stress reactions" among therapists; "compassion fatigue" in social work. I attend one called, "Vicarious Trauma: Creating a Resilient Workplace."

Vicarious Trauma? I've never heard that phrase. At the appointed time, all twenty-five of us in the room give the speaker our attention. "Trauma workers live in a world of charred skin, festering wounds, and shattered bones. We hear cries of suffering and smell the stench of decay. We witness injustice, anger, and grief. These images are burned into our psyches. Instead of fading from memory, they may accumulate over time and interfere with our own lives."

I poke myself in the ribs. *That's you, babe.* Every time I pass a certain spot on the Great Highway along Ocean Beach, I think about the eighteen-year-old bicyclist who lost his leg there and, further up the hill, the twenty-four-year-old motorcyclist who lost his arm.

The presenter describes how trauma workers often develop stress symptoms that mimic their patients' symptoms—paranoia, a sense of doom, numbing, hypervigilance, anxiety, nightmares, intrusive images of trauma, anger, fear, an inability to experience pleasure, and social withdrawal.

This sounds familiar!

Laurie, honey, cut the drama. You might have a touch of these symptoms but let's face it, you're not on the streets pulling people from fires or seeing bodies with blown-off faces.

"Vicarious trauma," says another person on the panel, "is an occupational hazard for empathic caregivers. Our exposure to victims and victimizers challenges our most basic assumptions about the world and disrupts our sense of safety, predictability, and trust. Vicarious trauma can cause us to question our effectiveness as caregivers, as people, even as partners in intimate relationships."

"Vicarious trauma" as in nightmares or the drum roll in my chest when I wake up in the morning or my incessant worry about my kids' safety, is that what they're talking about?

In response to a question, the main presenter talks about "pervasive institutional denial" that prevents agencies from acknowledging the toll that trauma work takes on providers. Antionette used the phrase "institutional denial" during our presentation in San Diego to describe the lack of metal detectors in the hospital. Janice thinks it's a factor in why my requests for process time, time to discuss our feelings about what we witness in our work, have always been rebuffed.

Another participant asks, "Isn't it cheaper for them to look the other way? If administrators were to acknowledge these symptoms, they would have to do something to help their employees!"

"I don't think it's cheaper to look the other way," says a panelist. "It costs a lot to replace highly experienced and trained staff. It would be far cheaper to offer supportive measures—a break from the front lines, debriefing groups, educational leave, as a few examples—than to have to replace burned-out employees."

The discussion makes me think about Ruby, the former trauma nurse coordinator on 4D, and the latest casualty, the art therapist on pediatrics who, like Ruby, resigned after feeling unraveled by the violence around her.

It has a name!

Another panelist takes the microphone. "A supportive work environment is one where time is set aside for staff members to share their feelings with each other about the work they do. In fact, according to a recent study, just offering time in weekly staff meetings to talk about how caregivers were coping with work was correlated with greater staff retention and higher job satisfaction."

Everyone in the room knows intuitively that this is so though it feels great to hear it said out loud by people who study these things. Inside, I'm rejoicing.

Hallelujah! Yes, feelings count. Professionals have them. If we share them, we feel better. Patricia, where are you? You need to hear this loud and clear!

On the subway ride home, I think about this new term, "vicarious trauma." Yes, the symptoms I've been experiencing — shortness of breath, nightmares, intrusive images, palpitations, paranoia — have a name! Suddenly I feel like Helen Keller in that moment when she made the connection between the fingers that Annie Sullivan pressed into her hand to spell "w-a-t-e-r" and the wet liquid she pumped from the well. I had begun to wonder if I was in danger of losing my grip; if the random trauma and human cruelty I've witnessed every day at work for the past four years has been affecting me because of some defect in my character. Now I know that it may have something to do with the dose of trauma I'm exposed to every week in the absence of enough support to ameliorate it. The fact that my symptoms have a name means that it happens to other people besides me, that I am not alone.

Still, I feel ashamed of not being more resilient. Why can't I let people's stories slide off my back? How do Janice and Antionette do it? Maybe they don't. The truth is that we don't spend much time talking about it.

When I return to work after the conference, I feel newly energized. Since they already call me the Process Queen, I've decided to live up to that name. Now that I've been reassured that it's normal for caring, sensitive people to experience distress after years of listening to others' pain, my mission is to change our "suck it up" culture.

"Patricia had to attend a meeting downtown," says Donald when all of us have arrived for psych-consult rounds. Just like old times, he takes the helm. "Any announcements?"

"I have a managed care joke," offers Barry.

"Maybe at the end," says Donald with a smile. "Any patients we need to discuss?"

"Mr. Savard died last night," says Antionette. Her voice, usually strong and resonant, conveys weariness. She casts her eyes downward.

"An hour before he died, he was pleading for his life. The docs refused to intubate him. They said there was no point because he would never get off the ventilator."

In the silence that follows, I recall prior discussions about this man. He had been a theater director of some renown in New York City. When his health started to fail, he moved to San Francisco to be with friends. Two months ago, he was admitted to the AIDS unit with breathing difficulties. Then his lungs collapsed. Each time chest tubes were placed to re-inflate his lungs, they clotted off. The treatment team recommended surgery. Mr. Savard wanted to try nontraditional methods of healing including hypnosis and meditation. The more the doctors pushed for a surgical solution, the more the patient was convinced he could heal himself through positive imagery and optimism. Although it drove his doctors crazy, members of our consult service who worked closely with him—especially Antionette, Donald, and Barry—marveled at his refusal to be intimidated and his insistence on remaining in control.

I sense that this is my moment. *Easy, girl. Don't come on like gangbusters.* "I never met Mr. Savard," I say, "but I've heard many people around this table talk about him. Something about this man was very compelling."

I was hoping that this comment would springboard us into an old style McLean Hospital process group. No such luck. Aside from Barry tapping the eraser end of a pencil on the table, everyone else seems to have traveled inward. What I know about achieving cultural change in organizations is that the proposed change must be embraced by leadership. Under Donald, we occasionally shared our feelings about patients, but he didn't allow us to dwell there for long. If Patricia were in the room now, there would be no opportunity for such a discussion. Patricia fills meetings with one announcement after the other. Then she passes out the weekly productivity reports where we see numerical evidence of our worth to the organization in terms of billable minutes. Today, with Patricia out and Donald no longer officially in charge, I decide to chip away at the status quo.

"I'm going to go out on a limb here. We don't usually talk in personal terms about our patients, but this patient seemed special. He was an educated, middle-aged, professional man with AIDS. For the last two months, you spent more time talking about him than any of our other patients. Right now, there's a lot of emotion in the room. I think it would be good if those of you who worked with him talk about the experience and how you feel about the way he died. Even I feel sad thinking about this man and I've never met him."

Silence. Of course, silence. Why did I think it could be different? Nothing's changed. It's my issue. I shouldn't keep pushing it on everyone else.

Barry clears his throat. He starts to say something, but backs off. He shakes his head and looks down at the table. More silence.

A voice, Donald's voice, low and thoughtful, slides into the silence like a canoe gliding into still water. *Donald!*

"I want to say that it's true; being with this patient in the existential sense was unnerving in ways I probably can't fully appreciate or articulate. I'm sure it has to do with the obvious fact that he was also in his fifties and overeducated. And that he represented the huge hit that the creative world has taken because of AIDS. But I suspect it also has something to do with my own mortality, which, like him, I don't want to face."

Donald! I would never have figured him to be the one to get the ball rolling.

Oops, strike that last thought. The ball is not rolling. We sit in silence. Janice's expression communicates that she would participate if she could. Like me, she never met the patient.

Barry tries again. "For me, it was hard to hear his desperation. It was really hard feeling helpless to do anything to change the outcome. Physicians are supposed to cure people but we can't cure AIDS yet."

Others speak of their frustration with the patient. The psychiatrists were called in to do medication evaluations but Mr. Savard wanted them instead to hold his hand. The neuropsychologists had been asked to do psych testing but Mr. Savard dismissed them when he understood the purpose of the visit.

"The interns and residents weren't too thrilled when Mr. Savard called them by their first names," says Barry. "It also didn't help when he assigned them to research medications and treatments on the Internet."

Everyone smiles at the role reversal scenario he describes. "We're just not used to patients like Mr. Savard who take charge of their own care."

"That's true," says Antionette, perking up a bit. "I encouraged him to assert his right to be an equal member of his treatment team. I respected his desire to use hypnotherapy and meditation to control his anxiety. It was OK by me because it benefited him."

Antionette pulls out a crumpled tissue and wipes her eyes. "Personally, I've never spent time with someone so close to death who held onto life so tightly. He knew it was his last act—the man was brilliant—but he constantly searched the literature and called the experts looking for a way to rewrite the script."

Antionette stops but she is not yet finished. She steadies her voice and continues.

"Maybe because I'm African-American, in his eyes he didn't need to compete with me or prove anything to me. I became his 'assistant.' It was OK with me. I went home and cried every night because I knew how tired he was, how much he wanted to live."

She pauses and bites her lower lip. "The thing that's hardest for me is that even though he refused surgery, Mr. Savard was clear from the beginning that if his oxygen level got too low, he wanted to be placed on a ventilator." Antionette's shoulders sag. Her eyes fill with tears.

"What I don't understand," she says, "is if the docs felt that mechanical ventilation was not an option for him, why didn't they tell him that earlier? Why did it come to a showdown in the eleventh hour?"

This time when no one speaks, it is because we've never seen Antionette be anything but controlled in meetings. In private and with patients, I have witnessed the depth of her caring, but in meetings she remains businesslike, speaking only when necessary as if she doesn't want to do anything to prolong the time she spends away from her patients.

Gordon, a psychiatrist who evaluates and treats AIDS patients and infrequently comes to these meetings, breaks the silence. "Mr. Savard's cognition remained intact throughout his hospitalization, which is unusual for our AIDS patients. Although wasting was evident in his face and his body, he still had a regal, imperious bearing."

Gordon unpeels a banana as he speaks. "The staff and even I, at times, felt impatient with his strong need for control. I understood their frustration with him. As far as my personal feelings, I don't allow myself that luxury. If I let myself get emotional about my patients, I couldn't do this work. So sorry, Laurie. I know that sharing feelings is basically a good thing but not in this case, at least not for me."

Ouch! I'm not going to argue with Gordon but I do wonder about the price he pays for walling off like that. I hope he has someone to turn to when he needs to talk. As a gay psychiatrist working exclusively with AIDS patients, he carries a heavier load than most of us.

After we listen to each other sigh for a few more excruciatingly long moments, another voice — soft, female, and rarely heard — enters the airspace. Megan, one of the psychiatric residents, practically whispers, "For me, it's hard to work with AIDS patients in general. So many of them look like concentration camp survivors. But, uh, I guess the real issue..."

Megan clears her throat. A pained expression seizes her face. "The real issue for me is that my brother was just diagnosed with HIV. So, it's really hard to listen to these cases."

We are again thrown into a centrifugal silence until Janice bails us out. "Oh Megan, that's so, so sad. It's especially hard because in the course of our work we witness all the stages of chronic illness. When someone in our family becomes ill, we know what's coming."

Megan nods and manages a weak smile. "That's all I want to say."

"It's true," says Barry. "We avoid talking about how our patients affect us but sometimes patients get to us for reasons that have to do with our own personalities or family dynamics. It would be nice to know we could use staff meeting as a place to sort some of that out."

Donald checks his watch. "It's time to end. I'd like to say this was a good discussion. Thank you, everyone."

Before leaving, Donald looks my way and nods.

On the way back to our office suite, Janice hugs me. "Congratulations! You finally did it. Let's hope it's the start of something new."

It has a name!

Barry gives me a high five. "Good going. Hope it sticks when Patricia gets back."

"Don't count on it," I say. "But let's hear the managed care joke Donald wouldn't let you tell."

As we walk down the long corridor from administration to our office suite, Barry holds forth. "So a doctor, a lawyer, and a managed care executive are all waiting in line to get into heaven. St. Peter says to the doctor, 'It's getting crowded in heaven. I need to make sure you truly belong here. So tell me, what good works did you do down on earth?'"

"Well," says the doctor. "I devoted my life to caring for the poor who otherwise wouldn't have been able to afford good healthcare. In fact, I set up free clinics all over the world."

"Very good," says St. Peter. "You may enter."

"And what about you?" he asks of the lawyer. "Why should I allow you in heaven?"

"I devoted my life to fighting for health-care benefits for people working in factories and in fields. As a result of my work, children of poor people now receive free immunizations."

"Excellent," says St. Peter, "You may enter heaven. But what about you?" he says to the managed care administrator.

"I set up an efficient system so that doctors could see five patients every hour. In addition, I made sure that no one stayed in the hospital longer than absolutely necessary thereby saving millions of dollars. In this way, I've made health care available to more people."

"I see," says St. Peter. "For you, I can authorize a 3-day stay."

"I'll have to tell my doctor that one," says Janice.

"I'll have to tell it to Brian. He'll appreciate hearing a joke where the lawyer actually comes off as a good guy."

Once inside the privacy of our office, Antionette squeezes my shoulder. "Thank you for pushing us to talk. I needed that."

The Comfort Garden

The next morning, I arrive before seven in order to talk to the night shift about dealing with personality-disordered patients. It's not "billable" time but I don't care. When nurses are skilled in managing the emotional needs of these patients, the patients are less likely to leave against medical advice, and less likely to erupt into violence when they hit a snag. Offering classes gives much-needed support to the staff nurses who, in my opinion, have the toughest job in the hospital.

Stopping by our office before the class in order to pick up some articles, I notice that Patricia's door is open. I walk over to say "good morning" and find her hunched over her desk, redlining passages of a report. Stacks of papers are piled everywhere. When she looks up, her face is pale and puffy as if she's been working through the night. The harsh florescent lights magnify the dark hollows under her eyes. We are both surprised to see each other here so early. I tell her about my class and ask about her excuse. She lists a number of projects she leads, all of which require her to write grant proposals and progress reports.

"I don't know how you do so much," I say.

"I really don't have a choice," she replies with a fleeting smile. "My boss has lots of ideas about new programs that he wants up and running and I'm the one elected to do it."

"So he gets the credit but you get stuck with the nuts and bolts?"

"Something like that."

"Do you get to take a vacation any time soon?"

"Va-ca-tion?" Patricia utters the word as if she were a foreigner learning the language, then laughs. "Oh, that. Actually, I'll be off for a month in January. It's just that I have so much to do before then." Her voice trails off.

I take an early lunch in The Comfort Garden. Even in November, a few things are still in bloom: the Princess Plant with its velvety purple petals the width of a human heart, and the brugmansia from which large bell-shaped orange blossoms spill like a display of birthday hats. When I sit on the bench in the middle of the garden and look closely, I see dahlias in decay and roses that look exhausted after a long performance season.

Is psychiatry also in decay? It feels as though we've abandoned something wise and precious, an essential ingredient in a time-honored recipe. We may know more about neurotransmitters and neural pathways, important in themselves and surely the key to our future understanding of the brain, but somewhere along the line in the quest for legitimacy, we've dismissed something warm and vibrant and connective. If we are not in touch with our own feelings, complex and contradictory, how will we gauge our patients' feelings? If we expunge shame, guilt, and anger from our own bodies, how will we respond to our patients when they grapple with these feelings, ones that pills cannot plumb?

I've worked in both professional worlds, psychodynamic and pharmaceutical, and both are needed, not one or the other. A psychotic patient responds to anti-psychotic medication. Lithium allows bipolar people to lead normal lives. In the absence of a therapeutic relationship with a caring and consistent therapist, however, these patients are far less likely to stay on their medications. The problem is that relationships are devalued in a "managed care" environment.

"I've had it with watching the clock," I tell Janice when I return to the office. "I'm going to do what I can for as many people as possible, but I'm not going to do a half-assed job just to keep my numbers up. They can't even bill for us nurses so what's the point in filling out the goddamn forms except to track us. What are they going to do—fire me? It's a civil service job! As long as I don't harm patients, I could be here forever."

"I know," says Janice. "The system is crazy and it makes us crazy too. But it's hard not to buy into it."

To feel good about the quality of my work, I will continue to give classes and set up care conferences. The system is wrong. Educating and training staff nurses how to better respond to their patients' emotional needs seems plenty productive to me. A mentor once told me, "Control is what you take."

20

The vacation

The bright-eyed young men and women funneling into the lobby this morning wear short white jackets identifying them as first year medical residents. They remind me that this week, the start of the new medical rotation, marks the beginning of my fifth year here at The General. I am envious of the excitement shining through their faces, the challenge of a new adventure, the knowledge that although the next three years will be difficult at times, completing a residency in their chosen specialties will launch them into a new and rewarding life.

Our annual Cape Cod vacation can't come soon enough for me. The trauma unit has been besieged by yet another bout of necrotizing fasciitis and with that, the predictable struggles of adequately medicating drug addicts. This time, to help the nurses empathize with these difficult patients, I taught a class on the family dynamics of drug addiction emphasizing that most prostitutes and many addicts are survivors of multiple episodes of childhood sexual trauma, neglect, and/or extreme emotional abuse and that these experiences corrupt morals and distort personalities. Understanding our patients' behaviors can help the staff to avoid judging their lifestyles.

One of the second-year trauma residents overheard part of the class and told me I should present it to the entire trauma department.

"Tell them to invite me," I replied.

My first patient of the day, a middle-aged guy found on the street with burns and lacerations all over his body, refuses to speak to me.

"I don't want to talk about it," he growls. "Talking won't help."

Something about his tone tells me I won't be able to convince him otherwise. I say goodbye and move on. The next patient creeps me out not only because of the teardrop tattoo under the far corner of his eye signifying that he has murdered someone, but by the furtive way he makes eye contact, the utter flatness of his voice, and the way he rocks his body throughout our conversation, all of which hint at horrors in his past. Small and slightly built, he talks about how powerful he is, how smart he is, how he will stalk his assailant and make him beg for mercy. If he knows his assailant's name, he won't tell me. I suspect he knows that I would be obliged to report such a specific threat to the police. I've met a number of shady personalities here but this guy induces nausea. I can't exit his room fast enough.

Prudence Weinstein is my last patient on my last day of work before we leave for Cape Cod. An 81-year-old woman with breast cancer, she is recovering from surgery that removed her left breast. Although medically ready for discharge to a skilled nursing facility, Mrs. Weinstein insists instead on going home. The problem, according to her social worker, is that her apartment is a public health nightmare, too stuffed with junk to accommodate the home health nurse who will need a modicum of space to change her patient's dressing. Given this patient's history of hoarding, the social worker has asked us to evaluate her mental competence. The psychiatrists usually take these cases, but today, I will screen her for them.

The three inches of Ms. Weinstein's wavy hair closest to her head are snow white. The next six inches, strawberry blond, curve into a pageboy around her wide face that is dominated by hawkish, deep set eyes and a slightly hooked nose.

Mrs. Weinstein tells me she worked "for decades" as an optometric technician. Her husband died thirty years ago; her only child, a daughter, died thirteen years ago of ovarian cancer. She becomes tearful when she mentions the recent deaths of friends and refuses to talk further. She perks up, however, when she recounts her days as a political activist.

"I always wore a full-length black coat covered with political buttons to the rallies," she says. "It attracted the attention of Charles Kuralt, the journalist. He interviewed me on TV."

Although she never attended college, Mrs. Weinstein educated herself by reading magazines and books. "I have piles of them at home" along with boxes of clothes she meant to give away but never did.

Mrs. Weinstein does not use the word "cancer." Instead she talks about her "failing health." When I tell her that the amount of things that fill her home makes it impossible for follow-up care, she admits to having a problem. She knows she risks eviction and loss of all of her belongings.

"Who would I be without my things?" she asks. "If I throw something away, it's like I'm throwing away a part of myself. Can you understand that?"

I understand that Mrs. Weinstein experiences her "self" in external things like her belongings whereas I experience my "self" in my role as a nurse, even more than as a wife and mother.

Is writing about my patients a kind of hoarding? When I'm old, I picture myself reading my journals, recapturing meaningful moments with patients, reassuring myself that I spent a big chunk of my life doing something worthwhile for others. Without my journals to document these moments, I too would feel bereft. What if I couldn't work as a nurse? Who would I be then? How would I define my "self?" Just thinking about such a loss makes me feel anxious.

In my note, I write: "The patient understands that her hoarding is pathological, unsanitary, and unsafe. However, her possessions help her to maintain a fragile sense of self-esteem and control, particularly in the face of many losses and deteriorating health over which she has no control."

I have no suggestions for what to do about the immediate problem. Forcibly separating her from her possessions seems cruel. Psychotherapy and anti-depressants could be useful, but they take time. I will ask one of the psychiatrists to evaluate her for medication. Maybe a student could follow her in the new outpatient clinic. That's about all that I can do for Mrs. Weinstein.

I say goodbye to Mrs. Weinstein and feel a pang of regret when I realize that most likely, we'll not see each other again. "I hope things work out for the best," I tell her, knowing that soon she will lose the glue that holds her together.

In the car on my way to the kids' schools, I think about how we know who we are. Most of us are defined by what we do or who we are in relation to others. We are nurses or cabinet makers or cops. We're someone's partner, someone's child, or someone's parent. What if, like Prudence, you are long retired and your family and friends have died? Absent a life filled with other people, or pets, or even plants to care for, maybe you know who you are by your stuff: your books, your hobbies, your collections. Without them, perhaps your feelings tell you who you are. What if feelings conjure too much pain?

On Saturday morning, the day before we leave, Brian plays with the kids in the backyard so that I can straighten the house before my mother and stepfather arrive. They'll housesit while we're away and stay a few days longer upon our return.

Before heading to the airport, I step outside to tell Brian that

The vacation

I'm on my way. On the grass, Danny is mixing dirt with water and passing drippy globs of muck to Corianne and Benny who are applying it to their faces, arms, and legs like war paint. A mud helmet covers Benny's blond hair. They giggle as Brian videotapes the scene. His voiceover mimics Marty Stouffer, the slow-speaking narrator on the TV show, *Wild America:* "Whenever possible, mud children roll in mud to camouflage themselves from their mothers."

"Jesus Christ, Brian! Why did you let them do that? I just got the house cleaned up!"

"It's fun, Mommy! Come be a mud person with us!"

"Arghh!!! Brian!"

Sometimes he of the brilliant mind has no common sense.

"Lighten up, honey. We're just having some fun."

Lighten up? All I can think about are walls with mud prints, the tub and floors I just cleaned, hair that will need washing, dirty towels that will need laundering and all this before my parents arrive. I slam the door behind me and bang my fist on the table. Goddamn right, I need a vacation.

With travel delays, we arrive at our Cape Cod cottage just before midnight. The moist air is thick with the odor of decay, signaling low tide on this moonless night.

This is the fourth year we've rented Mim's place, a rambling beach house on the street where Brian's mom lives and a short walk to the bay. In the morning, the boys make a beeline for the wicker toy chest where Danny spies the WW1 flying ace hat that he wore nonstop last year, grabbing it before Benny can lay claim to it. Later in the morning, he discovers the Power Ranger figure he left behind last year. No wonder the kids think we own the place.

By noon, all six of Brian's brothers and sisters and their families have gathered at Grammy's house for the annual reunion. All except one sibling have strong political views ranging from extreme right to extreme left and everything in between. While they debate in Grammy's kitchen, their booming voices drive their spouses outside. Meanwhile, the kids have a grand time playing in the sprinkler on Grammy's manicured lawn. As is our tradition, Grammy takes me on a tour of her garden where she points out vines with voluptuous tomatoes, a huge bouquet of basil, and the six-foot-tall stalks of white Casablanca lilies that perfume her screened-in back porch. Later, adults and kids head to the beach for a game of Frisbee. At low tide, we have the run of the beach as far as the eye can see.

Once again, my graduate school friend, Jeanne, is vacationing nearby. Early one afternoon she opens the screen door to our cottage.

"Hi, beautiful!" she cries. "I've missed you so fucking much! How the hell are you, honey?" Jeanne hasn't changed. She still swears like a sailor and has a heart as big as the sea.

The day could not be more perfect. We walk along the water's edge — our bare feet crunching into wet sand, our arms around each other, away from the crowds of vacationing families, and toward the creek that empties into the bay. A cadre of gulls swoops overhead scavenging for unattended food. Pea-green beach grass half-submerged in the oncoming tide flutters in the gentle breeze. On the way to the water, we pass a beefy young dad helping his baby daughter take her first steps on the sand.

"Remember those days?" asks Jeanne.

Her girls are eight and ten. Corianne, who is now nine, was thrilled to see them again.

"It all goes too fast, sugar. Way too fast."

Reaching the pool where the creek empties into the ocean, we wade into the cool water.

"Anyway, what's new? Still hanging in there?"

"I'm not sure."

"Why not, sweetheart?"

"Sometimes I think my mind has been warped by listening to

all these trauma stories. You know that dad and his baby girl we just passed? This is what went through my head: in a few years, he might be molesting her. How twisted is that? I can't help it. It's like I think the absolute worst about people."

Jeanne takes both of my hands in hers.

"Honey babe, you gotta take care of yourself. That's what I'm gonna do. Back to home and hearth for me."

"What are you talking about? You love your old folks. How could you leave them?"

"I reached the point of no return. Come, I'll tell you the story on the way back."

We towel off, reapply sunscreen, and begin retracing our steps back to Mim's cottage.

"Remember in school how we learned to re-orient demented elderly patients to the day, date, month, and year? Well, not any-more. There's no point. Now you gotta just go with them. If an old woman thinks I'm her mother, I'm her mother. If she's got to work out a conflict there—and you can tell because she keeps talking about the same thing—then I play the role of the person she needs to work it out with. Honey, I had an 86-year-old woman who regressed back to being a small, scared child. She asked me, 'Mommy, will you sleep with me?' And you know what? I did. I climbed in bed and put my arm around her and she calmed right down. Wouldn't you know it, my supervisor came by that minute and found me in bed with her and reported me to the director. The next day I had to meet with him, a sweet Jewish doc, such a mensch. I told him exactly what happened. I said, 'Jerry, do you understand why I did that?' He said he understood totally and that it was the best thing I could have done for that lady. I could have kissed him! However, the nursing supervisor was pissed when she found out that he agreed with me. And baby, that broad ain't going nowhere. She's been there for twenty-three years. She supports her mother and her disabled husband. She rides my ass whenever she gets the chance because I have a master's degree and make a few bucks more than she does. She graduated from a diploma school when God was in knee pants. I figure, fuck her. I don't need this job. I'm outta here as of next month. Outta nursing, honey. Too much crap. I'm gonna stay home with my girls and give 'em all I got."

I don't know what to say. Jeanne is one of the most passionate and dedicated nurses I've ever known.

"You mean you're leaving nursing?"

"Damn tootin', sugar. I've had it. You and I are the last of a dying breed. Who would want to be a nurse now when you could make twice the salary for half the shit, sitting on your ass somewhere in an office with a view?"

Last summer, Brian and I discovered that if we swim up the tidal creek during the last half hour of the incoming tide, we can float with the current back to the ocean during ebb tide. The day before we leave the Cape for New York City where Brian has to take a deposition, we leave the kids with Grammy and walk to the creek, the same spot where Jeanne and I took a dip.

Except for an occasional dive-bombing greenhead fly, we swim undisturbed deep into the salt marsh. Most of the time we breast stroke with our heads above water, listening to the birdcalls that replace the sounds of children playing on the beach. Suddenly, a school of small silver fish surfaces, glinting in the sun like coins tossed in a fountain. I feel myself relax in the moment, surrounded by blue sky and marsh grass waving in the slight breeze.

We float on our backs during slack tide and wait to be nudged gently toward the ocean. Slack tide is like nature's Sabbath, the quiet stillness between ebb and flow. I listen to my heart pumping strong and slow, the filling and emptying of air through my lungs and I'm aware for the first time in a long time that my body feels at peace.

The vacation

While I float in the buoyant water and absorb the sun's warmth, each breath deepens and draws me into a fathomless universe. Life happens, whether we want it to or not. The only thing we have some control over is the pace of life's energy as it moves through us. I want that pace to be this pace. I want to be attuned and awed as I am now. How can I bring this home with me?

"Let's make another baby," whispers Brian.

I know that he's remembering the night on the beach ten years ago when we conceived Corianne.

"Get yourself a younger wife, sweetheart," I laugh.

"Come on," he insists. "Let's try."

Drawing closer to the spongy banks of the creek, we notice dozens of fiddler crabs marching in unison among the stalks of marsh grass, a scene worthy of a Japanese horror flick. There will be no splendor in the grass on this day though. We head back to the cottage in time for a little afternoon delight before the children return from Grammy's. Cape Cod not only renews our spirits after a year of work and child-rearing, it renews our romance. It's good to know that while the spark that lit our way to each other may need a good dusting, it still glows bright.

21

The confrontation

Mr. Livermore sits on his bed cross-legged like a bloated white Buddha with finely chiseled features, hairless but for two manicured lines of gray moustache above his thin lips. Cool blue eyes with slightly raised eyebrows appraise me as I stand in the doorway awaiting permission to enter.

"A mental health nurse has been summoned to speak with me?" he asks in a tone of incredulity infused with a perfect Vincent Price articulation. "Have I done something to offend my caregivers or do they think I've lost my marbles?"

Mr. Livermore's pleasing features quickly lose ground to his acidic voice.

"I see lots of patients on this unit," I say in a cheerful tone meant to put him at ease and to avoid answering his question. "It's tough being a patient in the hospital. After a few days here, most people become depressed or frustrated or irritable—with good reason."

"Oh? And what might those reasons be?"

Oy, again with the stage speech.

He clasps his hands—both laden with silver rings—and sets them on his sternum. One eyebrow arches while the other one crouches down.

"To be honest with you Mr. Livermore, the only happy place in a hospital is maternity. Everywhere else, people are sick. They're in pain; they're lonely; they're frightened about the future. On top of that, the nurses are busy and patients have to wait a lot. Sometimes that's hard to accept."

"Congratulations," he replies, extending a multi-ringed hand that encases mine like a fox trap, metal against skin, jarring the bones in my fingers. "You're the first one who has made any sense to me. Indeed, the first person who has bothered to explain to me that I'm not even supposed to be happy here."

I am confused. Is he mocking me or can he be serious? And when is he going to let go of my hand?

"You see," he continues. "I've been quite miserable and it's helpful to know that my expectations of being well cared for here were simply too high. I thank you for setting me straight."

He squeezes my hand before finally springing it free.

No wonder the nurses feel defensive as soon as they walk through his door. Mr. Livermore repels people, not a good strategy for a hospital patient who is dependent on the nursing staff for care and comfort. He didn't help himself by telling one of the nurses that a monkey could change his dressing better than she did, or by remarking to another—an excellent nurse—that if she took care of him the way she took care of herself, referring to her obesity, his life would be imperiled. My challenge is to make Mr. Livermore palatable to the staff so they don't ignore him, or worse, abandon him. To do that, I have to find something likable about him, something that will make him a more sympathetic character.

"So how has it been for you to be cooped up here?" I ask.

"Do me the honor of sitting down and I'll tell you whatever you want to know."

In the manner of a stage magician, Mr. Livermore waves his forearms in the air and flicks his wrist at the chair across the room. I almost expect the chair to move itself close to his bed. With a heavy heart, I sit, knowing that I've committed myself to an epic when all I wanted was the CliffsNotes version.

"I am not a patient man to begin with," he says with a sigh of exasperation, "but this place is a model of inefficiency. This morning, it took three hours to complete a procedure that should have taken thirty minutes at best."

He checks my response. I consciously knit my brows together and nod, "Mmm."

Green light noted, he continues his soliloquy. "I have also suffered a number of unfortunate complications to the esophagectomy such that I no longer have trust in my doctors. Accordingly, I have requested that Dr. Price, the surgical attending, be solely responsible for my case. I simply can't have a different junior doctor every day. It is so tiresome. I'm here to recuperate, not to in-DOC-tri-nate, if I may use that word."

Mr. Livermore pauses as if dazzled by his own cleverness. "And, if things weren't already bad enough, they spelled my name wrong on the board in front of the nurses' station! I simply cannot abide such sloppiness."

"I can see why you would be so angry," I say mustering the sincerity of Barbara Walters in a celebrity interview.

"Angry? I didn't say I was angry. I don't get angry."

"Waiting three hours for a thirty-minute procedure would make anyone angry. So would having a new doctor each day."

"Yes, well, I am not just anyone."

"OK, then. Maybe you felt irked or peeved."

Mr. Livermore narrows his eyes and regards me for a few moments beyond what would be considered socially comfortable. I glue my gaze to his, refusing to be intimidated.

Eventually he says, "Yes, either of those words will do."

Just then, my beeper goes off. *Thank you, God!* Checking the number, I see that it is from the nurses' station. I explain to Mr. Livermore that I will need to take this call.

"And what would constitute an emergency in your area of specialization?" he asks.

There's no way in hell I'm going to tell you that, buddy.

"I need to leave, Mr. Livermore, but I'll try to come back later."

He frowns, "Promise?"

"Promise that I'll try."

Trudy stands at the entrance to the nurses' station, grinning broadly. "I thought you might need help extricating yourself from the Livermore. In any case, the other reason I called is to tell you about Mr. Avery. We just got him from ICU. He was there for six weeks with necrotizing pancreatitis, septicemia, and respiratory failure. He told me he remembers being intubated. He even remembers being resuscitated, and he's been having nightmares. Seems to me he was traumatized by the whole experience. That's why I thought of you."

I agree to see Will Avery but it will have to wait until after psych consult staff meeting which starts in twenty minutes, allowing me just enough time to finish with Mr. Livermore and write my notes, or have a cup of tea.

Don't be a wuss. If a staff nurse can tolerate him for a whole day, you can manage a few minutes more.

I opt to go for tea. While breathing in the orange spice of Constant Comment, I search for something likeable about Mr. Livermore. He's smart. He's articulate. But, the man is so cold I can almost see my own breath in his room. To feel something for him, I will need to find a capillary of blood hidden in that iceberg body of his. Warmed by the tea, I push against gravity and trek back to Mr. L's room.

The confrontation

"I hope whatever it was you were called out for was worthwhile," says Mr. Livermore who appears to be in the same position as when I left. He does not make eye contact with me. I feel his rage at being abandoned, that someone or something else mattered more than he did when I decided to leave. A therapist would focus on that moment because buried under layers and layers of sediment, is a psychological goldmine. However, he hasn't requested therapy and since such skills are beyond mine, we stay above ground.

"You know, Mr. Livermore, I was wondering about how you happened to be hospitalized in the first place."

"Yes, I suppose that would be of interest to you. First I must tell you that I am a man of excess. I indulge my appetites. All of them."

Oh brother! This guy puts the "pro" into provocative. No wonder the nurses avoid him.

"Unfortunately, I developed a hiatal hernia which caused me to feel much discomfort after my meals. Even so, I refused to give up my passion for fine cuisine. To relieve myself, I simply vomited my food. This worked quite well for a number of years until I developed esophageal adenocarcinoma"—he articulates the diagnosis with great care—"probably as a result of excessive vomiting."

Eeew, gross! Spare me the visuals. Do I have a geriatric male bulimic here?

"How did you react when you heard you had cancer?"

"I was excited!"

"Excited?"

"Oh, yes! I started attending cancer support groups. Through them, I've met so many interesting and important people. Two medical doctors are in one of my groups."

He watches my face for some kind of reaction. I nod and raise my eyebrows in a kind of 'You don't say' expression. Satisfied that I am impressed, he continues. "Yes, one could say that cancer has made possible a spiritual awakening within me."

"I don't think I've ever heard anyone say he is excited to learn he has cancer."

"You'll find that I'm a very unusual person."

"Yes, Mr. Livermore, I'm getting that picture although most people would say they feel horrified or sad or... ."

"Let me guess... annnnngry."

He stretches the word out like taffy.

"You got it."

"I can't stand people who are always emoting and never thinking."

"Whereas you do the opposite, I have to wonder, Mr. Livermore, is there any place for feelings in your life?"

"None at all."

"That's where we are very different. For me, life without feelings would be unbearable."

Ten minutes later in staff meeting, I remember that the Department of Consultation-Liaison Psychiatry has no place for feelings, either. However, even another discussion of billing procedures is preferable to hearing any more details of Mr. Livermore's vomitus operandi. He sure knows what to say to keep others out of projectile range.

After the meeting, I review Mr. Avery's chart over a strawberry yogurt. I miss my tamales but with Patricia on our tails about increasing billable hours, I can't give a plate of steaming chicken tamales smothered in salsa the attention it deserves.

Lunchtime peer supervision with Antionette and Janice has become a fond memory, a relic of the good old days before "mangled care," our pet name for managed care. I was hoping that the old-fashioned McLean Hospital-style process meeting we carried off after the theater director died would usher in a new era of staff support. But no. Apparently, that singular event was made possible by Patricia's absence.

The confrontation

According to his chart, Will Avery is an obese white man in his early sixties. During his six-week ICU stay, in addition to suffering necrotizing pancreatitis, adult respiratory distress syndrome, and septicemia, and being intubated and extubated four times, the surgeons removed his gall bladder and part of his pancreas. I'm no medical expert but I do know that the pancreas, part of the endocrine system, produces enzymes for digestion and regulates fluctuations in glucose and insulin, and that the gall bladder plays a part in maintaining acid-base balance in the body. Along with crummy lungs and a weak immune system, all this adds up to a tenuous hold on life.

Whereas Mr. Livermore is fine featured, Will Avery is a cross between Baby Huey and Mr. Potato Head with Lyndon Johnson sized ears, a fleshy nose, and a prominent jowl. After I review the events of his ICU stay with him, he growls in a raspy voice, "I feel like a goddamn guinea pig. Every time I close my eyes, there's a heavy slab of rock on my chest, squeezing the bejesus out of me."

When Mr. Avery coughs, he has chest spasms. Finally, he expectorates a yellow glob of phlegm. I stifle a gag reflex.

"You sound pretty upset."

"Upset? I'm goddamn furious at what they put me through."

Can you please give Mr. Livermore lessons in expressing feelings, or at least, anger?

Mr. Avery pauses and shakes his head.

"On the other hand, they saved my life and I should be grateful."

He motions me to wait while he coughs again. This time I avert my eyes when he coughs up thick mucous. Now I remember what I hated most about working in the ICU: suctioning patients' lungs and noses.

In the next moment, he revs up again. "But every time I asked my nurse what was happening to me she said, 'You need to rest,' and shot narcotics into me like I was less than human."

He lowers his head and rubs his eyes, then pinches the fold of skin between his eyebrows. "I don't know why they even bothered. I'm not worth it. Why didn't they just give up on me? I'm a nobody."

I watch as the anger that just melted into despair rises up again into a sturdy vessel of resolve.

"One thing I know," he says looking steely-eyed, "is that I will never go through that again. They will not take me back to the ICU."

Mr. Avery erupts into another coughing fit. I wait for it to subside before I speak.

"From what you describe, Mr. Avery, it's clear you had a terribly traumatic experience in the ICU. Have you experienced other trauma in your life as well?"

Mr. Avery squints at me. Then his eyes shift to a place I cannot see.

"Funny you should ask," he replies in a gravelly voice. "I was just thinking about it. When I was four—must have been 1939 or '40—my aunt... "

Mr. Avery's body shakes as he coughs.

"Sorry," he says when he regains his voice. "My aunt, she took care of me after my mother died. We were at some family get-together. She asked her brother to drive us home. Her husband—a drunken fool, like all the men in my family—he passed out in the back seat. We were on 101 driving to Redwood City, or so I was told."

Mr. Avery coughs so violently I worry something will rupture.

"Take it easy, Mr. Avery. I'm not in a hurry."

I pour some fresh water, which he sips after the coughs have calmed.

"I was on my aunt's lap," he continues. "Back then, cars had long door handles. I kept playing with it even when she told me not to." He pauses here and sighs deeply which sets off another round of coughing.

Such gunky lungs. I'll let his nurse know he'll need suctioning soon. He clears his throat and continues, his voice more air than sound.

"The door flew open. I bounced out onto the shoulder. My aunt fell out too. They brought us here, to this hospital. I was unscathed. My aunt, she broke her neck and died."

Mr. Avery coughs in spasms. I gently rub his shoulders until he leans back, drained of energy.

"Stay here," he sputters.

Mr. Avery tells me that for years he was passed around the family like a hot potato. At ten, he ran away from California, washing dishes for money or stealing food when he couldn't find work, hanging out with hobos but avoiding anyone who tried to befriend him.

Five years later, tired of surviving on his own, he returned home. The local officials declared him "a ward of the state" and forced him to live with his biological father, "a drunken brute of a guy" with whom he had little previous contact. He stuck it out and managed to graduate from high school after which he completed one year at the sheriff's academy. Mr. Avery ended up being self-employed as a bodyguard "for a lot of famous people."

"You didn't say how your mother died."

He studies me. Once again, his eyes look past mine through time and space. "She died giving birth to me. You see, by the time I was four, I had already killed two women. My family never let me forget that."

Although it is late October, we've had no rain. Until the rains come, it's clean up time in the garden; time to remove errant branches, sever stalks of faded dahlias, rake up and bag brown magnolia leaves, pull out poppies, and cut clematis vines to the ground. While I work, I think about Mr. Avery, killer of women and professional human shield.

Benny is four, the same age as Mr. Avery when his aunt broke her neck and died.

I pull out a rockrose shrub that fared poorly after I transplanted it last spring.

Benny is such a joyful little spirit. Maybe Will Avery was too, or might have been, if his mother hadn't died in childbirth.

I shake the soil from the plant's roots and cut off its half-dead limbs.

The longer I'm in this business, the clearer it becomes that a loving and secure attachment between a mother and child is the most important human relationship.

I throw the remains of the rockrose into the compost bin that Brian bought for me last Mother's Day.

Maybe Will floundered for a while until his aunt agreed to raise him. Maybe, in the time it took her to make that decision — when he should have been suckling at his mother's breast, looking up at her smiling face — a light inside him dimmed.

I lament the demise of the rockrose. I thought I had been so careful immobilizing its root ball before transplanting it. Some plants, especially the gray-greens, don't take well to transplantation no matter how carefully you tend to their roots.

Before bedtime, the boys and I clown around on the floor. I am the mommy elephant. Benny, a newly born baby elephant, creeps underneath my belly when I move. Danny, aka Tango, a lost orangutan, stands on my back, hoping to catch sight of his family. When the game ends with Tango's family joining him to live forever on the backs of elephants, I notice the "Emotions" poster I sent away for and hung in their room.

"OK, boys. How does Tango (the orangutan) feel before he

finds his family?"

Danny makes a face. "Stupid," he says and points to a goofy face on the chart. I think he's referring more to my effort at emotional education than anything else.

"I like this one," says Benny pointing to the "happy" face.

"I like this one," says Danny, pointing to the "proud" face. He imitates the expression and runs to show Corianne.

"I hate this one," says Benny, pointing to the face of a little boy who looks sad.

Wouldn't you know it, one of the surgeons nicked Mr. Livermore's bowel during one of his surgeries. The patient was remarkably undisturbed by the news. In fact, he almost seemed pleased by the prospect of spending more time on 4D, as if he hadn't tormented the staff enough.

Over the next two months, my days begin with the cold, irascible Mr. Livermore, who deflects my attempts to uncover his humanity, and end with Will Avery who plumbs the depths of his being asking why his life has come to this, why he has ended up with nothing and no one. In between, I listen to the pain and frustration of pedestrians, passengers, drivers, street victims, and wounded soldiers of drug and turf wars. I've heard their stories hundreds of times now, variations on the themes of trauma, poverty, neglect, addiction, mental illness, abuse, and rotten luck. After the surgeons patch them up, most limp out of the hospital within a week. Mr. Livermore and Mr. Avery have been here so many weeks that we are part of each other's lives.

Sitting with Mr. Livermore is like being in the presence of the Death Star. Whenever he senses my proximity to his heart, he activates its gravitational force to pull me toward the Dark Side. I fight the force of evil by reminding myself of my purpose: to provide an anchor for Mr. Livermore, to tether his destructive capabilities, and to prevent the nurses from killing him. To this end, while Battleship

Livermore fires off rounds of ammunition at the world, I dodge his bullets, occasionally firing off one myself.

At the end of each day, I see Will Avery. We talk about all kinds of things—politics, the NRA, eco-terrorism—and disagree on most things except how we are transported to heaven listening to Nina Simone sing "I Loves You Porgy." He reminds me of my wonderful Uncle Joe who was also big and overweight and never married.

Trudy says that Will's prognosis is poor. He still has fever, fatigue, and abdominal pain. Nevertheless, he will soon be transferred to the Skilled Nursing Facility, or "Sniff" on the third floor where there are fewer nurses per patient. Although he will have to say goodbye to the nursing staff on 4D who dote on him; the respiratory therapists, physical therapists, and I will follow him on his new unit. After eliciting Will's feelings about leaving 4D, especially about leaving a few nurses he is particularly fond of, I get more personal.

"What about relationships in your life?" I ask.

"I was married three times but none of them worked out."

"Three times? You never even told me you had married once!"

"Yeah. The first time at eighteen. I have a forty-five-year-old son somewhere. Six months ago, I wrote to his mother to ask if he wanted to talk to me. I haven't heard a thing. No surprise there. I walked away from him, gave him nothing all these years."

"Why didn't the marriages work out?"

"I could never get close to any of them," he confesses. "So I left. It was better that way. Basically, I'm a loner. I don't like people."

"Will," I say, for we have decided to call each other by our first names, "you are full of shit. I see how you relate to your nurses and your physical therapists. Forget what your family said, you are not a curse on humanity. You don't hate people. In fact, you enjoy them. I bet you're just afraid of killing off anyone who gets close to you, like your wives or your son."

In his silence, I can hear the wheels and cogs in Will's brain spinning.

"You're right," he says. "I know the truth when I hear it."

"And maybe you think you don't deserve to have anyone care about you. Does that sound right too?"

"Maybe," he says, pursing his lips.

"And is that why each time after we talk you tell me, 'Be careful out there' because you think you'll jinx my life like you've jinxed the others?"

Will nods.

"Well I hate to break it to you Will, but you just don't have the power you think you have. Sounds like a four-year-old child's fantasy to me, not a grown man's."

For a long moment, Will remains silent. Then he scrunches his face. "My God," he chokes, "I can see that now. I see why that became a part of me. I was only four. Small children can't murder people."

Oh Will, if only someone had helped you figure that out years ago, you could have forgiven yourself and found some happiness.

In our time together, he hasn't flinched in his desire to examine his life closely, to follow the strands of childhood into the flawed fabric of his adult life. Witnessing his struggle, I have come to care about him very much. The good news is realizing what I once knew: that burnout is caused not by caring too much, but by not being able to care at all. The bad news is that Will's prognosis is poor and I need to prepare myself.

Another month passes. Both men remain hospitalized. Will is not improving. With meticulous wound care, Mr. Livermore had been improving slowly and steadily until recently when his wound became re-infected. The doctors are stymied. The nurses are frustrated and defensive.

Will sounds terrible—constantly coughing, spiking fevers, and bringing up gobs of sticky yellow sputum. Although the nurses showed him how to suction himself, Will rarely does it. Lately he's been refusing physical therapy. For the first time, it's been hard for me to engage him in conversation. Now, when general questions go unanswered, I take a different approach.

"Will, are you having morbid thoughts?"

Slowly, he makes eye contact with me and nods.

"More than usual?"

He nods again.

"Have you been thinking about killing yourself?"

"I'm... a ward... of the state," he says through gritted teeth.

"I understand, Will. But I need to ask you, are you thinking about killing yourself?"

He nods, "If I could."

"How could you do that here?" Not so long ago, a patient on the jail unit managed to crush himself under a mechanized gurney.

"Not here. Too weak. Can't jump through the window."

"Will, do you have a gun at home?"

He nods.

"What's the chance that you would use it against yourself at home?"

"50-50."

I suspect he's been thinking this all along, but he's never admitted it to me. Last week he got his doctors to co-sign DNR papers telling them, "No more tubes! No more ICU. Just let me go."

Will reaches for my hand and grasps it tightly. His eyes are ablaze. "I'm scared, Laurie. I have nothing and no one. I have fifteen hundred dollars to my name, some clothes, a briefcase. That's it. I'm sixty-three years old. No one is going to hire me and I don't have the energy to start over. I'm a goddamn ward of the state—again!"

He coughs violently. Unable to stand the gurgling noises, I ask a nurse to suction him. Then I go to the nurses' station and call Barry. He wanted me to suggest a patient for him to see with a student. I'll suggest that he see Will.

The following Monday, I pass Will's physical therapist in the hallway. She extends her hand to me. Right away, I know something bad has happened.

"Laurie, did you hear? Will died over the weekend. Respiratory arrest. Sorry to be the one to tell you. He was such a nice guy."

I peek in Will's room anyway, just in case she made a mistake. Someone else is in his bed. A woman. *Where is Will?* I check the patient list on the dry erase board. His name is no longer there. *Where is Will?* Maybe he got transferred back to 4D. I'll look for him at our usual time, the end of the day.

In the hallway outside of 4D, I bump into Barry and the medical student, a tiny young woman with perfectly tweezed eyebrows, flawless skin, and flinty eyes.

"We just heard about Mr. Avery," says Barry. "I'm sorry. I know you really liked him."

I shrug. "I just can't think about it right now."

"You should have called us before you did," says the medical student. "He could have had a chance if he'd started on anti-depressants earlier."

When I don't respond she persists. "It takes a couple of weeks to reach a therapeutic level."

Do I need this from a little piker like her? What does she know about Will? Did she take the time to read my three months of notes?"

Barry looks embarrassed. "Laurie is a psychiatric clinical nurse specialist. She's very familiar with the way antidepressants work."

Maybe I should have gotten psychiatry involved earlier. Maybe their pills would have worked magic. But what would

*that have brought Will? Friends? Family? Health? Happiness?
A future? In my heart, I know that no pills, even magic ones,
can fill the void left in a young child when a mother disappears.*

"Will needed to mourn his life, not medicate it," I say, the edge
to my voice cutting my throat.

When a patient dies, his nurse is expected to continue caring
for her other patients without fuss. On autopilot, I prepare myself to
see Mr. Livermore whose medical condition has continued to slide.
Although he has spent months projecting his anger onto the nursing staff, reducing some of them to tears, they assure me that his
behavior is worse on the days I'm not there. The truth is, I'm pretty
much burnt out on Liverless.

"Well if it isn't my favorite mental health nurse," he says when
I enter his room. "My, don't you look upset! Would you like to talk
about it?"

The absurdity of his playing therapist causes me to smile. "I
don't think so, Mr. Livermore. I came here to check in with you.
How are you holding up?" His white cell count is up again today, a
sign of infection.

"I'm much more interested in knowing what's bothering you,"
he says with a smirk. "Perhaps something at home is awry?"

While I wait for Mr. Livermore to stop playing this ridiculous
game, I keep my eyes fixed on him and say nothing.

"Hmmm. I do believe Nurse Barkin might be feeling angry.
Am I right?"

If my instincts are telling me not to engage in this conversation,
my mouth is not paying heed.

"No, Mr. Livermore. If anything, I feel sadness for you. You
have cancer, you have a wound that won't heal, and no one has spot-
ted a visitor in your room since you got here. That's sad."

Mr. Livermore remains as still as marble.

No, Mr. Livermore, I don't expect you to feel anything.

The confrontation

Right now my chest feels full. My legs feel heavy. I'd rather be attacked by a cloud of mosquitoes than have to be here with you.

"I was wondering why you were so late this morning. I was beginning to feel 'abandoned.' How's that for a feeling?" Mr. Livermore smiles as he slides a silver ring up and down his middle finger.

"Feeling abandoned as a child or even an adult is a pretty awful thing. I don't know too many people who can joke about it."

Suddenly, it becomes clear to me where I must go in this conversation. "It's so devastating, Mr. Livermore, that some people will do anything to avoid feeling that way ever again."

"Oh, I understand, now. Is Dr. Laurie theorizing that abandonment in my past has caused me to erect psychological defenses which account for my immunity to human emotion?"

"I don't know, Mr. Livermore. You made it clear that I should not ask questions about your past and I have respected this but I can make inferences about your behavior. Your behavior tells me that despite your veneer, you do have feelings, like all human beings, even if you refuse to acknowledge them, and one of those feelings is loneliness."

For once, Mr. Livermore says nothing. While he glares at me, I weigh the wisdom of confrontation. If I say nothing, his behavior will continue with dire consequences. If I confront without proof, for all I have is strong suspicion, I risk rupturing our shaky alliance. I take a deep breath.

"Mr. Livermore, the doctors don't understand why your wound keeps getting infected. That's why I need to ask you—have you been infecting yourself?"

His expression remains placid, inscrutable. "What makes you think I could ever do such a thing?"

"Loneliness. I think you are a lonely person. I think that leaving here and being alone frightens the hell out of you."

Mr. Livermore's eyes are like slits high on a castle wall. I steel myself to hold his gaze as arrows of rage rain upon me. Then he lowers his eyes and pours himself a glass of water. Bringing the cup to his lips, he nods at the door behind me.

"You may go now," he says quietly.

When I don't move, he repeats himself, his voice slightly raised, his jaw muscles bulging.

He's right. I've said what I needed to say.

At the end of the day, I return to the skilled nursing facility where each afternoon for so many months I have visited Will. I stare at the woman in his room, a very old and feeble woman who sleeps sitting upright with her mouth open. Martina, one of the nurses who often took care of Will, comes over to me.

"On Saturday morning he turned his face to the wall. I've seen people do that before. He refused to suction himself. He didn't want anyone to touch him. He just wanted to die."

I squeeze every muscle in my face but it's no use. Tears escape from my eyes and drip down my face. Embarrassed by this outburst, I clap my hands over my face.

Martina hands me some tissues. "I know how much he meant to you."

Her soft words make the tears flow harder. My shoulders shake. Martina puts her arms around me. "He told me once that he wished he could have been one of your kids because they got to wake up each morning and see your smile."

Now I'm really a basket case. "Thanks for telling me that and for taking such good care of Will."

I blow my nose and try to compose my face. Then I give Martina a hug and walk out of the hospital as if it were just another day.

22

Nightmares

Minutes after waking up in the pallid light of November, I still see the carnage from my nightmare. Moving my body off the bed feels like a Herculean task.

Perhaps it will rain today. Although we've had our share of grey days, it hasn't rained more than a sprinkle since April. For the last few weeks, clouds have swelled to almost bursting. Then before releasing a drop, they've lumbered away.

I arrive a few minutes late for trauma rounds on 4D. When I enter the meeting, Caroline, the new trauma nurse coordinator, has just finished describing the latest gunshot wounds suffered by a certain Mr. Jones who I must know but can't conjure up at present. Next, she discusses a young woman who sustained ankle fractures after jumping from a burning building. Caroline wraps up rounds with an account of an elderly man whose schizophrenic grandson stabbed him in the flank.

"Those are the new folks on the unit now," says Caroline. "The recovery room should be releasing Linda St. John sometime this morning. Ms. St. John is a twenty-nine-year-old woman who sustained a broken femur and multiple contusions when she was hit by a truck that jumped the curb where she was waiting for the bus. Brace yourselves now—her seven-year-old daughter was thrown into the air. She died in the ambulance."

It just plain hurts to hear about kids dying. All of us seated around the table remain silent and still—praying, centering, breathing—each doing what we need to do to re-establish equilibrium and carry on with the day.

I force myself to leave the lounge and enter the nurses' station. Trudy emerges from the meeting with a stack of charts in her arms, which she drops on the counter.

"Some things you never get used to," she says, "and that's one of them. It made me wonder if I told my daughter I loved her this morning before she drove to school."

Trudy answers a phone and signals for me to wait. "OK, we'll be ready for her." She hangs up the phone. "Laurie, Linda St. John should arrive here in twenty minutes."

Trudy scans my face. "How old is Corianne now?"

"She's nine."

"Do you want me to call Janice or Antionette to see the patient?"

"No. I'll be alright."

Trudy cocks her head as if to say, "Are you sure?"

I nod, "It's my job."

She scrutinizes my face a little longer. "Well then, I've got to go to my CPR class. Good luck with Ms. St. John." She heads down the hall. A second later, she's at my side again.

"Hey! Did anyone tell you that the Livermore is gone?"

"What? He left?"

I recall confronting him about infecting himself.

Oh my God, what did I do?

"But his wound is infected!"

"He said it was time to go home. They gave him scrips for all of his meds and set him up with the visiting nurses. I don't know why they didn't do that months ago."

"Maybe because he threatened them with a lawsuit? If you remember, they nicked him in the OR."

Trudy lowers her voice. "Did something happen between you two yesterday?"

"I'm not sure. Why?"

"Because when he left, he said you'd be happy to know he was feeling a little bit angry."

I have to laugh. "Believe me, that's progress."

Trudy's face grows serious. She squeezes my arm. "I was so sorry to hear about Will. He was a special guy."

I tear up. "I know. He is."

She rubs my back. "OK, I'm off for real this time," she says and disappears down the hall. Every year, all nurses have to update their cardio-pulmonary resuscitation skills.

How about emotional resuscitation? If hands crossed over the throat is the universal sign for respiratory distress, maybe hands crossed over the heart should signify emotional distress.

In the middle of the nurses' station, I cross my hands over my heart just to see how it feels. Instead of inviting help, my arms feel like a shield. In my head, I hear myself say, *No more, no more, no more.* Alarmed, I drop my arms. I have work to do.

A group of medical students gathers around the dry erase board, snickering at a patient's name. "Wang Fat?" says one of them. "It has to be a joke."

Anthony Jones! Not again! You punky-assed, drug-dealing, arrogant, gold-toothed braggart. How many lives have you ruined since your last visit here?

"That's his alias of choice," I tell the students. "And no, he's no joke. Believe me, I wish he were." I add Anthony's name to the bottom of my list.

Listening to the story of the young woman who jumped from the burning building buoys my spirits. She was babysitting five children when the apartment building caught fire. Shaquonda threw each child to the firefighters below before jumping to safety herself, breaking her ankles in the process. Although in pain, she beams when I tell her she should win an award for saving five lives.

After leaving Shaquonda, I mentally prepare myself to meet with Ms. St. John. Even after centering myself, walking toward her room feels like walking the plank. Finally, I take a deep breath and knock on her door. When there is no response, I open it a crack. The room is dark and the lump in the far bed is motionless. Maybe she's asleep.

"Ms. St. John?" I whisper.

"Yes," she replies, barely.

I kick myself for not checking with someone first to find out if she knows about her daughter. Even though her roommate, an elderly woman, seems asleep, I draw the thin curtain around us. The dark space feels like a confessional. "I know you were in the recovery room until this morning. If you'd like to rest I can come back."

"I just need to know—why did God take her? Can you tell me that? Why? Why?"

She looks deeply into my eyes for answers. "How could God take my baby from me?"

She cries from a place of unfathomable pain. I pull a chair to her bedside and sit, saying nothing because nothing I say will be helpful. I clasp my hands together as hard as I can to distract myself from an emotional surge that threatens to burst my chest open. After a few minutes, she looks up and asks, "Are you a mother?"

I nod.

"So you understand."

I understand nothing about losing a child.

She wipes her eyes with the back of her hands. "We were just standing on the corner waiting for the bus. She was telling me about a boy in her class who could wiggle his ears. I said, 'I bet you could wiggle your ears if you really put your mind to it' and she shut her eyes to concentrate when all of a sudden I see a truck jump the sidewalk in front of us. Oh my Lord Jesus, he's hit my baby! My baby. Help me, Jesus. But I know she's gone. I know my baby girl is dead."

I do not want to cry in front of a patient. Repeat. I do not want to cry in front of a patient.

Sometimes I can distract myself but right now, it's a lost cause because tears are streaming down my face like Yosemite Falls in spring despite my best effort to suck them back into my eye sockets. Oh, what the hell, it's not working and it's so goddamn sad that I almost can't bear it until I realize that she must bear it, not I. She must endure this sorrow while I get to go home and hear my children's laughter and feel their kisses and hugs. Life is not fair.

I sit with Ms. St. John who sobs softly and soon drifts back to sleep. Maybe it's the pain meds or the residual effects of the anesthesia or the wish that the next time she wakes up, it will all have been a bad dream. I watch as her breathing slows and grows heavy. Then I tiptoe out.

Wimp.

In the bathroom, I splash cold water on my puffy face. While I wipe it with a scratchy paper towel, my beeper goes off. I recognize Tamara's number.

"Do you have time to meet for a cup of coffee?"

"Is something up?"

"Just something I want to run by you."

"Sure. How about now?"

We meet in the cafeteria. "I'm glad you could get away," she says. "I needed to talk to someone who will understand why I'm feeling homicidal. Hey, are you all right?"

"Yeah. I just heard another sad story. Comes with the territory."

Tamara and I sit in a far corner. Even though we're quite alone she practically whispers. "I'm having serious concerns about Patricia's clinical judgment."

"Is that new?"

"Unfortunately, no. But it came up again because she's still insisting that the outpatient mental health clinic offer therapy to offenders as well as victims of domestic violence."

"In the same building, or in a different location?"

"In the same building! She still doesn't get that these guys are lethal. Diana, the D-V social worker, told her the same thing but she won't budge. Her exact comment was, 'They've been hurt too. Most of them were victimized as children.'"

"How did you respond?"

"Diana and I told her once again that we're not against offering perpetrators treatment as long as it's on another planet or at least across town. Separating the victim from the victimizer is the most basic concept in the field of domestic violence. For the life of me, I can't figure out what goes on in that woman's mind!"

Tamara crunches on a wheat cracker and takes a swig of tea.

"That's not all," she continues. "For a few months, Diana had been helping one of her clients to leave this really abusive guy. Then the same guy shows up in the clinic, stalking Diana and her client, scaring them both to death. Diana was relieved that Patricia was in the clinic at the time and witnessed his being there. But in a meeting in front of everyone, Patricia called Diana 'paranoid' and said she was blowing the whole thing out of proportion!"

I flash on the day when I heard the news that a psychiatrist at Boston State Hospital was killed by a patient during an office visit. A psych nurse I know who was working there said that the psychiatrist had minimized each of the many threats the patient had made against his life.

"It gets worse," says Tamara. "Last weekend security apprehended a different guy with a gun in the clinic elevator. You should excuse the pun but Patricia blew that one off too. She actually laughed when she heard about it."

I remember looking at the hospital from my living room during my last maternity leave and comparing it to a chaotic family with parents who are unable to cope with caring for so many kids. Patricia is like one of those well-meaning parents — too busy to notice that the kids are trashing the house and skipping school, or maybe too overwhelmed to do anything about it.

"One last thing," says Tamara. "Patricia passed out in a staff meeting last week. When she came to, she refused to go to the Emergency Room. She even refused to let us get a wheelchair for her."

"Was she sick?"

"Who knows? She said it was nothing. Here she is setting up programs right and left, working crazy hours, doing everything but taking care of herself. I swear I heard her wheezing the other day."

Tamara brushes crumbs from the table, then pushes her chair back.

She arches an eyebrow. "She sets a lousy example for us all. Speaking of counterdependence, tell me what's going on with you. You're looking less than perky today."

"I guess that means I can't say I'm fine."

"Nope, not an option."

I want to tell her that Will died yesterday and that Linda St. John's daughter died this morning but I don't want to boo hoo here in the cafeteria. I also feel a little embarrassed, as if something is wrong with me when there shouldn't be. I may have a touch of vicarious trauma but blessed as I've been, I should be able to handle the stress of my job.

"OK, I'm less than fine."

While Tamara waits for me to formulate the words, my heart pounds so hard I feel it thumping in my ears.

I've heard that talking helps.

The other eyebrow arches. "So?"

"So lately I feel irritable, easily pissed off, on edge."

"Is everything OK at home?"

"Well it doesn't help that Brian has had to travel a lot lately and when he's home, he's preoccupied with work but that's nothing new. I know it will pass. It's more about wondering how much longer I can go on listening to these stories. There's just so much sadness in the world."

Why don't you tell her that you wake up feeling like someone's been playing a game of handball inside your chest?

"And of course no time is allotted to process any of it. How about Antionette and Janice? Do the three of you talk?"

"Not much lately because they feel pressured to increase their productivity numbers. Frankly, I don't give a shit anymore."

"Sounds to me like you need a couple of weeks on Maui."

"Didn't doctors used to prescribe that kind of thing?"

Tamara smiles. "Those were the days. Look, whatever you do, don't let this crazy place stop you from taking care of your own mental health."

She runs her hands through her short curls. "I'm serious. Take care of yourself. I need you here."

The door to Ms. St. John's room is closed. Just before knocking, I exhale fully and take a deep breath in. When there is no answer, I carefully push the door open. This time, a flimsy light blue curtain is drawn around her bed. Stepping softly and closing the door quietly behind me, I can see the silhouettes of women wearing hats standing shoulder to shoulder around her bed. Then I hear their voices in chorus:

> *What a Friend We Have in Jesus*
> *All our sins and grief to bear*
> *What a privilege to carry*
> *Everything to God in prayer.*
> *Oh what joys we often forfeit*
> *All because we do not carry*
> *Everything to God in prayer.*

Ms. St. John's roommate, an elderly woman in the bed close to where I stand in awe, hums along. Her eyes shut as she nods her head and says under her breath, "Yes, He is. Thank you, Lord. Mmmm. Yes, Jesus."

One of the women in the circle speaks like a woman used to being on a pulpit.

"Sister Linda, we must trust in God's wisdom. He is here with you now and He knows how you are suffering. He has called his child back for a reason. God is almighty. We must trust in Him."

When she begins to sing, "I Will Trust in the Lord," other voices fold in, blending with hers, creating layers of harmony and love. I turn to leave and close the door behind me. Outside, I imagine Ms. St. John being lifted into the air, held aloft by the faith and traditions of her community. They will help her more right now than anything I could do or say.

Faith is a powerful pill and I envy those who possess it. Growing up in a liberal, Jewish family that attended synagogue only on the High Holidays, I was taught self-determination. Believing in God was presented as an option. The God I grew up with didn't seem to hear His people's cries for help when it really counted. Or, if He did, He was not so powerful that He could stop atrocities from happening on earth. I have a sense of God as a creator. I do not have a sense of God as a savior. I wish I did. In times of trouble, strong faith is the best and sometimes the only medicine.

At the end of the day, I see Anthony Jones, aka Wang Fat. This is Anthony's third hospitalization for gunshot wounds. He's been supporting his mother and sisters by selling drugs since he was twelve, just after his father deserted the family. The last time he was here, I walked into his room as he was showing his newest gunshot wound to his five-year-old son. Later, after the boy and his mother had left and I had stopped seething, I suggested to Anthony that showing off his fresh gunshot wounds might frighten his son instead of impressing him with his father's toughness. The idea had never occurred to him. After some discussion, he could see my point. Now, even before I knock on Anthony's door, I am aware of feeling pissed off that he is back again.

"How's it going?" says Anthony when he sees me. He lies flat on his back with his knees bent. His hair is braided in tiny cornrows. A thick gold chain hangs around his husky neck. According to his chart, Anthony was shot in the right thigh and testicle.

"Better for me than for you, I think. So I see that you're still conducting business on the street."

"Aw, it ain't nothing. The other guy got it worse'n me."

"Is that right? Is he dead?" I can't help the hostility in my voice.

Anthony shoots me a hard look, one that lets me know I've ruined any trust we might have had between us.

You bastard. Does life mean so little to you? Don't you have feelings? You kill someone else's son, someone's father, someone's brother and it means nothing?

"How's your son?" I ask.

"He be fine. Tough little dude."

"Uh huh. Did you show him where you got shot this time?" The words are out before I can catch them.

Anthony's eyes narrow. "Hey, I thought nurses were supposed to care about their patients, not beat them up when they be down."

I look at this man who might have killed another man and maybe even others. One who has been dealing crack cocaine to mothers with children and to fathers who should be paying child support. I look at him and I feel sick inside.

"You're right, Anthony. I should care more than I do. This is your third hospitalization with bullet wounds. Why should I care about you when you don't care about yourself?"

I tear out of the hospital and drive to Benny's preschool. I want to take in his smile when he first sees me. I want to feel his body in my arms. Not just want. Need. When I arrive, earlier than usual, he is busy building something with large interlocking plastic pieces and barely looks up.

"Hi, Mom. See what I can do? I can make it taller than anything!"

When it falls, I put my arms out to comfort him but he ignores me and runs to his cubby to get his things.

"Bye Brandon," he calls. "Bye, Tony. Bye, David. Bye, Allison. Bye, Reiko. Bye, Travis. Bye, everyone!"

We walk across the street to Safeway where I throw Benny into a shopping cart that rattles as I push it over the asphalt parking lot toward the store entrance.

"Faster, Mommy, faster," says Benny, giggling.

Once inside the store, Benny urges me on. "Go fast again, Mommy," he pleads until I find an empty aisle to speed down. We zoom through the rest of the store, slowing only when we pass people reading labels and searching for the right spice. After selecting strawberry yogurt for Benny, two six-packs of apple-raspberry juice, pretzels, sushi for Corianne, French bread, cheese, peanut butter, a couple of soups and milk, I head for the checkout lane.

Ten minutes later, we're at the kids' school. Although Corianne and Danny are relieved to see us; they can't imagine how relieved I am to see them.

At home the kids and I sit down to one of my basic working day dinners: bowtie pasta in tomato sauce, pineapple chunks from a can, frozen peas, cucumbers, and chocolate pudding made from the week's leftover milk.

"Stories of the day time!" exclaims Corianne.

I started this ritual hoping that the kids would recount funny stories from school. When they started asking me about stories from my day, I had a problem. Trauma units aren't exactly bursting at the seams with comedic moments, at least not the kind they can hear. Recently an elderly woman tearfully confessed to me that she has been "a crotch watcher" for most of her life. Another time, one of the nurses found a giant dildo when going through a young female's belongings. Keeping a straight face the young woman said, "They told me to pack only what I need."

Today, in lieu of an age-appropriate funny story, I have an uplifting one to share with them.

"One of our patients is going to be on the ten o'clock news tonight because she did something very brave."

The kids become quiet and give me their full attention.

"Shaquonda was babysitting five kids when she smelled smoke in the apartment building."

Benny claps his hands over his ears. "I don't want to hear bad things!"

"It's OK, Benny. The story has a happy ending."

"Go on Mommy, I want to hear," says Corianne.

"Me too," says Danny.

Benny keeps his hands over his ears while I continue. "She

knew not to open the door because it was hot and because smoke was seeping under it. When she looked out the window and saw fire trucks, Shaquonda yelled to them that she had five kids with her. The firefighters put something like a trampoline below her and told her to toss each kid out the window. The kids were really scared and struggled against her but she did it, and because of her actions, she saved all five of them."

I don't tell the kids that Shaquonda broke her ankles when she jumped.

The kids' eyes are wide. I can see they're picturing the scene.

"After I heard the story, I told Janice about it and Janice called someone at the hospital who called the news station. They sent a reporter to the hospital. That's why it's going to be on the news tonight! Isn't that great?"

Everyone is quiet. "Mommy, could our house catch on fire?" asks Danny.

Benny, who had taken his hands off his ears, covers them again.

"Guys, this is a story about a girl who is a hero because she kept calm and saved those kids."

"But Mommy," says Corianne. "What if it happened here?"

"It won't happen here."

"Do you promise?" asks Danny.

Can I promise that we don't have a neighborhood arsonist or that the cat won't knock over a Shabbat candle? Can I promise that nothing bad will happen to them? Shit. I opened up a door I did not mean to open all because I wanted to share something positive about my day. Now I have to conduct a drill and deal with their fears of fire for the next week.

On Saturday, the kids' friends are here. The boys play with gas masks from the Army Navy store and plastic rifles that we seem to collect despite my disapproval. Dressed in camouflage clothes and sunglasses, combinations of GI Joe and James Bond, they scream at each other, "Take cover! Let's get him! Run!" Someone hurls his body over the couch and another skids across the floor. Next, the inevitable confrontation: "I got you. No way! Yes way! You're dead! Am not!"

"Who wants a popsicle?" I ask, to interrupt the showdown.

"Me, me, me, me!" They throw down their weapons and crowd around the freezer. If only popsicles could tempt grown men in the same way.

While the boys play, Corianne and her friend are shut up in her room choreographing a routine to "Who Do You Think You Are?" by the Spice Girls. Brian decided to work today instead of Sunday, as he usually does, in order to go to a birthday party at his secretary's house to celebrate her son's first birthday.

I feel stuck. I must be available to make lunch and snacks, to put on Band-Aids, to moderate stand-offs and tell them, no, they cannot watch TV when their play gets mired down. With all the racket, I can't concentrate enough to read a book or a journal article. God knows I don't feel like cleaning a drawer or the refrigerator. I stand in front of the glass door to the backyard as I often do, entranced by the rain that has finally arrived, thinking deeply about nothing in particular, then about Will Avery.

Benny tugs on my pants. "Mommy, are you death or someping?"

How long has he been trying to get my attention?

I reach up into the closet to retrieve a board game for him and think about everything else I've been spacing out on lately: bills, burning quesadillas, forgetting to sign yet another form from school. Last week I forgot about my dentist appointment.

Alone again at the window, I remember a patient I saw a few weeks ago who was crying and cursing as transporters wheeled her gurney to 4D from radiology. When I got her to calm down, she told me that all four of her kids had been taken from her and that last year, in prison, she was diagnosed with HIV. Every day she feels empty and abandoned. Every night she dreams of people chasing her, trying to kill her. She wants to be left alone. No one will just let her die.

Fueled by her screams—part terror, part fury—that ring in my ears, I imagine myself jumping onto my spade and feeling it sink into the ground; pulling up dense root balls of shrubs no longer in their prime; pulverizing those irritating clumps of arum, errant blackberries, dandelions, oxalis, and wild onion that invade every year even though plenty of them will survive to mock me in spring. I imagine my victims pleading with me for their lives. As I sever the last root of life, they will ask, "Why?" I will look at them with cold, unfeeling eyes and answer, "Because, children, life is not fair."

Earth to Laurie, Earth to Laurie. We seem to have lost contact.

When I refocus on the backyard, my eyes alight onto the plum shrub. Once again, I kick myself for saving it when we re-landscaped the backyard six years ago. Moving it to a sunnier location in the hope that it would bear fruit has failed; no blossoms have appeared on its barbed, whip-like stems. Tomorrow, if it's rained enough to loosen the soil, I'll dig it out by the roots for good.

23

"Who will take care of the caregivers?"

On Sunday morning, I decide I can't go with Brian and the kids to his secretary's party. I feel too anxious, too much in my own head to be able to make small talk with people I don't know. As soon as they're out of the door, I have second thoughts.

Maybe I should force myself to socialize.

No, talking to me would be a downer for anyone. I need some time to wring myself out.

Will Brian be able to handle all three kids at the same time? He doesn't get nearly as much practice as I do.

He'll get help if he needs it. Women fawn over dads left in charge of their kids.

From the third floor window, I watch the van pull away and head down the hill. Seconds after it disappears I panic. It's drizzling outside and the streets are slick. When was the last time I had the brakes checked? The tires? I think about the father and his two sons who were killed by a drunk driver on their way back from a ski trip last year. The mother and daughter had stayed home. How do they get through the day? What if... .

Stop right now! You have precious time alone. Uninterruptible time, reading time, singing time, gardening time.

I stand immobile in front of the window. The house itself seems to be in a state of shock. What, no clamoring? No whining? No crying? What's going on? I anticipate a child wailing or the crashing of block towers on oak floors. In the silence, my heart pounds.

Do something! Clean the kitchen. Turn on the music.

My mental condition improves as soon as I begin wailing with Chaka Khan. While I sing, I fill the dishwasher, scrub the counters, and put away toys. Then it's down to the second floor to make our bed and down again to the basement to throw in a load of laundry. After that, I run back up to the kitchen to clean floors sticky with juice and spilled pancake syrup. When Chaka has sung herself out, I vocalize with Dusty Springfield singing about "a little lovin' early in the morning."

Those were the days! Clearly, Dusty didn't have young kids.

Although out of practice, my voice doesn't sound half bad. Vocalizing has always been a tonic for me, a way of releasing my feelings. Singing along with Dusty, I'm aware of how much I've missed it.

Too bad we don't have a soundproof room with a lock on it. Maybe I should join a church with black gospel singers. I'd love to let loose like that every week.

The church ladies stood in a circle around Linda St. John. Their hands were clasped together; their eyes were closed; their soft voices melded into a lullaby.

> *What a friend we have in Jesus*
> *All our sins and grief to bear*
> *What a privilege to carry*
> *Everything to God in prayer.*

My baby, she said, my baby's been taken from me. Why did God take my baby from me?

How will Linda get through the day? How would I get through the day if it were my daughter?

Don't go there. How about the garden? Weren't you going to dig out that plum shrub?

I pull on my jeans and boots and walk out into the drizzle. What was I thinking when I transplanted it? At the time, it seemed right and respectful. Now, the idea of preserving something from the original garden seems silly and sentimental.

The vertical branches that form the shape of a tall birdcage have grown thicker since the last time I moved the plum shrub. Nasty barbed whips grow out from the sides and tops of each branch. Undaunted, I begin to slice the earth around the roots with my shovel. Yesterday's two plus inches of rain have softened the ground enough to loosen the top layer of soil. Under it, a network of thick and gnarled roots pushes deep into the clay soil instead of spreading wide on the surface, making my task much harder than anticipated.

Repeatedly, I pierce the earth and hurl each shovelful of soil against the fence. After twenty minutes, I still haven't made much progress. Determined, I jump on the spade and push my body against the shrub's major branches to help crack open the soil. Not so much as a rootlet snaps to reward my efforts. When a barb hooks my forearm skin, I curse and change tactics. Gripping my pruner, I begin to sever the five to six-foot whips on each branch, removing most of them by the time the drizzle turns to rain. Taking care to avoid the barbs, I bundle and tie the whips with jute rope. After tying the last batch, I stand up and feel my head spin. Kneeling, I wait for the feeling to pass.

After a shower, while waiting for my tea water to boil, my head starts to spin again. I forego the tea and lie on the couch with a wool blanket stretched over me. Listening to the patter of rain hitting the skylight, I drift off.

When I awaken, it's dark outside. Where's Brian? Did he leave me a phone number? Damn, what is his secretary's last name? I'm not even sure where in the East Bay she lives. A search for her phone number comes up empty. It would be like Brian not to call. During the workweek, he rarely calls during the day. He is so focused and has so little down time that the thought just doesn't occur to him, even when the kids are sick. I make a cup of tea and carry it over to the piano.

It's been a long time since I've accompanied myself singing. In an old ritual that stopped when breastfeeding began, I exhale completely, then inhale, relax my jaws, close my lips and hum, exhaling slowly while ascending three notes of the scale and back, holding the last note until it fades like the last rays of sunlight. After a deep breath and another sip of hot tea, three more notes, beginning and ending a half step higher. At the high end of my range, when my throat strains, I begin the descent, slackening all my muscles until I've reached a low C at which point, tone disappears. Warmed up, I sit on the bench and play one of the few songs I know from memory, "Like a Lover," a bossa nova, barely hitting the high E flats I used to make with ease. Rummaging through my Laura Nyro songbook, I turn to "Billy's Blues," embracing the song like an old friend.

When I sing, "Billy's down, he was born, he was bound to lose," Will Avery's face appears in my mind's eye. Before I finish the last note, emotion rises up in my throat. This time I give in. No one's here. No one to upset but myself.

He really got to you the most. Why?

Because he was so alone in the world.

And?

And because he had spent a lifetime blaming himself for things that were beyond the control of a child.

I am full out crying now, so this must be the mother lode. I mix myself a vodka and tonic. When I am cried out, my head throbs and my skull threatens to burst open. I take two ibuprofens and try to read but my concentration is shot. It's after six.

They left before ten this morning. Why aren't they home?

By seven o'clock, I'm pacing and wondering if I should call all the emergency rooms between here and Contra Costa County.

Maybe another drink will help me not bite Brian's head off when he walks in. But the alcohol unleashes my worst thoughts.

I didn't tell them that I loved them this morning when they left. What was the last thing they heard me say? "Make sure there's enough gas in the van? Or worse: "Mommy needs some time to herself." When did I start putting my needs above my family? If they come home, I swear I will never separate myself from them again. I just want to feel their arms around me. Then, another dizzy spell sends me downstairs to bed.

"Mommy! Mommy!"

Lights snap on.

"There she is! She's hiding!"

The boys jump on the bed. "Let us in!" They move their hands between bed and bedspread looking for an opening.

I groan, "Mommy is sleepy. Where's Daddy?"

The boys free a corner of blanket and tear it away from my body. Chilled, I tuck it back in. Uh oh. A game has begun. They free another corner and pull it from my body. Finally, they wriggle in next to me. Danny pulls the bedspread over the three of us.

"Mommy is the Mama bear and this is our cave," announces Danny.

"Hey, Laur. It's only eight o'clock. What's up?" Brian drops his backpack and takes off his leather jacket.

"It 'pooky in here," whispers Benny as he cuddles into my body.

My headache is better but my body still feels heavy. "I'm just beat. Could you pop the kids in the tub and put them to bed?"

I hear exasperation in his breath—he's been watching the kids all day—but I can't force myself out of bed.

"Mommy, where's the gold marker?" demands Corianne. "I NEED it for my Victorian house project."

I try to answer but something triggers a coughing fit. She stares at me as if I were withholding vital information from her.

"In the telephone drawer," I sputter.

When Brian throws the boys in the tub, I kill the lights and slide back under the covers. Cocooned, I listen to the chamber music of my lungs and heart. The tempo is too fast.

Re-arranging positions and pillows to find a combination that quiets my lungs ends in failure. I cough through the early morning hours before finally falling into a dead sleep.

Brian's heels click on the hardwood floor. I turn toward the fuzzy half-light of November and crack open my eyes.

"Bye, Honey," he says, "I've got to get in early for a conference call. See you tonight." Heels click down the stairs.

Wait a minute!

The door opens, then closes.

What about me?

I will myself up, roust the kids, make breakfast, pack lunches, drop the kids off, and collapse back into bed.

Get up and call work.

Antionette asks what's wrong. Before I can answer, my lungs spasm.

"You need to see a doctor," she says in her military voice. "Today."

I just want to sleep. My ribs ache, my chest hurts, my head pounds, I have chills. But I know she's right. I call. Yes, I can be there in an hour. I drive, knowing I shouldn't. The X-Ray confirms the diagnosis.

"You've got pneumonia, my dear."

"Allergies?"

"Pharmacy number?"

"Go home and rest."

I leave a message on Brian's voicemail asking him if he can leave work early to pick up the kids and my prescription. Then I curl up under the covers.

The phone rings. The house is dark. "Mommy, aren't you going to pick us up?"

Moving through disorientation, I pull on my sweats and arrive at school two minutes after closing time. When we pick up Benny, the last child to leave, he bursts out crying when he sees me. I apologize for being late, for being sick, for making them worry. Once we're home, I remember that Brian never called back. I call his office.

"Sorry, honey. I was in Oakland all day for a deposition. Even if I'd gotten your message I wouldn't have been able to get away early. Not with the trial coming up."

Who will take care of the caregivers?

Brian comes home after the kids and I are already in bed. Then, before any of us gets up the next morning, he's gone. Sometimes his work is like this, especially if he is pre-trial. Even though most of his cases settle before they actually go to trial, the work and the pressure leading up to the decision are intense. During these periods, even when Brian is home, he is preoccupied. Although he does makes a conscious effort to spend what time he has with the kids, especially if it coincides with baseball or soccer games, our marriage takes a back seat. Usually, I understand. But this morning, when I wake up and see that his briefcase is gone, I feel abandoned. I suck it up and get the kids ready for school. Later, I pick up my prescription myself.

The kids know I'm sick and do their best to comfort me. After I pick them up from school, Corianne makes me tea with honey, Danny draws me a picture of a beautiful day, and Benny climbs on me as I lie on the couch, desperate to find somewhere to snuggle out of coughing range. Corianne reads to the boys at bedtime so that I can turn in early. She promises to make them brush their teeth before they turn out the lights.

Hours later, I feel Brian slip into bed.

"What time is it?"

"After midnight," he says. "We had a filing. Did you get your medicine?"

"Yeah, but it takes a while to work."

"I'm so tired," says Brian. He turns over and goes to sleep.

In the darkness, I cry. Something in me has changed. I am not the person I thought I was—self-reliant, independent, strong, a person who takes care of others but needs no caretaking in return. The fact is I need my family. They ground me. They soothe me. It shocks me that I've come to depend on them as much as they depend on me.

24

"If I am not a nurse, who am I?"

Yesterday, a man on the ICU hovered between life and death after a branch of an old cypress tree fell on his car during a storm. Today, an eighteen-year-old boy fractured his shoulder when his car skidded on a flooded street, then rammed into a light pole. He will be told that his passenger, his best friend, died during surgery.

This morning, the sun hides under a blanket of clouds. Oh, to be a momma bear hibernating in a cave, cuddling with my brood instead of waking in the dark from nightmares that make my heart race. The good news is that Brian's case settled instead of going to trial. To spend more time together, we've signed up for a theater series.

My head is filled with dream fragments. In last night's feature dream, I was stabbed. Thick sticky blood oozed from a wound in my abdomen, the same story I heard last week from a patient's sister who came to my trauma group. Elena was walking with her twenty-year-old brother on Market Street when he was eviscerated by a man with a knife. She held him until the ambulance came. Now he's in the ICU.

On the way to the hospital, I have the urge to turn around and go home. Even though I've been back at work for a month since I was sick, I still don't feel quite right. It's not anything physical, just a feeling that something has shifted in my body and brain.

When I arrive, Janice and Antionette are already in the office talking about a nurse who was recently diagnosed with cancer. That makes four nurses and a social worker with breast cancer, one nurse with liver cancer, and one with brain cancer. Several weeks ago, a substance abuse counselor committed suicide.

Who will take care of the caregivers?

On 4D, Trudy looks grim. In a hushed voice, she points to the room across from the nurses' station and tells me about its latest occupant, a nineteen-year-old prostitute who was beaten over the head with a hammer, stuffed into a plastic garbage bag, and flung into the bay.

"Boy is she lucky," says Trudy. "The neurologist says she'll probably make a full recovery. I hope they find that guy and cut off his balls."

"He's still out there?"

"So I hear."

Trudy picks up the phone. "My daughter has a class this morning. I know it's silly, but I just want to be sure she got there."

While Trudy punches the numbers on the dial pad, I remember that her daughter is a freshman at a local college. "The police will be coming in later to interview the patient," she says. "She's awake and alone now. Do you have time to see her?"

"Sure."

I knock gently and open the door to Krista's room. The head of her bed is raised thirty degrees in order to decrease the pressure of fluid in her brain. A swath of bandages covers her shaved skull.

Bruises and abrasions mar her slender arms. Krista's eyes are swollen shut, awash in blue and gray splotches.

I take a moment to steel myself against the story I will hear. For now, Krista will know me by my voice alone. Assuming a childhood history of abuse and neglect so prevalent among prostitutes, I don't expect her to trust me. Nevertheless, I need to evaluate how she is coping and how we can best support her in the hospital.

Due to her head injury, Krista may have difficulty understanding my questions and organizing her responses. Accordingly, I speak slowly and carefully in short sentences with spaces between them. Although moments pass between my questions and her responses, I am relieved when her answers are clear, appropriate, and organized. She speaks without an accent or any trace of regionalism. Her use of language—grammatically correct and precise—and her soft voice convey a delicate soul, not the hard veneer of a longtime prostitute.

I start by explaining why it's important to talk about what happened. So it does not become unspeakable; so her feelings are allowed to course through her body instead of being lodged within; so she can organize the memories of her senses into a coherent story to be told repeatedly until it can be bunched up and tossed into a corner of her being.

Krista says she understands and will walk me through the minefield of her memory.

In a measured voice, Krista tells me that three days ago, she got into a stranger's car on Capp Street, a known venue for prostitution less than a mile from the hospital. The man drove her to a place behind an abandoned building on Bayshore Avenue, a building I pass by on my way home from work each day.

"He told me he wouldn't hurt me, that he wanted me to kiss him. When I wouldn't, he stripped me and bound my hands with a telephone cord. I told him my wrists hurt. He took it off and used bungee cords instead."

After sipping some water, Krista tells me that the man orally raped her—sucking hard on her genitals—before pushing her naked body out of the car and onto the ground.

"Then he took out a hammer and pounded my head. I begged him to stop. I told him, 'I'm a mother. Don't do this to me.' But he kept hurting me. I felt myself get weak so I played dead hoping that he would stop. He got back in his car and drove away. Then he came back. He got out of the car and stuffed me into a garbage bag. Then he threw me into the trunk."

While Krista stops to take another sip of water, I fight the impulse to clap my hands over my ears like Benny and scream, "No, no, no! I don't want to hear about bad things anymore!"

Instead I ask, "How are you doing so far?"

"I'm OK," she answers. Her voice sounds flat and tired.

"You must have been so scared in the trunk."

"No, I just kept planning how I was going to get out alive."

As she speaks, I notice that her fingers have curled under like claws.

"He drove for a while. Then I think he backtracked. When he finally stopped, he opened the trunk and picked me up."

For the first time Krista's voice falters. She pauses to wipe away a tear. "Then he dropped me. When I hit the water, the bag ripped open. I got myself free of it and started swimming."

"What about the bungee cords around your wrists?" I ask.

"I got them off when I was in the trunk. I had to punch a hole through the bag so that I could breathe."

"How did you get out of the bay?"

"I looked up and swam toward a structure. There was a fence I had to climb. I wasn't sure I could do it, but I told myself I had to."

Again her voice breaks. "It was hard to pull myself up. I was so cold. When I got over the fence, the people driving by stared at me because I was naked."

Krista's body shudders. When the shaking stops, she sighs deeply and collects herself. "A woman pulled over and gave me a jacket. She's the one who called 911."

Krista does not curse, cry, or even whimper. She moistens her lips and asks me if I can refill her water pitcher. Outside her room, I am aware of feeling drained. I am also in awe of how Krista survived her ordeal; how she willed herself to survive the cold depths of anonymity and clawed her way back into the world of the living. I pour her a fresh glass of water.

"You saved your own life, you know. Not too many people can say that."

She doesn't answer. I hope she doesn't think I'm being flippant.

"You survived because of your own actions. You played dead; you made sure you could breathe; you swam to the structure, and you climbed to safety. You kept your wits about you the whole time. Your children still have a mother because of that."

"I guess so," she whispers.

"It's true. How were you able to play dead when you were in so much pain?"

"I let my body go limp. I kept my eyes open and rolled them back into my head."

Probably, she dissociated.

I understand why Trudy looked so shaken. Krista could have been her daughter. She isn't a hardened, foul-mouthed crack queen. She had been working the streets for three months before this happened. She did not use drugs or even drink alcohol. She had been a good student and graduated high school. She worked as a lifeguard during the summer. I wish I could understand why Krista ended up on Capp Street getting into cars with strange men, risking her health, her life, and her children's future. What went wrong?

I ask Krista whether I should return tomorrow. She says yes and thanks me although I don't know why. I fear that revisiting the scene of the crime has depleted her. Perhaps the police will be delayed, allowing her a bit of sleep.

Before I leave, I feel compelled to ask Krista one more question. "If they find this guy, will you testify against him in court?"

She hesitates. "I don't know."

I bite my lip. *You don't know? How could you not?*

"Well, think about it this way. You and you alone, have an opportunity to put this animal in a cage before he does the same thing to someone else."

When Krista doesn't answer, I continue.

"In fact, some might say you have an obligation to testify against him for that reason."

With this last sentence, I know that I have overstepped a boundary. I've imposed my feelings on her. For the sake of other women, it had to be said.

I leave her room and go into the nurses' lounge, thankfully deserted, where I sit with my head in my hands.

For a long while, my body feels as heavy and immovable as a boat stuck on a sandbar. Then anger rises in my chest. Suddenly the boat becomes an airplane engine gearing for take-off.

I see him on the runway waving his arms wildly, screaming for us to stop. The plane gains momentum and heads straight toward him and then it's too late. We feel a slight tug as he is sucked into an engine and chopped into bits by cold metal blades that spit him out in small pieces. The ground crew rushes over, removes the pulverized human particles, and gives us the OK to resume our take-off. Everyone cheers. We are finally on our way to Bali.

I look up at the clock and rise, startled. Where did the time go? I'm going to be late to psych-consult staff meeting. When I rush in, Patricia is talking about the latest possibilities for new office space, a perennial problem with our expanding programs. Taking an empty chair, I'm aware that my colleagues are looking at me. Patricia stops speaking mid-sentence.

"Sorry I'm late. Could I have some time at the end of the meeting to talk about a patient I just saw?"

Patricia looks uncomfortable. "Maybe we can check in with everyone next time. Meanwhile, Laurie, I appreciate your bringing it up. I know we're all working really hard but there are some other things we have to get to."

She returns to the topic of office space. Then it's the usual pep talk about beefing up our billable hours.

I am not able to listen. My legs are shaking; my head is heavy, and I feel slightly nauseous. I practice every relaxation technique that I know without being obvious. Instead of closing my eyes, I focus on the Norfolk Pine in the corner of the room. After reaching the ceiling long ago, it bent at a forty-five degree angle and has been growing horizontally toward the window ever since. Someone must be watering it. Hasn't that person noticed that it's outgrown this room? While Patricia drones on, I fantasize about smuggling it out of the hospital and replanting it in my backyard to grow unimpeded. Would it eventually right itself or would it always look misshapen?

On my day off, my friend deposits her son at my house so she can run some errands. The boys rummage through toy boxes in the family room and pull out action figures and dinosaurs. They take turns shouting: "And then this guy morphs into a velociraptor with a gazillion arms. Then Nick Nitro comes and blows up the world. But he doesn't know about the transformer's magical powers or that the Tyrannosaurus Rex knows where he is. Then the Power Rangers jump on top of Nick Nitro."

I clean up the kitchen, half-listening to the kids but preoccupied with the fact that, at sea level in San Francisco, I'm breathing as if I'd been whisked to the top of Mount Whitney. My heart is beating ninety-two times a minute instead of the usual sixty-six or seventy.

What is wrong with me?

After a while, the boys abandon their fantasy and decide to draw monsters, an activity that lasts for less than fifteen minutes. I search the cupboards for snacks.

"Mo-om," Benny intones after handing me his picture, "Can we watch a movie? You said it's gonna rain."

Aladdin will give me a chunk of time to myself. Like all modern four-year-olds, Benny knows how to work the VCR. When he and his friend have finished snacking, I give them permission to turn it on.

"I'll be in the backyard. Call me if you need me."

Dark clouds have gathered over the city, although rain has yet to fall. Inhaling the clean smell of earth, I experience a moment of peace that devolves into a million mini-explosions when I exhale. Perhaps a more gifted person could harness this energy into writing a symphony or a passionate poem. Such energy has also fueled the hand of suicide. Being neither so gifted nor so troubled, the energy in my body impels me to dig, cut, or chop.

I choose my weapons from the oak barrel under the deck: a spade, an ax, and a tree saw. This will be the end of the plum shrub. I'm in the mood to scrape and debride, amputate and decapitate, maim and batter, torture and bully. I want to hear the limbs split and crack before they hit the ground with a heavy thud.

If only the plum shrub were a young rosebush easily lifted out of the soil in its dormancy. But no, even though I've already dug down more than a foot around the roots, it stands firmly entrenched. Stepping inside the birdcage structure of its branches, I rock it back and forth hoping to hear the popping sounds of rootlets giving way. Nothing gives. A light rain begins to fall as I jump on the spade and remove more mud. After exposing another few inches of roots, I hurl my body against the bars of the birdcage. This time, something does give way but a powerful elastic resistance bounces me backward and off-kilter, causing my foot to slip and lodge tightly under the tangle of roots. I yelp in pain. When no amount of manipulation releases it, I sink to the ground cursing.

During the next few minutes, the rain picks up, wetting the root ball enough to extricate my throbbing foot. Having declared war on this beast, I ignore the pain and attack the roots with renewed vigor. My offensive is barely underway when my foot slips once again. Frustration mounting, I switch tools. This time I pick up the ax and hack at the roots. I hack as if I were the psychiatrist who axed his lover in a methamphetamine rage. I hack with all my strength as if I were the animal who hammered Krista's skull until it broke open like a filbert or Mrs. Holloway's assailant who sliced her neck after she refused him sex. Punch drunk with fury, I keep swinging and hacking, slipping in the mud, righting myself, swinging and hacking again. I am tormenter, basher, stabber, and slicer, trysting with murder and liking the violence storming through my body.

The ax is too dull to sever anything. Determined to remove the hated shrub, I widen the battlefield with the spade and hurl heavy chunks of clay soil behind me like a gravedigger. The shrub lists to one side. Working the spade into the soil alongside the roots, I feel their depth, their tenacity, their imperviousness to my will. Success will require more strength and time than I have.

Defeat weakens my muscles. Rain and mud have soaked my clothes. My shivering body sinks into the cold dark mud where tears mix with dirt.

Five years has come to this. Five years of hearing stories of men who violated children and mothers who pretended it wasn't happening; five years of hearing about pimps who enslave girls, husbands who beat wives, and young men who shoot at people as though they were cans for target practice; five years of seeing the fractured souls of grown-up children whose parents tried to "beat some sense" into them.

I need to talk about how awful it is to come face to face with evil in the world. I asked for what I needed. That was hard enough. Did I violate a taboo by asking? How can those of us who bear witness to trauma make sense of the violence, inequity, injustice, and waste of human potential that confronts us daily? What should we do with the feelings we feel? Other trauma programs incorporate time each week for staff to talk about such things. Why can't we?

For twenty-two years, I have helped steer patients through emotional crises by listening deeply to painful feelings, offering validation and perspective, challenging misperceptions, and encouraging change and growth. On inpatient psychiatric units, I worked with people who mutilated their bodies or refused to eat, people who scrubbed their hands until they bled or heard voices telling them they deserved to die. In my trauma work, I've been more like a scoutmaster: teaching patients survival skills, cheering them on during their uphill climbs, supporting them as they cross raging streams, and pointing out the blazes on the path toward recovery.

It feels like I've come to the end of a twenty-two-year backpacking trip. My shoulders ache. I feel depleted.

What would happen if I took off my pack?

As I lay back in the mud, the rain slackens and the ground beneath me warms. I stop shivering and relax into the same earth that supports redwoods and rivers. I sense my insignificance, my true self stripped of title and degree.

The fact is that I am replaceable. Other shoulders can lift the load for a time. New ones join in every day while weary ones take a break. I just need to step out from under the shadows for a while and feel the sun on my face. It's that easy. Is this what my body has been trying to tell me?

If I am not a nurse, who am I?

I look at the plum shrub, which lists slightly but remains firmly rooted despite my hard labor. Without the camouflage of spring's leafy plumage, its strong and sturdy limbs look dead, etched like bold charcoal lines against the grey sky. A part of me feels dead too, like a pine tree skeleton after a fire, only instead of being consumed by flames, I feel ravaged by overexposure to human cruelty and suffering.

Perhaps I am, by nature, vulnerable to other people's pain. Images of trauma become lodged in my psyche, standing in the wings when I am awake and moving to center stage when I dream. If there is a way of listening to others' feelings without being touched in return, I cannot imagine it. To me, giving and receiving human emotion is as visceral as sharing food. If the food is fake, both of us will starve.

The plum shrub may look dead but I felt life in its roots growing like branches underground, anchoring it to the earth. So too do I sense my roots as a nurse, deep and unscathed. Come the next rain, I know I will rebloom.

But will I rebloom as a nurse? And if I am not a nurse, who am I?

I grow anxious thinking about this question. I've wrapped myself in a nurse's cloak for so long that I'm afraid to take it off. What if I don't exist without the nurse's cloak? What if the sum total of my self-worth is invested in my professional identity?

Maybe I'm asking the wrong question. Maybe the real question is: "What do I need?"

I need to immerse myself in beauty. I need to feel joy. I need to float in a slack tide, neither coming nor going, just being. I need a prolonged Sabbath with wine, fresh baked bread, candles, prayers, and family. I need to sleep peacefully. I need to be touched, physically and spiritually. I need to drop my backpack, sit on a high peak, and gaze at where I've come from and what lies ahead. I need to laugh with friends. I need to take care of myself. I need a break.

I need a break.

Although the mud feels strangely caressing, I pull myself out of its warm stickiness and put away my implements. Then I sit on the steps of the deck and remove my mud-caked boots. In front of the glass door that leads to the kitchen, I strip down to my underclothes. When I enter the kitchen and peek inside the family room, the boys are still riveted to *Aladdin*. They are seated at an angle such that I could sneak by without their noticing. If they look up, I will joke that I am a mud person and that I have just taken a mud bath. That will make Benny laugh, which, in turn, will make his friend laugh. They take no notice as I tiptoe behind them to the bathroom. Silently, I close the door behind me and turn on the shower water. Judging from the scene of *Aladdin* that I saw as I walked past, I have twelve or thirteen luxurious minutes in which to bathe.

When the water runs hot, I step inside and rinse the mud from my hair and body. After scrubbing, shampooing, and conditioning, I stand with my back to the downpour while wet heat pummels my muscles and opens my lungs, filling me with a new sense of purpose and possibility. A rumbling erupts in my chest. It pushes upward until it uncorks streams of uncontrollable laughter that rise above the rush of water and reverberate in the small curtained space. I ride the waves of giddiness until they dissipate and deliver me to an island of calm. Then I hear the pounding on the bathroom door.

"Mommy!" yells Benny. "Maaaaaahmeeeeeeee!"

I shut off the water, wrap myself in a towel, and open the door.

Benny eyes me suspiciously. "It's over, Mommy. The movie is over."

I smile at my future. "So it is."

25

The last stroll

When I tell Antionette and Janice that I am leaving The General, they are not surprised. They know I haven't bounced back since Patricia's unwillingness to give me time in staff meeting to discuss what happened to Krista.

"I'm not happy about it but I understand," Janice says.

Antionette asks, "How are you going to explain your decision to Patricia?"

"I will tell her the truth."

Except that when I deliver the news to Patricia, she does not ask why I'm leaving. She says she appreciates the work I have done, adding, "I can't imagine working and having three kids at home. I don't know how you've been able to manage it all this time."

With that, she excuses herself, gathers an armful of folders, and hurries to a meeting.

Later at a staff meeting when I announce my intent to leave, Barry appears surprised.

Donald asks, "What are your plans?"

"I don't have any plans. I just need to take some time off."

Around the table, a few heads nod slightly but most of the psychiatrists and psychologists adopt well-worn masks of neutrality.

Over the course of three weeks, I share my news with individual nurses and social workers on 4D. Most assume I am leaving to spend more time with my kids but Trudy pulls me aside.

"Our patients' stories can tear your heart out. You know that better than anyone. Take good care of yourself and your kids, and come back when you can."

We hug.

At first, Tamara feels abandoned.

"What? You're leaving me?" she wails, then, lowering her voice, whispers, "This place is killing me. I'm on your heels as soon as I figure out my next move."

A week before my last day, I send out fliers to past members of my trauma support group, encouraging them to attend my farewell party. Current members are invited to come and meet the new facilitators, Antionette and Janice. My former co-leader, Ilan, moved back to Israel a few months ago.

At home, I call Jeanne and tell her of my decision.

"It's about fuckin' time, sugar," she says. "I've been worried about you."

When Jeanne presses me for details, I tell her about being denied staff time to discuss the Krista affair. "You must have felt terrible," she says, "and pissed off."

"Yes, because I really did need help. Here I was sitting in a roomful of psychiatrists and psychologists and no one responded."

"It's a symptom," says Jeanne.

"Of what?"

"Of what's happened in psychiatry since you and I began. Even before I left, everyone avoided talking about real issues like childhood abuse or fucked-up family dynamics. They were too afraid patients would regress and need more treatment than insurance would pay for. That's why trainees aren't learning how to listen and respond to emotional pain. These days they shove a few pills down patients' throats and kick 'em out the door with a list of coping strategies."

"It's happening in Connecticut, too?"

"Bet your ass it is. It just hit us a little later. No one's doing the deep work of therapy anymore. When you want to talk about how hard it is to listen to trauma, you're shot down because it's too uncomfortable to hear and because it's not a 'cost-effective' use of time. That's the trend, sugar. It's over for people like us. You and I are relics."

The evening before my last staff meeting, I take the kids to their swim lessons at Baby Baleen Swim School. My kids, old hands here, are stationed at the opposite end of the large indoor swimming pool from where we parents sit in yellow plastic chairs. Across from us, a group of dads stands in the pool holding their babies, all born in the last year. A slender, middle-aged woman with a pixie haircut directs the activities, encouraging the dads to scoop water onto their own heads before gently wetting the heads of their babies.

"Have fun," she says. "See if you can make your baby laugh. Remember, your baby will be watching your face for cues, so look confident, even if you're not."

When a baby starts to cry, she advises the dad to hold the baby close before trying to distract him with one of the toys she hands him for that purpose. "Respect where your child is at. Read her feelings and respond to them. Don't be in a hurry. This is not about accomplishing a goal. It's all about play and trust."

I had hoped to use this time to think about what I'm going to say in tomorrow's staff meeting. Now I wish I had a video camera. This is the cutest thing I've seen in a long time. Looking around, I notice other parents are equally enchanted by these dads and their babies. On the other side of the pool, I make eye contact with my kids. They wave before returning their attention to the instructor.

In the dad and baby group, the teacher passes out small floating mattresses and instructs the dads to place their babies on top of them. Each baby takes time inspecting the new object and checking dad's face before deciding whether to cooperate.

It feels so good to see dads having fun with their babies. In the next moment, I feel sad knowing that it's going to take many experiences like this to outweigh the horror stories that clutter my mind.

Walking into my last staff meeting at SFGH, I remember when I felt that I could stay in this job forever. In our meeting room, pastries, fruit, and bagels have been laid out on the table in my honor. Janice and Antionette are setting up coffee, cups, saucers, and napkins.

When the meeting begins, Patricia runs through the agenda, leaving me for the last topic of discussion. With twenty minutes left, she smiles and formally acknowledges my last day on the service.

"I'd just like to thank you for your hard work on 4D and your dedication to the trauma support group," she says. "I've enjoyed working with you."

"Thank you," I say.

"Does anyone have anything to add?" asks Patricia.

Barry tells me how much he's enjoyed our collaboration. "By the way, how is the woman whose throat was slashed?" he asks, referring to Mrs. Holloway.

"She's OK. I'm hoping to see her at the trauma support group party later today."

After a few other people wish me well, Donald clears his throat. "I want to compliment you on your effort to incorporate staff processing time into our meetings. We didn't take it too far, but not for lack of trying on your part."

"And now we're losing our Process Queen," Barry quips.

I recognize this as my moment to address the issue.

"When you call me that, I have to laugh. I sure didn't start off that way. I used to dread those groups because I didn't know how to express my feelings back then. But I could see that talking openly about feelings or staff conflicts deepened our relationships and increased the feeling of trust among us. I wanted to bring that here because our patients' lives inevitably evoke reactions in all of us, not just me. I regret that I wasn't a more convincing salesperson."

I stop talking. In the silence that follows, I notice that the Norfolk Pine is still alive and more in need of transplanting than ever.

Donald breaks the silence. "So, what are your plans after you leave us?"

Thirteen pairs of eyes focus on me. I sip my tea and decide to speak from the heart.

"First, I want to be clear why I am leaving."

Looking directly at Patricia, I speak in even tones. "It's not primarily about my kids although they will benefit by my being home. I am leaving because since managed care, the quantity of patients we see takes precedence over the quality of patient care we provide. I'm leaving because I hate feeling like I'm in a horse race, because I started to feel like a machine, because I need support to do trauma work as I think everyone does, and because I don't see that happening here anytime soon."

Taking a deep breath, I continue. "I have absorbed too much trauma in this job. I need to leave to take care of myself before I become a basket case."

No one responds except Janice who winks at me. I thank everyone for listening and for bringing the fruit and pastries. Looking up at the clock, I am relieved that it's time for the meeting to end.

At lunch, I tell Janice and Antionette that I feel bad for having the option to leave when others don't. Janice assures me there's no reason to waste time feeling guilty about my decision.

"You'll be glad you're home when Corianne hits middle school next year."

Antionette tells me that although other people have expressed interest in taking my position, she knows it will be hard to find someone with my experience. "Not to mention, someone who's as easy to work with as you."

It is clear to me that the three of us will be staying in close touch.

When the time comes, we head to the medical library for the trauma-support group party. Not expecting a big turn out, I am pleased when ten former patients come to say goodbye. Mrs. Holloway is not among them. She lives more than three hours away and I didn't count on her coming. I make a point of introducing people to Antionette and Janice as the next group leaders. They are pleased when some of the patients recognize them from their hospital stays and fill them in on their lives since then. When the party winds down, I say goodbye to my group members, knowing that I'll lose track of their lives. When some of them hug me and thank me for leading the group, I tear up.

In our office, while I finish packing my things, Antionette plays the messages that have accumulated on our message machine. I recognize Mrs. Holloway's voice right away, asking me to give her a call should I have a moment.

I dial her phone. "I'm so glad you called to say goodbye."

"You know that you saved my life."

I feel stunned. "I did?"

"Yes, you surely did. That day after group when I told you my assailant had been released because they had never charged him with attempted murder? I felt crazy inside. If you hadn't convinced me not to go back there, I would have done something bad. I'm so glad I didn't."

"I'm glad, too."

The last stroll

"That's what I wanted to tell you, Laurie. You made a real difference in my life."

I am so choked up that I can barely thank her for telling me.

Antionette asks, "What did she say?"

As I tell them, each of us reaches for the box of tissues.

Leaving San Francisco General Hospital for the last time, I stroll through The Comfort Garden before heading home. Already the light is fading through the mist of this winter's day. The garden is lush with foliage but few flowers are in bloom.

Mostly I will miss the meaningfulness inherent in my work as a nurse. Not many people get to make a difference in other people's lives. I believe in the power of human connection. Resonance between people—the warm and responsive embrace between two souls—protects and heals us from the world's ills and makes possible its greatest bounties. Over the last few years, I have mourned the shift away from this knowledge. Maybe it will be temporary, until science finds a way to prove what many of us know about the primacy of emotional communion.

For now, I need to figure out how to heal myself. If I were my own nurse, I would advise doing what feels good: take the kids to the park, dig in the garden, make love, cook good meals, write, sing, spend time with friends, and choose movies from the comedy section; and try new things: meditation, exercise, and yoga. We caregivers must find ways to take care of ourselves so we can continue doing our work.

Near the end of my stroll, I stop to look at the rose bushes. So resplendent in spring and summer, the roses now resemble sticks stuck in the mud. Observing them more carefully, I notice swollen buds of new canes about to burst open just under the pruning cuts. I smile. It has always been like this. Year after year, following a season of dormancy, roses leaf out and bloom. I wish I could be so certain of my future; certain that I, too, will experience a spring renaissance after shutting down for a season.

I leave the garden thinking about how much I will miss my work here and wonder what will take its place. On the way home, driving past the parking lot where Krista was beaten and stuffed into a plastic bag, I shudder. Will I always have this reaction? Will the trauma lodged in my mind and body ever disappear?

I don't know the answer to that. But the answer to another question I've been asking myself becomes clear: just as a rose will always be a rose, I know I will always be a nurse. My roots in nursing are strong and deep. Like the roots of a rose, mine will continue to support me through a period of dormancy, until I am ready to bloom again.

acknowledgments

This book took nine years to write. For eight of those years, Giana Miniaci, Pamela Reitman, and Mary Hower—members of my writing group, along with Daniel Drapiewski—patiently tutored me in the craft of writing. Without their expertise, encouragement, and commitment, this book would never have progressed beyond an idea.

My former colleagues, Antionette Griffin RN, MSN and Janice Papedo RN, PhD, set the gold standard for psychiatric consultation-liaison nursing practice. They are a gift to the patients and staff at SFGH. I treasure their ongoing support and friendship.

I am indebted to Barbara Hayes, DNSc, for reading an early draft of this book and for calling me from Australia every Thanksgiving for the last 23 years without fail, "enthusiastic as evah!" Andy Barkin, Ted Barkin, Sylvia Hahn, Roberta Richards, Bethe Austin-Natkin, Ann Doherty, John Ladd, Margo Perin, Carol Davies, Cynthia Becker, Ann Lange, and Jonathan Lange donated their time and attention to reading and critiquing my drafts. These pages contain many of their thoughtful suggestions. I am grateful to Jo Anne Childress for the hours she spent reformatting and cleaning up my manuscript.

David Watts MD, founder of the "Healing Art of Writing" conference, has created a community of nurses, physicians, family members, and patients committed to capturing in poetry and prose the moments of grace and fear, strength and vulnerability that we are privileged to witness or asked to bear. Through this conference I met Penny Wolfson, whose journalistic ear helped shape this book, and Jack Coulehan MD, who helped me talk through my concerns about releasing it.

Thank you to June Komater for her photography and for translating my vision of a book cover into reality. Thanks also to my son, Danny Brosnahan, for his insightful comments. The contents of this book have been greatly enhanced by Bonnie Britt's careful editing and personal integrity, her clear-mindedness, and her enthusiasm for this project.

Throughout the writing, my family's love and humor have nurtured and sustained me. My husband, Brian Brosnahan, made it possible for me to write. Without his support, his love, and his humor, this dream would not have materialized. Furthermore, his loyalty and passion for the San Francisco Giants and the Boston Red Sox—which he has imparted to our children—gave me many hours of precious, uninterrupted writing time. Thank you, darling. You are my rock.

To my patients: although I am unable to thank you by name, I want to express my gratitude for having known you, even for a brief moment in time. I will remember what you have taught me.

14601195R00223

Made in the USA
Lexington, KY
12 April 2012